CONTEMPORARY EUROPEAN CINEMA

CONTEMPORARY EUROPEAN CINEMA

MARY P. WOOD

Hodder Arnold

A MEMBER OF THE HODDER HEADLINE GROUP

First published in Great Britain in 2007 by
Hodder Arnold, an imprint of Hodder Education and a member of the Hodder Headline Group,
an Hachette Livre UK Company
338 Euston Road, London NW1 3BH

www.hoddereducation.com

Distributed in the United States of America by
Oxford University Press Inc.
198 Madison Avenue, New York, NY10016

British Library Cataloguing in Publication Data
A catalogue record for this book is available from the British Library

Library of Congress Cataloging-in-Publication Data
A catalog record for this book is available from the Library of Congress

ISBN 978 0 340 76136 6

1 2 3 4 5 6 7 8 9 10

Typeset in 10/13pt Adobe Garamond by Dorchester Typesetting Group Ltd, Dorchester, Dorset
Printed and bound in Malta

Contents

Acknowledgements **ix**
List of figures **x**
Introduction **xi**

1 European cinema at the barricades **1**
The global reach of Hollywood 1
How big is the market and who are the main players? 3
Structures of the European film industries 5
National initiatives 8
The development of EU legislation 10
Co-production agreements and Eurimages 14
Playing the local and global cards 15
Conclusion 17

2 Art cinema, a cinema of *auteurs*? Low- to mid-budget authorial film-making **24**
What is an *auteur*? 27
Portugal 28
Eric Rohmer and the middle-class audience 29
How has Godard survived? 32
Agnès Varda 34
Dogme and the Danish bid for power 35
Other models of authorial control: Italy 37
Authorial control: the UK 38
Michael Winterbottom 39
Conclusion 40

3 The evolution of the 'quality' film **43**
The evolution of the quality film 44
Miramax 44
The Italian case 46
Lars von Trier 50
The *cinéma du look* 52
Pedro Almodóvar 54
Conclusion 58

4 Outclassing Hollywood at the box office? 67
Co-productions with the USA 68
High-concept co-productions 69
Event films and national stereotypes 72
French cinema: style and spectacle 75
Roberto Benigni and the dreadful case of *Pinocchio* 80
European stars 80
Conclusion 82

5 Popular cinema and local stories 83
Appealing to the young male audience 83
The gangster genre 86
Broadening the borders 88
Middle-class tastes 89
Local tastes: comedies which make it within national borders 92
Horror audiences 95
Soft porn: a parallel universe 97
Conclusion 97

6 Cultural identity and the importance of television and satellite co-productions 99
A complex media map 100
France: vertical integration and a differentiated slate 101
Who will be part of the family? 107
Children's films 109
Conclusion 114

7 The irrelevance of borders? 115
Global and local 116
British multiculturalism interrogated 117
The difficulties of marking difference: Italy 121
The irrelevance of borders 125
Turkey: meeting of East and West 126
Balkan directors 128
Conclusion 128

8 Theme park Europe? 134
The heritage film and the British costume drama 134
Sex and violence and the past 142
Constant engagement with history: Italy 143
The Eastern European epic 145
War films and the attempt at closure 145
Conclusion 150

9 Case study: Ireland **152**
Colonial and postcolonial 153
Contemporary Irish cinema and its past 155
Creativity and difference 158
History or heritage? 160
Television and low-budget film production 164
Conclusion 166

Conclusion **169**

Bibliography **174**

Index **192**

Acknowledgements

The publishers would like to thank European Audiovisual Observatory for permission to reproduce figures on page 9, 10, 20–23, 25, 26, 60–66, 100–101 and 131–133.

Every effort has been made to trace and acknowledge ownership of copyright. The publishers will be glad to make suitable arrangements with any copyright holders whom it has not been possible to contact.

List of figures

Figure 1.1 Number of feature films produced in the European Union, Japan and the USA, 1990–2004 9
Figure 1.2 Admissions in the European Union, 1996–2005 10
Art cinema/auteurist films by admissions 20
Figure 2.1 Average cost of production of feature films: 1992–2004 (in US$ millions) 25
Figure 2.2 Comparison between the number of films produced and the number of films released in the European Union (EUR 25): 1997-2003 26
Box-office hits 60
Figure 6.1 Channel supply by genre in the European Union (January 2006) 100
Figure 6.2 Sources of finance for French films in 2005 (%) 103
Top-earning European history films/costume dramas 131

Note

In the figures listed above, please note the following:

a) EUR 15 relates to members of the EU prior to 1 May 2004
b) EUR 25 relates to EU 15 plus the expanded membership including Eastern European states post 1 May 2004
c) EU 29+ relates to the 25 states of the EU, plus other European states currently outside the European Union such as Switzerland, Iceland, Norway, Romania and Turkey

Introduction

In the late 1950s the idea that something called European cinema existed seemed incontrovertible. There were great directors, great national movements and a territory for study which stretched from Ireland to the Urals. After 1956 came the clampdown which cut Western Europeans off from the majority of the cinema of what was generically designated Eastern Europe; Europe shrank and European cinema became just the cinema of Western Europe. Not until the breaching of the Berlin Wall in 1989 did knowledge of the cinema of that area increase. In the aftermath of the fall of state socialism in Eastern Central Europe, formerly state-supported film industries faced with American competition provided powerful examples of the fragility of national production for all of Europe.

In this book I will consider European cinema after 1990 when changes in the film industries, and their political, social and cultural context, accelerated. I will raise the following questions: What are the modes of production and cultural spaces which allow European film-makers to engage with their own national and European realities? What sort of films does European cinema do best – not just the films which are exported, but those which are very successful on their home territory? What measures have been taken to ensure the survival of the cinema industries of Europe and how effective are they?

In addressing these questions I will be considering the institutional, economic and commercial as well as the social and cultural contexts of European cinema. At the beginning of the twenty-first century, it makes no sense to study films in isolation. We live in an era of rapid technological advances and equally rapid changes in social habits, particularly in the use of the media. Technological changes are not neutral events but the result of commercial and political forces. To ignore the work that creative people in the film and media industries have to do to get films made, and seen, is to construct a restricted context for understanding both their artistic input and their professional expertise. When the European Union's MEDIA programme was set up in the early 1990s, it had 15 countries from which to gather statistics and the numbers have increased at regular intervals to 25 and 33. There is no question that the context of European cinema is now global and that it is important to explore the complex interactions between American commercial practices and those of Europe if we are to understand why certain films get made and why others are blighted by difficulties of investment and distribution.

Globalization

The economic, social and political consequences of globalization will inform my analyses of successful areas of European production and my analyses of individual films. Why does so much European cinema retain an epistemological agenda, that is, a desire to represent some sort of truth about history and daily reality, when theorists of the postmodern such as Jean-François Lyotard (1984) suggest that the loss of faith in the grand narratives which offered explanations of who we are and our place in the world has eroded the idea of the availability of any objective truth? In a situation of postmodern distrust and rejection of the grand metanarratives of Christianity and communism, race and patriarchy, those overarching explanations of who we are and our place in the world, some understanding of the global forces which attempt to shape our lives is necessary. Globalization is often reduced to the simple, unproblematic consequence of space–time compression, that is the experiencing of other cultures and events via globalized communication systems, the huge increase in air travel and the presence of people from other cultures within old national borders. Yet the generous responses of individual Western Europeans, watching the devastation of the Asian tsunami of 26 December 2004 and feeling empathy with populations thousands of miles away, conceal the fact that lack of technology, political will and territorial importance meant that an earthquake early-warning system did not exist. Areas, peoples and regions 'which are non-valuable from the perspective of informational capitalism' are excluded from flows of wealth and information (Castells 2000b: 72). Space–time compression and postmodern art and media forms cannot be separated out from their economic, cultural and political context. Indeed, identification of some of the characteristics of postmodernity have been framed or 'enfolded' by explanations of the nature of globalization (Edwards and Usher 2000: 2). It is no coincidence that these attempts to understand the contemporary world were set in motion by the experience of economic recessions, the movements of populations from the old European colonies and the opening up of Eastern Central Europe. Effectively, concentration on the symptoms of change diverts attention from underlying shifts in economic and political power.

There are many definitions of globalization. Anthony Giddens links it to the modes of social life and organizations of modernity, whose four dimensions include the world capitalist economy, the nation-state system, the world military order and the international division of labour, and he makes the point that there is considerable 'push and pull' between the transnational economic imperatives of the first and the centralizing tendencies of the second (1990: 1, 70–3). The conflicts between these two will be visible in chapters exploring the different production models of European cinema. The globalization of capitalism is key, involving the media and communications industries not only in the pursuit of profits but also in the control of information and social supervision. Another view is that the promotion of the ideology of consumerism lies at the heart of the global capitalism perspective of globalization (Devereux 2003: 33). More to the point is the recognition that capitalist corporate culture favours the expansion of market opportunities in order to maximize profits and in order to control and minimize the risks involved in operating in an extended economic sphere. In a prescient 1989 article, Anatole Kaletsky suggested that

Western Europe itself precipitated the internationalizing of Hollywood (1989: 7). Television deregulation stimulated commercial growth and a youthful, educated generation was perceived to be 'significantly altering the types of entertainment and information in demand'. Beyond the immediate bonanza, Europe was seen as a competitive threat and the big, American media conglomerates added 'global reach' to their management objectives in order to preserve their market dominance. Kaletsky's comments smack of blaming the victims for their plight, providing a smokescreen for the fact that even successful US blockbuster films no longer cover their costs on their domestic market, hence the imposition of a delay between the theatrical release and television release, and high prices for pay-TV releases and 'most favoured nation' agreements. A European cinema release became a significant revenue source (Rampini 2003: 26). Companies have had to expand, grow larger and absorb and merge with other companies controlling areas perceived as important. Research on American corporate practices identifies the persistence of a culture of buying and selling and, as Devereux points out (2003: 33), transnational media companies may represent only one sector in the commercial interests of global industrial conglomerates.

Effectively, this means that strategies of vertical or horizontal integration are used to hedge risks. Vertical integration involves 'owning assets involved in the production, distribution, exhibition, and sale of the single type of media product' (Croteau and Hoynes 2001: 94), while horizontal integration involves the control of a wide variety of media companies, such as newspapers, publishing, broadcasting, film production.

The mid to late 1970s was the watershed moment for European cinema. The pace of technological change hotted up, setting in train the phenomena now labelled as typical of postmodern society and globalization – space–time compression, using media representations to make sense of our lives, increase in media products and developments – all of which are still evolving in the contemporary world. The explosion of commercial television channels, the development of synergy between media interests combined with the maturing of the baby boom generation stimulated demand for different types of products. The long period of postwar economic boom had faltered in the early 1970s with a recession which was brought on by the rigidity of what David Harvey suggests was a 'Fordist–Keynesian' configuration of political and economic power whose mass production systems, labour markets and power elites could not react quickly enough to competition' (1990: 124, 142). The social conformity necessary to drive such a highly controlled system received a severe knock in the uprisings and revolutionary movements of 1968, which were a sign that both young people and workers felt excluded from power and that 'knowing their place' and bland acquiescence were not what a world war, education and consumer aspiration had led them to expect. Having been given some access to prosperity, young people wanted more. One effect of the expansion of higher education was the growth of the middle classes. Far from being a mass entertainment medium, by the 1970s the film industry had conducted audience surveys which identified the average cinema-goer as educated and middle class. What the film and media industries needed for continued expansion was the rapid development of new products and new opportunities for media consumption. There was a point in the 1980s when it seemed that a good cinema release was unnecessary for a film co-produced by a large, vertically integrated media company.

Production costs could be amortized through the sale of advertising slots interrupting the broadcast of the film, by sales to terrestrial and satellite channels, videocassette pre-sales, and through spin-offs in the form of books and records. However, the value of a good cinema release for generating a film's subsequent exploitation opportunities was swiftly recognized. The shift in commercial practices necessary to respond swiftly to global changes has been defined by Harvey as 'flexible accumulation' (1990: 147). This includes the greatly intensified pace of technological innovation typical of the media hardware and software industries, the rise of new products and ways of using them and new commercial opportunities. The growth of companies specializing in production of the add-on features accompanying the film on DVDs is an example. The flexibility with respect to labour markets and changes in production processes deriving from new technologies results in uneven development. The exploitation of one geographical area, and its abandonment in favour of another, often results from large-scale film productions switching locations to take advantage of tax breaks, subsidies and trained personnel. European film studios vie with each other to attract blockbuster film productions; European countries lucky enough to include mountains, coastlines and different climatic regions advertise themselves as a 'one-stop shop' for film productions whose stories cross the globe.

The economic measures taken in the west to combat recession involved the now all too familiar downsizing of companies' full-time labour forces, the casualization of labour through the out-sourcing of services and the tacit acceptance of the marginalizing of sectors of national economies. What Mattelart calls the 'technoglobal representation of the world's destiny' promotes the idea that the weakening of nation-states goes hand in hand with the formation of a worldwide, global community in which poverty would have no part (2002: 591–3). For Mattelart, managerial-speak conceals the fact that global capitalism is unaccountable and that citizens have not scrutinized its implications. However, in spite of globalization theorists' stress on the weakening of the nation-state through the commercial interests of multinational corporations, European states, whether democratic or not, use their power to protect what they perceive is in their own interests, and the preservation of elements of national culture is perceived as important.

The history of some recent, European, vertically or horizontally integrated media companies illustrates these phenomena. Media globalization is by no means a one-way process from the USA to Europe and elsewhere in the world. American companies have proved to be just as vulnerable to takeover in the competition to colonize and control. The pattern for European media companies has been to struggle to achieve tight, capitalist business practices (identified as close attention to costs and revenues – the significantly designated 'control sheet' of PolyGram (Kuhn 2002: 127)). In PolyGram's case, the achievement of vertical integration, allied with its pre-eminence and business practices in the music publishing sector, led to a turnaround in its fortunes and an increasingly high profile for the company in terms of films' success and profits generated. This led to its vulnerability to takeover and PolyGram Filmed Entertainment (PFE) was bought out by the Canadian, horizontally integrated multinational company Seagram. PolyGram was left wide open to takeover by the decision of the majority shareholder, Phillips, to sell its holdings, in spite of the fact that (or because) *Notting Hill* (Roger Michell, UK/USA, 1999), *Being John*

Malkovich (Spike Jonze, USA, 1999) and *Plunkett and Macleane* (Jake Scott, UK/Czech Republic, 1999) were ready for exploitation. Seagram bought PolyGram for $10.4 billion in December 1998 and promptly sold off PFE's library to MGM for $250 million. In June 2000, Vivendi announced the merger/buyout of Seagram for $30/34 billion. In this respect, Manuel Castells provides a convincing explanation of the shifting power relationships in the contemporary world with his idea of global flows which takes account of regional hubs of the production of decision-making, financial and information services in areas other than North America (2000a: 446). Powerful institutions, political and cultural elites in Europe, the Far East, Australasia and South America carve out spheres of influence on the global media map, treating media products and companies as valuable commodities. The rights to exploit the titles in a company's film library are regarded as a particularly tasty morsel.

Arjun Appadurai's model for understanding global cultural flows is useful when discussing the complexity of audiences and markets for contemporary European cinema. To consider British cinema as peripheral to Hollywood, or subsidized Welsh or Scottish cinema as peripheral to 'mainstream' British cinema, is too simplistic in the contemporary situation. Britain is a diverse, multicultural society. The top 20 foreign-language films released in the UK in 2001 included 11 Indian films, and *East is East* (Damien O'Donnell, UK, 1998) makes a reference to Bollywood films' dance sequences; the networks of diffusion of British cinema in countries of its former colonial influence is a two-way process. There are large audiences for British films on television and Welsh- or Gaelic-language films are not ghettoized in regional channels. As Crane suggests, 'cultural influences move in many different directions' (2002: 3). Appadurai's framework consists of five dimensions: ethnoscapes, mediascapes, technoscapes, financescapes and ideoscapes (1999: 297). Ethnoscapes, the shifting groups of immigrants, tourists, refugees, exiles, guest-workers and others, and the 'odd distribution of technology' in technoscapes, are crucial to understanding the complex relationships between money flows as people move to work where needed. Mediascapes refer both to the distribution of 'electronic abilities to disseminate information' and the images of the world which they create. Thus European immigrants influence the money flows of remittances 'home' and the banks of videotapes in London's Iranian supermarkets attest to the importance of the Iranian mediascape to that community.

Ken Loach's films from the 1990s onwards also provide examples of film-making which has a small appeal in Britain but are part of the mediascape of other European countries. Jacob Leigh suggests 1990 as a turning point in Loach's career after lack of success in the 1980s (2002: 169). He developed a more accessible film-making style to combine the political realism for which he was known with comedy and melodrama to punch home his messages. Significantly he also formed Parallax Pictures with his regular production collaborators, Sally Hibbin and Rebecca O'Brien, producer Sarah Curtis and directors Les Blair and Philip Davis. A production involvement gave him more control over his career, a path which many other film-makers have taken. Loach's films are successful on the festival circuit, which assigns prestige to serious themes and means that they are picked up by art-house distributors. Their subjects have contemporary relevance. *Hidden Agenda* (UK, 1990) was a conspiracy thriller raising the spectre of right-wing elements meddling in British politics; *Riff-Raff* (UK, 1991), *Raining Stones* (UK, 1993) and *Ladybird Ladybird* (UK, 1994), made for Film on Four television, explored the effects of Thatcherite economic policies in the growth of an underclass excluded from the flows of wealth of global capitalism and denied dignity in its dealings with the state. Loach returned to this theme in *My Name is Joe* (Spain/Italy/France/UK/Germany, 1998), punching home the message of class solidarity across borders in Joe's (Peter Mullan) football team's shirts. The links between the underclasses of the first and third worlds are suggested in *Bread and Roses* (UK/France/Germany/Spain/Italy/Switzerland, 2000), charting the progress of a strike to improve living conditions of illegal immigrant cleaners in Los Angeles, while *The Navigators* (UK/Germany/Spain, 2001) shows the failed attempts of British Rail unions to safeguard the jobs of skilled workers when the rail network is privatized. Political struggle is set in the context of competing ideologies in *Carla's Song* (UK/Spain/Germany, 1996) and *Land and Freedom* (UK/Spain/Germany/Italy, 1995), while *Ae Fond Kiss* (UK/Belgium/Germany/Italy/Spain, 2004) is an inter-racial romance narrative. On a personal level Loach's career is at the interstitial margins between mainstream and alternative, political film-making, while his subjects reflect the realities of globalization. Although not in the blockbuster league, or in the annual top-50 tables of European films, Loach's political stance and subjects find a financial and critical response across borders.

The spatial metaphors which Appadurai uses help us understand that the European films which at first sight may appear to have an extremely small audience have, in fact, been made as a result of economic and commercial decisions based on assessments of aggregations of fragmented audiences. Gurinder Chadha's *Bend It Like Beckham* (UK/Germany, 2002) has the appeal of a strong story of a girl's aspirations to play amateur football and interest for diasporic Asian communities in Britain and outside. It also did extremely well in India. Although criticized for the 'universality' of its story of female struggle (Monk 2002), the film achieved over 4 million admissions in the 29 countries of the EU (EAO 2004/3: 54). The production arrangements with German public bodies and Wim Wenders' company, Road Movies, and with Helkon certainly assisted its wide diffusion.

Another view is that the global and the local are relative terms: 'what is considered local, is produced within and by a globalizing discourse which includes capitalist marketing and its increasing orientation to differentiated local markets' (Barker 1999: 41–2). Robertson (1990) coined the term 'glocal' to describe the process by which American cultural forms took on the guise of another culture's artefacts in order to make themselves more acceptable and vice versa, or the local appropriation of American culture by another. Traces of the glocal can be seen in the barrow-load of poinsettias in the snow in the long montage sequence in the market in *Notting Hill.* This is an American, not British, version of Christmas. The films of Gurinder Chadha and Ken Loach appeal to fragmented, niche audiences identified by the media industries, but the cross-over potential of *Bend It Like Beckham* lay in its aspirational comedy, shorn of overt anti-racist politics, allowing it to become the eleventh most successful European film of 2002. Loach's appeal to a political activist and/or tertiary educated, left-leaning audience limits both his budgets and his films' earnings, but not their financial success in relation to their budgets.

The reality of contemporary film production is that it is no longer narrowly national.

Appeal to diaspora communities outside Europe is also important for European cinema. Australia's SBS (Special Broadcasting Services) was set up to cater for the needs of Australia's diverse cultural communities and to reflect that country's move from the 'White Australia' policy to a multicultural and pluralistic profile in the postcolonial age. SBS Television is a typical market for European films, showing seasons of films of interest to different language groups and claiming in one month in 1999 to have reached 94% of Spanish, 92% of Polish, 88% of Greek and 84% of Italian speakers (SBS 1999). Films which reflect the multicultural nature of Europe resonate in countries such as Australia which makes available state funding to reflect its contemporary image of a 'dynamic, evolving society where diversity is embraced as the cultural mainstream' (SBS 2002).

Disjunction and chaos

Life in contemporary Europe involves the familiarity of personal routines, but also the awareness of forces outside our control, 'the influence of distant happenings on proximate events, and on intimacies of the self' (Giddens 1991: 4). Giddens identifies a sense of disorientation as the result of the perception many people have of being 'caught up in a universe of events' which it is impossible to fully understand (1990: 2). Robertson and Appadurai both identify uncertainty and instability as characteristics of globalization. Robertson places the contemporary world in the fifth phase of global density and complexity, starting with a heightened awareness of the Third World in the late 1960s (1990: 26–7). Individuals' conceptions of their identity are rendered more complex through experience of other gender, ethnic and racial identities either on their home territory or through the experience of deterritorialization and constant exposure to global institutions, events and movements. Appadurai identified deterritorialization as one of the central forces of the modern world 'because it brings laboring populations into the lower-class sectors and spaces of relatively wealthy societies', contributing to instability in both the original and new home society and at the core of a variety of fundamentalisms (1999: 301–2). The global cultural flows which he identifies are not unidirectional and impinge on each other in unequal ways.

I will argue that the prevalence of crisis narratives in American and European cinema suggests the psychic importance of making sense of these anxieties. Disjunction and chaos are characteristic of the forces operating in contemporary commercial, financial, cultural and political life. Carl Boggs and Tom Pollard argued that the aftermath of the 9/11 terrorist attacks on the World Trade Centre and the Pentagon started a cycle of US militarism and international terrorism, 'reinforcing conditions of postmodernity exemplified by a world of heightened atomization, chaos, violence, and dystopia – themes that for many years have been salient to postmodern cinema' (2003: 248). The duality which they identify in postmodern cinema derives from the profit motive of large American media conglomerates, whose obsession with the mass markets, necessary to amortize the costs of their blockbusters, leads to formulaic, spectacular films. But the perils of staleness, which the ideological blandness of blockbusters threatens, open up spaces for experimentation, diversification and new influences. Chaos, instability and changing social identities, violence and the hyperreal can also be regarded as the working through of alternatives to conformism and traditional values. In the case of American cinema, ultra violence, conspiracy thrillers, fears of disaster and being taken over by aliens, war films whose mass armies are generated by computer-generated images (CGI), represent some of the expressions of anxiety.

The contemporary cinemas of Europe provide a much more nuanced response to the social and political complexities of globalization and postmodernism, which is characterized by the obsessive revisiting of past history and by visual excess. Omar Calabrese attempts to explain the strong presence of excess, which he identifies as virtuosity, the monstrous and grotesque, violence and disruption, in cultural texts as reflecting a drive to restore complexity and ambiguity and to combat the certainties preferred by those wielding political or economic power. He defines these disruptive and destabilizing elements as neo-baroque, by which he means that they reject the stability, order and closure of modernist and classical works, preferring disruption and open texts. He suggests that they form part of the contemporary postmodern rejection of the grand metanarratives (1992). Both he and Christine Buci-Glucksmann (1994) typify these Baroque elements as co-existing with simple, ordered structures, representing the struggle between conservative social relationships and new ways of making sense of the world. I will argue that the oscillation between disruption and order is expressed narratively, structurally and visually in much European cinema. The huge social and political changes after the Second World War, the political instability which has resulted in changes of government, threatened or actual *coups d'état*, scandals, unexplained bombings, terrorist attacks, threatened or actual civil wars in Europe, corporate malfeasance and, more recently, mass immigration, legal and illegal, from the 'Third World', mean that elements identified as postmodern are visible in European cinema from the late 1940s onwards. Western Europe has a long acquaintance with chaos. This book will take the view that uncertainty and chaos engender interesting films in which the changes and predicaments of contemporary life are rehearsed at a distance.

Methodology

Culture itself is a slippery term among theorists, and John Tomlinson's stress on the importance of its key purpose as 'making life meaningful', individually and collectively (1999: 18), is useful because it allows us to examine films in order to see how they are organized and what meanings are being suggested. This approach is more fruitful in the case of multiple national attributions to a film, or where there is a mismatch between national attribution of director and film, or where the content may be nationally specific but the financing derives from outside Europe. I will, therefore, be giving attention to the commercial and industrial context, as well as to the textual analysis of my chosen examples. In the five years between 1999 and 2003 alone, 4,120 films were produced in 34 countries of Europe. It is impossible to be comprehensive and my choices of films to analyse are inevitably limited to those which interested or intrigued me, and which I have been able to see in the London Film Festival, on the large screen in cinemas, on terrestrial and satellite television, and at other cultural events in the capital. My aim has therefore been to select representative films from my own viewing to illuminate different modes of production, appeal to particular audiences and opportunities to communicate aspects of life in contemporary Europe.

What is European about contemporary European cinema?

In this book I will be addressing different aspects of European cinema in each chapter in order to suggest ways of understanding the contemporary context. The interaction between global and local, the conflicts between nation-state and supra-state organizations and the big business interests of communications corporations will be examined in Chapter One. I will explore the local initiatives of the European Union's film and media programmes to ensure the production, distribution and exhibition of films reflecting contemporary European realities. Contemporary European cinema has to be understood in the context of the EU's MEDIA programme, which has aimed to create a new idea of the cultural and commercial market and its opportunities. As Chapter One will explore, the European Union has played an important role in trying to overcome the difficulties of pan-European cooperation and in attempts to contain the domination of American cinema. The proliferation of languages and cultures within Europe is regarded as a barrier to the full exploitation of the films produced, and Hollywood domination of national cinematic space is considered a threat to cultural expression.

The local, European response to competition from Hollywood will be examined in Chapter Two. The art and authorial film sectors are regarded as quintessentially European areas of production but they have changed considerably in the last 20 years, and I will examine how film theory has attempted to account for this. The release onto the European market in war's aftermath of the backlog of American films had a huge impact on Western European film industries, in particular threatening to swamp national productions in formerly occupied countries. Individual states were not slow to react to the perceived cultural imperialism of Hollywood and successive European governments put in place a series of more or less generous measures to support their national film industries, in the form of tax breaks, production incentives, festivals and prizes. The Cannes film festival was set up in 1946 and has been held annually since 1951; the prestige of its prizes conceals the fact that it has always had a commercial function. State support identified types of cinema which enhanced cultural prestige, although some films now regarded as classics (such as neo-realist films) were held to be undeserving of the approbation of festival judges at the time and to be giving an unfavourable image of the country abroad. A number of state institutions were set up to promote or preserve national production, such as the CNC (Centre National de Cinématographie) in France, the Export-Union of German Cinema in 1954, the National Film Finance Corporation (1949) and the Eady Levy (1950) in Britain, and many national film institutes in Scandinavia. Government support meant a level of political control and the placing of arrangements for financial support under ministerial direction. Besides showing that the establishment of a healthy film industry was not the main priority of recently liberated mainland European countries in the postwar period, these political moves indicate the importance that nation-states attached to a unitary image of national identity in the cinema of the 1950s and 1960s, and the difficulties of imposing or maintaining such ideas in a time of massive social change.

Ironically, the desire to preserve mainly conservative views of national identity, which were expressed in state funding for opportunities to display national creativity, was instrumental in favouring the development of authorial film-making which often challenged the status quo. The inevitably limited funds available supported modestly budgeted films. The consolidation of the European art film sector was also assisted by the growth of an army of critics, specialist journals and magazines to award critical approbation, specialist cinemas and a cineliterate public who were able and willing to appreciate the films. Authorial film-making, developed as a strategy to compete with American cinema, became the cultural space for experimentation with new techniques and ideas, eventually feeding into mainstream, commercial cinema and engendering new waves all over the continent and beyond in the post-Empire world. Chapter Two will challenge accepted definitions of authorial cinema by following the careers of two survivors of the 1950s *politique des auteurs*, Eric Rohmer and Jean-Luc Godard, both of whom have had to adapt to changing global circumstances by maintaining and nurturing their constituency. By concentrating on authorial intention in analysing films, *auteur* theory masked the commercial realities of film-making. By examining the work of Kenneth Branagh, Lars von Trier, Nanni Moretti and Gabriele Salvatores, the contemporary strategy of combining the actor/director/producer role is revealed as a career move to retain artistic control over production, and as emblematic of how to use the available European Union subsidies. Michael Winterbottom's cinema also shows the difficulties of achieving authorial status with a thematically inconsistent filmography.

One result of the internationalizing trends described in preceding sections is the development of quality cinema based on art cinema practice. Chapter Three will show how this sector of the film and media industries evolved and the key roles that television and specialist companies have played in its establishment. The filmographies of established Italian film directors will be used to illustrate the processes by which certain film-makers are identified as competent to deliver complex, spectacular films with international box-office and subsequent exploitation potential. The careers of Lars von Trier and Pedro Almodóvar will be used to illustrate the importance of national and pan-European circumstances, financial opportunities and organizations in the move into the quality film sector. Definitions of quality cinema will also be tested against the spectacular qualities of French *cinema du look*. I will also examine the use of national stereotypes and the cinematic means whereby complexity, disturbance and a sense of risk can be engendered in the face of film industry expectations that big budgets inevitably mean increasingly Americanized, homogeneous and conservative films on the high-concept model (Wyatt 1994).

There exist a number of European films which outclass American films at the box office and whose appeal is exhaustively analyzed in film trade publications in the hope of defining the elements necessary for future success. These films, conceived of as movies for the mass audiences of the global media markets, will be the subject of Chapter Four. Ironically, although they may look like the products of distinctive national traditions, they are very often made with American finance. A feature of globalization is the 'glocal', the product which has been carefully constructed to look local, but which, nonetheless, may be the result of an American corporation's product differentiation in order to reach new markets. Big-budget British and French movies will be examined as 'glocal' products and as evidence of American use of Europe as an R and D (research and development) laboratory, and I will be particularly interested in how European craft expertise (set and costume design, cinematography and CGI) has become an essential factor in these films' success, whereas the fame of European actors generally has not. I will also examine Roberto Benigni's *Pinocchio* (Italy/France/Germany, 2002) as an example of a film which aimed for massive, international success but failed to achieve it.

The attention of Chapter Five will shift to the popular genre films which indicate that European audiences still prefer stories in their own voices. Only from the 1970s onwards have critics, historians and academics researched and given value to popular cinematic forms, in spite of the fact that they have been the bedrock of national production. European cinema colonized those spaces which American cinema could not reach, either because US production was ineligible for European state subventions or because Western European cinema could make money from subjects which the American studios could not touch or low-budget genres reflecting national tastes, aiming to make money in small markets.

European culture is still diffuse, regional and varied, and American economic and political power has not been accompanied by a cultural domination displaying American attitudes and values and, by its pervasive nature, leading to cultural homogenization (Crane 2002: 3). Moreover, the centre-periphery model of cultural transmission, which assumes that there are central, generally accepted ideas of nationhood, politics, myths and stereotypes, is very complex. Chapter Five takes account of the role and power of the film audience, local resistance and complexities. Although power has been attributed to capitalist economic structures in their potential to order human experience via the commodification of cultural artefacts, European nations' insistence on national content and the input of national creative teams in order to qualify for subsidies are key factors in combatting cultural imperialism. Moreover, cultural exchange works both ways. American independent cinema has regularly been influenced by European realism and its new waves and has influenced European cinema in its turn. Creative people talk about each other and to each other. My examples are drawn from German, Italian, Scandinavian and French comedies, British gangster films, Spanish and British excursions into horror, mapping out the typical budgets, audiences and success of these popular genres.

From the statistical evidence, co-production partnerships with television and satellite companies have been life-savers for the European film industries. Chapter Six looks at the opportunities, and drawbacks, of this production model for both sides of the partnership. Television co-production is symptomatic of yet another polarization in Western European media which started in the 1970s when a few key players – Silvio Berlusconi in Italy, Kirch and Bertelsmann in Germany, Havas, Vivendi and Hachette in France – took their lead from American models and started to develop vertically integrated media networks of their own. In doing so they took account of the growth of terrestrial television channels, plans for satellite broadcasting and video technology, which took off in the 1980s. Colour television reduced the visual gap between cinema and TV and rejuvenated TV viewing figures. Commercial television channels developed all over Europe, often making state TV look rather staid. Film production which put itself in competition with Hollywood became increasingly expensive, leading to the evolution of new genres. Big-budget films were therefore obliged to take account of the synergy outlined by Harvey – the marketing of the film as product, and the book, vinyl or CD soundtrack recording, laserdisk, videotape and now DVD as products. At the same time, control of two or more of the production, distribution and exhibition sectors enabled some producers to limit their investment risk. From the late 1970s onwards there have been constant takeovers in the media industries for the above reasons. The traditional breakdown of cinema sectors into production, distribution and exhibition can currently more realistically be conceptualized as media-wide production, distribution and exploitation. The big European media conglomerates have fought over the acquisition of newspaper and book publishers, bought into cinema chains and satellite channels, advertising and PR companies, and engaged in political battles with state and supra-state bodies to ensure favourable legislation for their activities. Western Europe is both an agent in the globalizing process and affected by it.

In the 1990s terrestrial television companies funded increasing numbers of European films, enabling small-scale films exploring European issues and realities to reach a much wider audience than they would have conquered through cinema exhibition alone. Made-for-television films could therefore claim to be central to national production by virtue of their audience reach, while still being peripheral in terms of their recognition at the cinema box office. The aggressive marketing of satellite channels has altered this picture. I will examine the case of Canal Plus and state television channels and the threats and opportunities they offer for experimental and popular film production. Although television provides a space for local stories to be told, legislation limits the diffusion of controversial subjects to specialist channels or late-night slots. A case study examines both the issues which TV films about children allow to be explored and the aims and institutional support for films for children.

Chapter Seven examines the interesting example of the eruption into mainstream cinematic space of representations of the Balkan conflict and how these have evolved to include concerns about mass immigration of populations from Eastern Central Europe. The postmodern legitimation of histories and stories of minority communities has disturbed unitary notions of national identity. In his study of imagined communities, Benedict Anderson suggested that nineteenth-century print language and the dissemination of newspapers and other printed artefacts allowed an emerging bourgeoisie to imagine 'in a general way the existence of thousands and thousands like themselves' (1991: 77). It is doubtful whether there were ever unproblematically accepted notions of national identity. It is common now for ethnic identities to be experienced across borders. European nations contain mixtures of ethnicities, of which the fragmenting of the former Yugoslavia is an extreme case. Britain comprises four nations; regional affiliations are strong and the country has famously absorbed linguistic elements from former invasions and influences from its colonial adventures. Switzerland is a federation of cantons with strong identities and four national languages. Minority languages survive in Britain (Gaelic, Welsh), France (Breton, Basque, Provençal), Switzerland, Spain and so on. With the lessening of the old authorities and ideas of nation and identity, value is given to events and identities at the borderlines, shaking the old certainties of national and gender identity. Globalization theorists identify the persistent presence of local interests as a counterbalance to cultural homogenization and global economic power, although the reasons suggested for the flourishing of local culture vary. On the one hand nation-states resist the perceived threat of global culture by supporting (and even inventing) national traditions, social and ethnic groups. On the other hand, the fragmentation into regional and other identities generates uncertainties about one's place in the national scheme of things, as does the presence on television screens and on national soil of peoples from other countries and cultures. This chapter explores the sorts of narratives which Balkan stories enable and how much of an investment in multiculturalism they reveal. Inevitably in these narratives, *mise-en-scène* and performances show in varying degrees the disjunctive elements typical of cultural texts which attempt to engage with globalization.

Historical films, adaptations of literary texts and films set in a European past are considered to be what Europeans do best and will be the subject of Chapter Eight. Their success, box-office appeal and longevity as marketable products have made them the source of film critics' special fascination. As Julianne Pidduck has observed, recent cinematic costume drama has been 'routinely dismissed by critics, most damningly as an ideologically conservative mirror of glorious national pasts' (2004: 4). In Britain the development and consolidation of the heritage industry identified by John Corner and Sylvia Harvey (1991) raised critical questions about the commodification of historical experience and the suppression of negative aspects of the past. The picturesque aspects of working-class homes and of nineteenth-century industries were stressed, concealing the realities of exploitation and poverty and leading to the criticism that the past was being sanitized in a theme-park concentration on superficial appearances. With their tendency to use historic houses, particularly National Trust properties, British costume dramas, so praised by conservative Prime Minister Margaret Thatcher, were dubbed 'heritage films' or 'the National Trust school of film-making'. However, what makes contemporary costume dramas such interesting sources for analysis is the identification of conflicting discourses within these films which reveal the presence of beliefs about the past and the present.

This chapter will examine two types of costume drama: firstly those which, on the surface, appear to be portraying a static, conservative idea of society and social organization, but where visual richness and visual and performative excess generate disturbances which suggest the considerably more complex interplay of aspirations and beliefs about gender, class and social mobility; secondly, a group of disparate contemporary war films set in the historical past. By definition, war films are conflict narratives, pitting representative characters against each other. The violence and chaotic worlds of war films are the counterpart of the visual and performative excess of the gentler family dramas examined in the first half of the chapter. As Guy Westwell has observed, war films have many functions, providing opportunities to rehearse different political positions, moral choices, questions of identity and gender, and 'one of the primary ways in which past wars are recalled, re-enacted and rescripted' (2006: 113). In analyzing some recent European war films, I am particularly interested to explore re-evaluations of historical conflicts in the light of current experience and changes in the formation of cultural memory. In the period after 11 September 2001 these European films work through conflicting discourses about military and civil power, and it is possible to identify critical perceptions of the military violence which accompanies economic globalization.

In a final case study, Irish cinema is the subject of Chapter Nine. The Republic of Ireland has been chosen as an example of a small European country which has been particularly successful in carving out a cultural space for the growth, maintenance and survival of its film industry, but its relationships with the province of Ulster, which is part of the United Kingdom, cannot be divorced from this study. My aim is to apply the categories explored in previous chapters to Irish cinema to obtain a snapshot of its distinctiveness. The effects of local legislation in attracting big-budget productions, the accessing of European Union and UK subsidies, auteur and quality cinema, popular genres and partnerships with television will be examined, much of which is also marked by the push and pull of conflicting interpretations of a complex history.

Conclusion

European cinema has always sought to play to its strengths – national stereotypes, characteristic landscapes, cultural traditions, high-culture texts, exotic stars, a rich creative cinematic tradition. Globalization has been perceived as both a threat and an opportunity. It is difficult for European films to find a place in their own market and thus act as part of the consciousness formation of its populations. At the same time the fragmentation and small size of European film industries have provided a space for creative experimentation and renewal. Although European cinema is still typified as a collection of national cinemas, contemporary European films are more global in their subject matter and funding arrangements than in the past, reflecting the circumstances of life in the late twentieth and early twenty-first centuries. Successful film-makers, cinematographers and writers, however, find a lucrative career difficult in Europe and have been absorbed into Hollywood. Lasse Hallström, Julio Amenábar, Ridley and Tony Scott, Michael Apted, Jean-Jacques Annaud, Vittorio Storaro have all revitalized Hollywood film by inflecting standard genre forms with their European sensibility. The production models and genres which will form the subject of the following chapters allow tensions between the global and the local to be brought into the open and the parameters observed. The activities of the European Union provide an example of cultural flows which sweep in the opposite direction to American corporate media culture and their potential to help or hinder European film production will be explored in the next chapter.

chapter one

European cinema at the barricades

European nations have reacted differently to what is perceived as the cultural imperialism of American film and media, sometimes putting in place quotas to protect the domestic industry, generally favouring tax breaks and subsidies, but often still courting American investment at the same time. The European film industries currently present the paradoxical situation of having, or choosing, to take account of the European Union's MEDIA programme, which encourages cross-border collaboration, while still legislating on a national level for favourable conditions for their domestic industries. There are multiple tensions between the overarching, global industrial practices of multinational media corporations, the globalizing forces of the European Union, and the national and the regional. National and pan-European measures to support European cinema are effectively barricades erected to ward off predatory exploitation by strong global media interests. This chapter will examine the nature of the threat and will outline and assess the national and EU mechanisms aimed at building and maintaining strong European film industries. Knowledge and understanding of the support available provides a bigger picture of the work which film-makers have to do to get films made and seen and is essential to understanding the different production niches of European cinema.

The global reach of Hollywood

What is Hollywood now? Since the 1960s, protectionist measures by the Motion Picture Association of America (MPAA),[1] as well as the language and look of European films, have limited their access to North American markets while the big, vertically integrated American studios adopted aggressive policies of ensuring markets for their own films. From the 1920s to the 1960s the American majors[2] could cover the costs of a mid-budget film production during its US distribution, sales to overseas markets representing the icing on the cake. Rising production costs coupled with expansionist business practices meant that the European markets (and now the lucrative markets of the tiger economies of Asia) were crucial for the generation of profits (Miller et al 2001: 4–5). European films still have difficulty in gaining access to North American markets, although most nation-states have flirted with measures to tap into American distribution networks.

The Hollywood majors have transformed since the 1960s and now consist of Sony

(Sony Classic, Columbia Tristar), Time Warner (Warner Bros, New Line, Fine Line, Turner Classic), Disney (and its distribution arm, Buena Vista; and until recently Miramax), Fox, Viacom (Paramount), Universal, MGM. These are vertically integrated multinational corporations, controlling production, financing and distribution of a variety of media, the majority of whose interests may not be in film production. They have their own worldwide distribution channels, enabling them to dominate the cinema industry. In 2001 they were credited with generating $8,413 million of US film revenue and $3,859 million of European film revenue (Lange and Westcott 2004: 165). Almost half their income therefore derives from Europe. Embedded as they are in multinational corporations, coupled with their rich assets of portfolios of film and media rights, the majors have constant access to lines of credit. From the late 1990s they have increasingly taken advantage of 'substantial financial flows' from European funds, tax incentive schemes and deals with European banks (Lange and Westcott 2004: 165). A wide release in the USA can involve 3,500 screens, and exceptionally up to 7,000, and marketing budgets reflect this. Lange and Westcott give the average cost of a film released by the seven US majors in 2002 as $30.6 million (2004: 159).

Although large independent production companies and distributors do exist, most independent production is low to mid budget and relies on the majors for distribution. Since the late 1990s, however, there has been a significant power shift away from the majors due to the increase in split-rights deals, in which international rights to exploit American films are allocated to non-MPAA distributors, and to the increasing power of sales agents (*Screen International*, 28 July 2000: 6). The American Film Marketing Association (AFMA) is not restricted to US sales agents and its members sell to television, video and DVD as well as earning theatrical revenues. Europe is now considered an integral part of an American film's financing and release, allowing vast advertising budgets to achieve maximum impact, and returns, within a short space of time. By contrast, European films cost a fraction of an American film's advertising budget alone, are financed by often precarious packages of funds from a variety of sources, and have limited access to distribution and exhibition channels dominated by the American majors. European successes have to be seen in the context of the global domination of US media interests.

American cinema dominates European cinemas (the traditional exhibition sector), the small screen, the video shop and the racks of DVDs. It is tempting to regard American cinema as the ghost at the feast when discussing contemporary European cinema. In fact, as Ib Bondebjerg says, the ghost has its feet well and truly tucked under the table, for the mass media audience is not concerned whether American media pose a threat, 'but simply accepts the American way of life and its culture as something fundamental and well-known' (2001: 55). American narratives are the *lingua franca* of cultural globalization.

European national and pan-national concerns coincided in 1993 in the negotiations at the Uruguay round of the General Agreement on Tariffs and Trade (GATT) when Europeans campaigned for the exclusion of film and audio-visual products from the agreement. The lobbying of the MPAA had resulted in American claims that films 'were merely commercial products', whereas the French led the European opposition, claiming 'that film quotas were a legitimate means of cultural protection' (Ulff-Møller 2001: 107). The European Parliament enshrined the freedom of action in the sphere of audio-visual policy in its Resolution of 18 November 1999, in which it reiterated the European audio-visual sector's special role in sustaining cultural pluralism, drawing the lines for subsequent standoffs between what is perceived as the American capitalist view and the European belief that film and audio-visual products perform a cultural service for a healthy economy, freedom of expression and cultural diversity. The difference between the two philosophies or ideologies can be summed up in the position of the American, multinational corporations which wish to expand their operations while limiting those of another continent, and the position of the European Union which has opened up its MEDIA programme to European countries which are currently outside the EU, but which are considered to be an integral part of the European audio-visual area. This epitomizes the commercial versus the cultural remit of the parties concerned.

Opposing philosophies and semantic fields continue to generate contemporary divisions between the USA and Europe in the audio-visual sphere. The recent development of simultaneous film release in the North American and European markets confirms Kevin Robins' claim that the multinational, 'Eurovision' zone is treated in terms of a local marketing segment by global media companies (1997: 33). However, as he points out, 'local' is perceived differently in the corporate lexicon than it is 'in the regions and small nations of Europe' where the particular, difference and diversity are seen as precious commodities worthy of being defended (1997: 37). This could, of course, happen only once American companies had succeeded in dominating the distribution sector in most European countries, effectively relegating local distributors to small niche markets (for American as well as non-American films). This is the contemporary situation against which European media institutions have to be seen. This chapter will start to explore the European film market and consider the idea of audio-visual space as political metaphor for the operation of cultural power.

How big is the market and who are the main players?

The population of the 15 post-1995 member countries of the European Union is over 380 million, slightly larger than that of the USA. A market containing countries with a high national gross national product (GNP), it has been attractive to large media companies and US companies in particular have bought into the film distribution sector in order to ensure maximum exploitation of American films. In economic terms, the size of the audio-visual market of the 25 states (15 plus the new accession states of Eastern Central Europe) of the EU was estimated as €104,790 million in 2003 (EAO 2005/1: 31).[3] This estimate included public television and radio broadcasters, private television companies, home shopping, pay-TV premium companies, TV packagers, thematic channels, film theatre gross box office, VHS software, DVD software, records and leisure software.

There are several geographical spheres in which European companies operate with competence and success, making an advantage of the linguistic differences usually considered a barrier to competitiveness. The German language has a large satellite 'footprint' in Central Europe, and markets in Germany, Austria and parts of Switzerland. Italian film production has markets in Italy, Switzerland, Italian diaspora communities worldwide, Spain and South America through Mediaset's satellite interests, and a history of co-production agreements with France. Although the sheer size and global presence of the US film and media industries leads that country to be perceived as dominating worldwide cultural economies, there are in fact many other global players in the media and information sectors.

The EAO statistics implicitly chart typical characteristics of the global capitalist economy, showing the cycles of new media launch, exploitation and decline. In this unstable situation of frenetic activity to develop new media, saturate the market and move on, Coopers and Lybrand predicted in 1992 that four scenarios for development of the European film industry were possible, resulting in varying levels of domination by North America (1992: 28–31). If the European film industries did not work together, then a reduction in government funding would result in increased US dominance and reduced production and audiences for European films. Without pan-European integration, but with increased local funding, US dominance would continue but the output of European low-budget films would increase. Yet significant integration would at worst hold US dominance at bay and at best challenge it. Some European majors would emerge and the production and distribution cycles would become more commercial. In the event, greater coordination of funding and cross-border initiatives in the last 14 years has resulted in the emergence of European majors and a greater commercial culture. However, US dominance still obtains and the allure of the markets of Eastern Central Europe has led to increased competition between the USA and Europe.

European majors are in constant danger of being absorbed into US conglomerates when they become too successful. By adopting American business practices they become visible and recognizable to US multinationals, which then seek to pick them off. In 1995 the main European players were ARD (Germany), PolyGram (Netherlands); KirchMedia (Germany), Bertelsmann (Germany), Thorn EMI (UK), while the world's top-20 multimedia groups included Bertelsmann, Havas (France), Matra Hachette (France), PolyGram, Thorn EMI, BBC (UK), CLT (Luxembourg), Fininvest (Italy). European television companies featured large in the ranking of world-leading audio-visual companies (EAO 1997: 51–5). The spate of mergers and bankruptcies since 1995 has pushed European companies down the list, below the Disney Corporation, Viacom, Time Warner, Sony, News Corporation and NBC. However, European companies have fought back with Vivendi (which owns Canal Plus) and Bertelsmann remaining major players in spite of corporate and financial difficulties, and Lagardère Média having a dominant position in broadcasting, cable and publishing (EAO 2005/1: 27). Terrestrial television companies have diversified and moved into satellite and service industries in order to play to the strengths of European national media in a global context.

The European media industries are given depth by the presence of many large to medium-size companies whose specialist knowledge of local markets gives them an important position in each nation's cultural space. However, the fragmentation of the distribution sector in particular into many companies, each with a market specialism, is regarded as one of Europe's weaknesses (Hoskins et al 1997: 63–4). Whereas the vertically integrated US majors each have a distribution network which enables them to carry large production slates of films which then reach exhibitors, the fragmentation of European production and distribution means that specialist knowledge is not shared and much effort is wasted as individual companies negotiate the rights to different parts of European territories.

Although overall the audio-visual sector has grown 1.9% from 2002, there are interesting fluctuations within it. The pay-TV sector is currently in gentle decline. The gross theatrical film box office, which in 1999 was €4,393 million (compared with €5,835 million for VHS rental and retail video), gradually increased to a high of €5,624 million in 2002, but declined by 5.3% to 5,326 million in 2003. In the same period the VHS market, which peaked in 2000, dramatically declined to €2,810 million, a decrease of 39.3% on 2002. The DVD market has grown by 40–50% a year and now stands at €9,014 million.

Behind these statistics lies evidence of the instability of the media markets worldwide. The first DVD players came on the market in Europe in 1997 and it has rapidly become possible to bypass the regional chip in a DVD player. In effect big global media interests were seeking to maximize profits by dividing exploitation rights into world sectors. In doing so they ignored one of the facets of globalization, that is, the transnational spread of language or cultural groups and the power of the internet to satisfy demand across the artificially created zones of North America (region 1), Europe (region 2) and Australasia (region 4). The number of language subtitle options available on a DVD provides evidence that distribution companies have to assess possible sales before negotiating the rights to exploit a film on DVD in several territories. The vertically integrated French company Gaumont has had a policy of making films by established directors and exploiting them in depth. Francesco Rosi's *Carmen* (France/Italy, 1984) has had a lifespan of over 20 years, first on celluloid, through many video windows (from rental, sell-through, premium satellite, terrestrial broadcasters, low-budget cable and satellite companies, budget re-releases), on videodisk, and released on DVD in the early 2000s with 20 language subtitle options.

European distributors would also benefit from the digitization of cinema through the saving of the costs of providing celluloid copies for the exhibition sector and through the digital format's possibility of multilingual and multisound support (Perretti and Negro 2003: 206–10). The production sector would benefit from speedier access to markets, but contemporary wrangles indicate that the exhibition sector is unwilling to shoulder the burden of re-equipping film theatres which, for the USA alone, was estimated to cost the equivalent of around 73% of total gross revenue from cinema exhibition. As with all new technologies, progress is likely to be both slower and more complex than its promoters claim. The difficulties of arriving at a pan-European consensus indicate that the size of the European media market works to the advantage of American media interests. European production is also at a disadvantage because it mainly takes place in small companies without the cushion of financial resources or large corporate structures.

Structures of the European film industries

Up until the later 1970s, it was relatively easy to determine how a Western European film was made, how much it might have cost and its box office returns. Eastern Europe was another matter as it lay outside the capitalist system of supply and demand. Film production is a high-risk business and all production areas devise strategies for the limitation of the risk involved in high investment over several weeks or months on a promise of financial return perhaps a year later. For commercial cinema, this might involve analysis of statistics of the success of previous productions involving particular genres, stars, directors, screenwriters and cinematographers. For art cinema, an additional calculation of film festival impact, prizes and state subsidy might be involved.

If a production company decided to self-finance a film, 'all the risk of the project is borne by the production company' (Lange and Westcott 2004: 157). Film production was more generally financed by a combination of bank loans, private investment and investment by distributors on the basis of assessment of future revenue (the 'advance on receipts'). As Lange and Westcott have detailed, involving commercial lenders in film financing follows the model of obtaining pre-sale agreements in determined markets from distributors and TV companies as a condition to the finance package. Once the finished film is in the market, the rights on additional, secondary markets or windows of exploitation can be sold, the loan being repaid from these earnings (2004: 158). As Gillian Doyle explains, once a film starts to earn money:

> The cinema-owner takes a cut directly from the gross box-office receipts to cover the costs of running the venue. After deduction of these expenses ... the remainder is divided between the exhibitor and the distributor. ... but the exact terms on which net box-office receipts are shared between the cinema and the distributor vary according to the film, the duration of the theatrical run and other circumstances. The 'distributor's gross' goes back to the distributor, who deducts commission and costs, including all advertising and promotional costs. Anything left after this is then passed on to the equity investors or financiers who have covered production costs, and who deduct a premium for covering risks ... Finally, any profit remaining goes back to the producer and (if appropriate) the production studio.
>
> (2002a: 108–9)

This was the model for Western European film production which, modified, still obtains today and it is easy to see that, since the majority of a film's costs are incurred in its production stages, investors might be wary of venturing into the industry. Putting together the financial package for a European film involves hedging risk, usually by accessing several sources of funding, such as tax incentive schemes, national public support, and considering entering into co-production agreements. Assembling these often complex packages of financing constitutes part of the development stage, which now implies substantial costs in terms of work time, legal fees and interest on loans. Producers generally include their fee in the film's initial budget, otherwise there would be no incentive ever to make films. A feature of the last 15 years has been the rise in importance of the sales agent who puts together significant amounts of a film's budget by arranging foreign sales. The bulk of the $19.8 million budget for *Gosford Park* (Robert Altman, UK/USA/Germany/Italy, 2001) was generated by foreign sales deals arranged by Jane Barclay and Sharon Harel at London's Capitol Films, but these were predicated on the domestic, North American deal, which

Altman had to put together by drawing on his personal contacts (Hofmann 2002: 11). The film went on to make an estimated $87.7 million worldwide, but would not have got off the ground without sales agent input. That the role has become increasingly important can be judged from Nielsen EDI's 2005 Gold Reel Award for surpassing $100 million in the non-US box office in the last year, indicating that there is a 'growing category of films for which US box office is almost an irrelevancy' (Gubbins 2005). *Kingdom of Heaven* (Ridley Scott, UK/Spain/USA/Germany, 2005) cost approximately $130 million and generated box-office gross of $47 million in the USA and $152 million in non-US territories and is one of several historical epics in the Gold Reel category, which includes *King Arthur* (Antoine Fuqua, USA/Ireland/UK, 2004), *Alexander* (Oliver Stone, France/USA/UK/Germany/Netherlands, 2004) and *Troy* (Wolfgang Petersen, USA/Malta/UK, 2004). All of these are films whose big budgets ($150–190 million) involve complex packages of funding, justifying the fees of sales agents. *Bridget Jones: The Edge of Reason* (Beeban Kidron, UK/France/Germany/Ireland/USA, 2004) made more money in the UK than in the USA and is clearly packaged as an international film. The IMDb (Internet Movie Database, www.imdb.com) and Lumiere (http://lumiere.obs.coe.int) figures for gross box-office returns do not, of course, tell the whole picture of video/DVD retail and rental income, games sales and television pre-sales. Television can also act as producer, distributor and/or exhibitor.

Most European production companies do not have the resources of the American majors, which are able to bear the costs of a slate of six fairly unsuccessful productions through the financial success of one blockbuster. Large budgets are not necessarily the answer for European cinema; revenue might not amount to much more than the production cost. Terry Ilott's case study of the commercial journey of *Il ladro di bambini* (*The Stolen Children*, Gianni Amelio, Italy, 1992), a low-budget film, concludes that, although it made 'a very respectable return for its investors' and could not have been cheaper, it needed additional marketing support to generate extra income from international markets (1996: 95–100). It repaid its Eurimages loan and subsequently profited from an Entreprise de l'Audiovisuel Européen (EAVE) grant for video distribution. The tiny budget ($2 million) even covered Amelio's well-known slow-shooting strategy, resulting in a visually interesting, well-plotted film whose narrative premise of following the protagonists (a young carabiniere, a 13-year-old girl who has been prostituted by her mother, and her brother) down the Italian peninsula allowed contemporary social problems to be laid bare and for Amelio to comment on the state of Italy. However, the ideal for European productions has to be represented by *The Full Monty* (Peter Cattaneo, UK, 1997), which covered its costs many times over.

The key players in financing a contemporary European film are therefore the commercial bank, the completion guarantor (who confirms the budget in order to issue the insurance policy and adds contingencies in view of any risks involved), the sales agent (who represents the producer in negotiating distribution for various territories, charging a commission on sales), the distribution company (which purchases rights for each territory where it has planned to exploit the film in cinemas or TV), TV channels, collection agents (contracted to producers and sales agents to maximize income), private investors and lawyers (Lange and Westcott 2004: 160–10).

The cycles of exploitation of a film vary from country to country (Italy has a window for sales to daily and monthly newspapers for example), but the general pattern is for a film to have a release in the exhibition sector, then video/DVD sales and rental, pay-TV window, free-to-air TV, terrestrial and cable syndication, relicensing and archive exploitation. These windows of exploitation make it much more difficult to assess the success of a contemporary European film on the basis of the box-office receipts alone. And, for researchers, much of the information which might be supplied by the above players is regarded as commercially sensitive and therefore made difficult to access. In contrast, national funding mechanisms, mainly funded by the state from their tax payers, are models of transparency and will be considered next.

National initiatives

Uncertainty has been a constant feature of film-making in Europe and a raft of support for national film industries has characterized the sector. All those involved in the industry are adept at playing 'the system'.

National support for the film industry started in the 1930s with the coming of sync sound, the majority of funds being set up after the Second World War. It includes the pan-national support of alliances based on language and/or geography. In the contemporary situation these national funding mechanisms play an absolutely crucial role in complementing those of the MEDIA programme. In the arcane language of the European Union, 'subsidiarity' refers to the practice of encouraging nations or national enterprises to match or complement funding from MEDIA. The majority of funds derive from state funding, with other income from taxes on television, cinema receipts and, in the case of the UK, over 90% derived from the National Lottery (EAO 2002/3: 103).

Catherine Bizern and Anne-Marie Autissier identified several phases in the postwar development of aid to the film industry (1998). The first wave of regional development occurred in the 1980s, then the emergence of aid for audio-visual production, marked by measures to balance economic and cultural aspects of the film industry in the 1990s. The postmodern unpicking of the centralizing tendency of monolithic nationalism and the consequent valorizing of alternative cultural identities can be observed in these measures. Cultural arguments are overwhelmingly behind national governments' allocation of tax payers' money to the film industries and usually include the defence of minority languages and culture, the necessity of speaking with one's own voice about the contemporary world, the employment potential of national film production and the advantages of a healthy national economy. The larger European nations have devolved funds to regional bodies, such as the *Länder* in Germany, the National Arts Councils in the UK and the *Départements* in France. However, the older and traditional form of conduit for supporting the film industry is the administratively and financially independent national public body. The French CNC was set up in 1945 with financial independence based on levies on the income of various branches of the industry (EAO 2004/3: 94). Film institutes channel support in Austria (Österreichisches Film Institut), Denmark (Danske Filminstitutet), Sweden (Svenska Filminstitutet), Spain (Instituto del Cinematografia y de las Artes Audio-visuales) and

Portugal (Instituto do Cinema, Audio-visual e Multimédia). Other countries have autonomous public bodies to oversee funding and development: the German Filmföderungsanstalt, the Irish Film Board, the Film Funds of Iceland, Norway and the Netherlands, the Polish Film Production Agency, and so on. The European Union's Korda database also gives details of pan-European film organizations. In addition to the MEDIA programme and Eurimages described below, the Nordisk Film and TV Fund reflects the interests of Denmark, Sweden, Norway, Finland and Iceland, the Agence Intergouvernementale de la Francophonie supports France's postcolonial networks and diasporas, and Ibermedia links Spanish and Portuguese-speaking countries in Europe and Latin America, joined in 2001 by the Baltic-Russian Development Fund for Documentaries and from 2003, the Balkan Fund.

In 2002 public funding of the film and audio-visual industry in the 30 countries of Europe amounted to €1,162,230,000, of which €1,084,169,000 was devoted to the 15 older EU countries (EAO 2004/3: 96). These sums have to be put into context – 623 films were produced in the 15 countries of the EU in 2004. The majority of European films have small budgets, the average being about $4 million. With the exception of the UK, this average has not increased greatly since 1991, whereas production budgets of the US majors increased exponentially from $25 million to over $60 million by 2003. The combination of the predominance of small companies and the small size of the public funds available has encouraged an increase in the production of low-budget films, the effect of which can be judged from Figure 1.1.

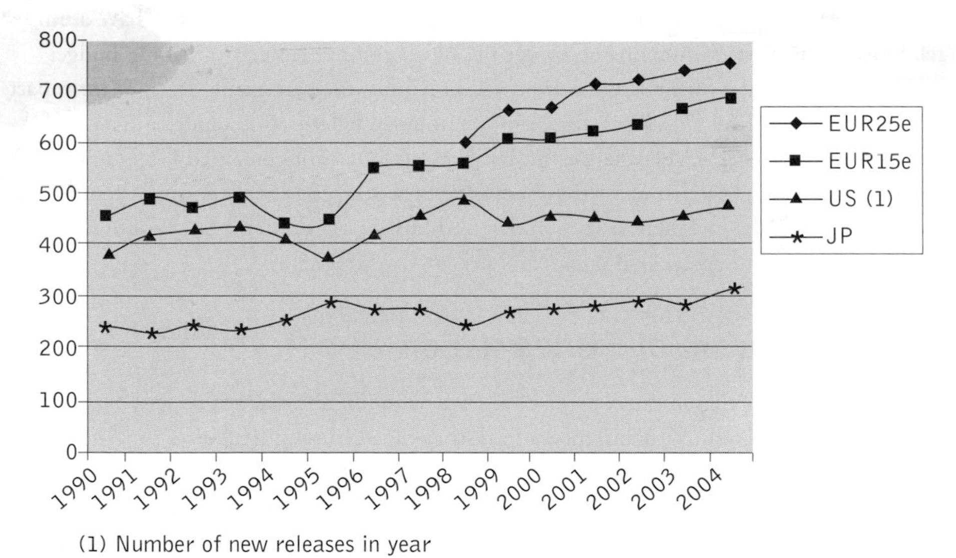

Figure 1.1 Number of feature films produced in the European Union, Japan and the USA, 1990–2004

Source: European Audiovisual Observatory Yearbook 2005/3: 14

In 2004, 449 American films were in distribution in Europe, the majority of them being big-budget films, released with multiple prints on the circuits controlled by the majors and profiting from the publicity campaigns already devised for their North American release, with some tweaking for local conditions.

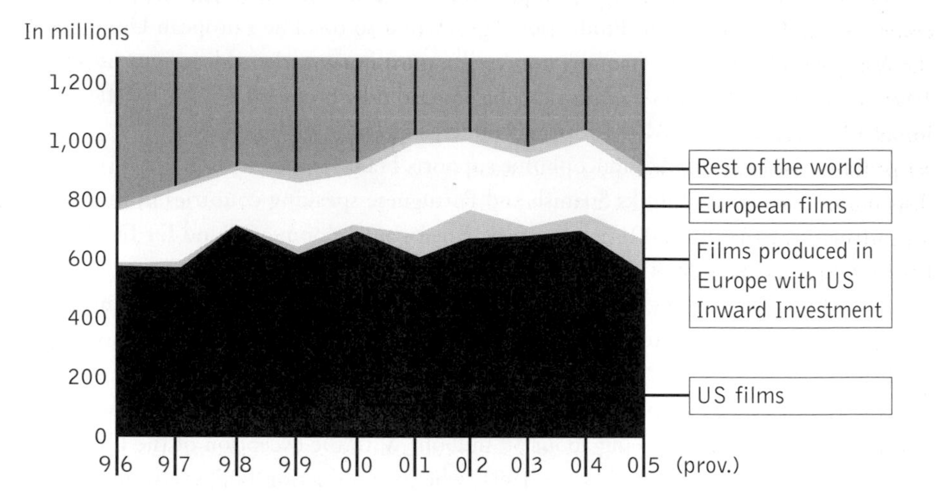

Figure 1.2 Admissions in the European Union, 1996–2005
Source: European Audiovisual Observatory *Focus 2006: World Film Market Trends*

By contrast, an increasing number of low- to mid-budget European films have a limited release, sometimes with only one or two prints. They compete directly with big-budget American films in the prime, city-centre cinemas. Unless they are genre films, or form part of a popular series (the *Taxi* films, for example), their publicity campaign is a one-off and may not even be repeated in other territories if the film has not generated foreign sales. Figures 1.1 and 1.2 together show that buoyant European production does not result in increased market share. The next section describes institutional attempts to address European films' poor returns on public and private investment.

The development of EU legislation

The EU's MEDIA programme consists of a series of funding initiatives designed to strengthen the European film and media industries by addressing structural problems and encouraging media professionals to think in pan-European terms. Since the end of the 1980s and the beginning of the 1990s the European Union has taken decisive steps to support the European television, film and media industries. This was, of course, not just as a result of the year-by-year decrease in the box-office share of European films in each national cinematic space, although that was one of the signs that intervention was necessary. The impetus derived both from European Union commitment to support minority cultures and languages and from the big European commercial interests, reflecting the symbolic significance of film as a cultural text and the desire not to be left behind in the digital age (Hoskins et al 1997: 3). The programme, devised in four phases, has been ambitious and although compared with US production budgets the funds available have been small, their effect has been considerable (in spite of criticisms).

The pilot phase of the MEDIA programme ran from 1986 to 1990, involving 2,000 companies and organizations to prepare MEDIA-financed projects which were accepted by the European Commission in 1990. In the next phase 12 projects, to run from 1991 to 1995, were initiated, 'valued at 200 million ecus (£140 million)' (Jäckel 2003: 68). The initial 12 projects included support for film development and production (the European script fund, animation production, documentary, and the use of archive material), distribution (assistance with a cinema or video release, presence at film festivals and support for independent film circuits), dubbing and subtitling, professional training and the MEDIA Business School. An additional seven projects were added to support exhibition (Media Salles, EUROPA CINEMAS, and EFA, European film awards), the stimulation of financial investment, conservation and restoration of films, development and production (Jäckel 2003: 68–9).

A flavour of the work which had to be done can be gained from the report in 2001 by Jens Rykaer, the President of Media Salles, in which he describes their first task as mapping out the European cinema exhibition sector (2001: 1). This had never been done before. The resulting yearbook deals with all aspects of the cinema exhibition sector, a database of films and their distributors, and a network of cinemas specializing in showing children's films, the Euro Kids Network. Through the subsequent MEDIA programmes, Media Salles developed its promotion of European films at industry conventions and started training events for cinema exhibitors. Funds also became available for the updating and safety elements of film theatres. The MEDIA Business School in Madrid was set up in answer to pressures for more training and research resulting from EAVE workshops for the training of young entrepreneurs (Vicente Gomez 1990: 7). An early example of the usefulness of MEDIA funds can be seen in initial phases of *Rob Roy* (Michael Caton-Jones, USA, 1995). Development funding from the Scottish Film Production Fund (£15,000) and British Screen (£5,000), and a repayable loan from MEDIA's SCRIPT fund (£12,000), were crucial to the writing phase, and together with the attendance by the producer, Peter Broughan, at an EAVE workshop all enabled the progressive refining of the project as a big-budget, international production (Finney 1996a: 192–202). Thus, although these national and European subventions enabled the project to get off the ground, providing work in Europe, it is clear that, in *Rob Roy*'s case, they also provided cheap pre-production funding for a US film.

The MEDIA programme was reviewed and modified in 1995 and MEDIA II was put in place to run from 1996 to 2000 with a larger budget, reduced number of projects, but a continued remit of training, development and transnational distribution. It was also enlarged to include the countries of Eastern Central Europe and the islands of Cyprus and Malta. Addressing the problem of the small size and precarious existence of European media companies, the 'slate funding' mechanism was launched in 1999. This aimed to build up the overall profile of film companies chosen from independent production companies 'with a proven track record of developing and producing projects with potential to sell on the international marketplace' by entering into a medium-term relationship (*MEDIA Programme*

Newsletter 2000: 15). What the 40-odd companies chosen all share is an active production profile and plans to diversify their operations, but they are as varied as the sector itself. A Lab (the Netherlands) was a group of five independent companies creating a vertically integrated structure to make documentary and TV drama; Alia Film (Italy) planned to make art-house films and TV drama, while Fandango (Italy) would make TV series for Berlusconi's Mediaset companies and continue to make feature films. Several companies associated with well-known directors and producers such as Revolution Films (Michael Winterbottom), X Filme Creative Pool (Tom Tykver), Zentropa Entertainments (Lars von Trier, Peter Aalbæck), Working Title 2 (Tim Bevan and Eric Fellner), Cargo Films (Jean-Jacques Beneix) planned higher-budget, international feature films. Companies associated with television planned to increase production and include features. Documentary production and its pan-European distribution featured in many plans, the results of which, such as *Être et avoir* (Nicolas Philibert, France, 2002) have had an impact with theatrical as well as TV release. From the 1950s onwards, many medium- to large-size European film companies had gained a high level of professional expertise in developing varied annual slates of films, hedging the risks of art film production with popular genres. The progressive domination of European distribution and exhibition by US interests had made the varied slate more difficult to achieve, but slate funding to a very limited number of companies was hardly likely to address the causes of the problem.

The report detailing the number and scale of the productions and interventions supported by MEDIA II justified the continuation of the programme from January 2001 to December 2005 with a budget of €400 million (£240 million) (Jäckel 2003: 75). The parallel MEDIA training programme was given a budget of €50 million. The MEDIA Plus programme increased the funds available for development and included promotion as well as distribution. Coordinating information and arrangements for the transition to digital technology was also a prime concern. It is interesting at this stage to see what the report identified as the main problems facing European cinema. There was more emphasis on the commercial viability of applications, although the difficult economic conditions of the period were acknowledged. These included an economic crisis characterized by increased difficulty in gaining access to finance following the world slowdown in growth after the events of 11 September 2001 (*COM(2003) 725 final*: 4–6). This was compounded by the development of cheap television programming (reality shows and national fiction) and the consequent reduction in the number of European films pre-financed by television. The structural difficulties still giving cause for concern included insufficient attention to project development (writing, financial packaging and drawing up the marketing plan); the very diversity of European regions which inhibited the movement of films outside regional spaces; the 'dichotomy between countries with low production capacity and/or a restricted linguistic and geographical area, where production volume is naturally limited by the size of their markets; and countries where production capacity (production volume in relation to the population) exceeds that of others' (*COM(2003) 725 final*: 5). To this were added concerns about the much lower levels of investment and public support in the film industries of the ten Eastern Central European countries shortly to join the EU. The fragmentation of the distribution sector along national lines was also identified as a factor in the competitive disadvantage of European distributors compared with American film distributors.

Having identified the structural problems of European cinema, MEDIA Plus targeted the specific weaknesses listed above, aiming to make interventions in areas which would complement national funding opportunities. The programme also included incentives to work with European countries not yet members of the EU, European Free Trade Association (EFTA) countries and Turkey, and co-production arrangements with non-European countries if this would enhance the work's prestige. Industry pressures insisted that the funds disbursed, although small in comparison with American film and promotion budgets, be regularly checked against their objectives. The European Audiovisual Observatory's monitoring of the operations of the different MEDIA Plus funds appeared to confirm their success, judged by the increasing number of applications and the high rate of entry into production of supported projects. EU bureaucrats hailed the number of projects which the MEDIA Plus had been unable to support as an indicator of success because it showed the increased awareness of the programme, whereas industry professionals bemoaned it as proof that the budgets were too low to achieve the objectives of training and cooperation. MEDIA disbursements were intensively debated in the trade press, with impassioned criticism of the high level of red tape which often resulted in budgets not being spent (Drinnan 2001: 1–2). The emphasis of training events on considering the European dimension generated a perceptible increase in co-production agreements or cross-border partnerships. The report also recommended raising ceilings on the percentage of MEDIA Plus aid to reflect changes in the industry, such as the significant increase in the number of copies required for a film's launch.

Monitoring the results of disbursements enabled MEDIA to identify a slow-burn effect often overlooked by administrators seeking immediate outcomes from funding. The writer/director of *Summer – 27 Missing Kisses* (Nana Djordjadze, Germany, 2000) met her producer, Jens Meurer, during a MEDIA programme in 1994–95 and they started working on a feature film which was polished during an Ateliers of European Cinema (ACE) event. At an EAVE event in 1998, the associate producer won the support of the Filmstifting Berlin-Brandenburg and a MEDIA development loan to Egoli Films enabled it to complete pre-production and financing. Constant seed funding enabled the small production company to diversify from documentaries and after another EAVE training, Egoli Films became part of the pan-European DNET consortium responsible for a digital catalogue of documentaries (*MEDIA Programme Newsletter* 2000: 6).

Film industry professionals might be thinking transnationally, but European public awareness of the MEDIA programme as a guarantee of quality and Europeanness has been slow. There may be some knowledge of the increase in 'world cinema' in video/DVD shops, but even those drawn to those shelves would be unlikely to know the meaning of the different logos on the back of their videos or DVDs, or even wonder at the presence of Maurizio Nichetti's *Ladri di Saponette* (*The Icycle Thief*, Italy, 1988) (subtitling supported by EVE), Eric Rohmer's *L'Anglaise et le Duc* (*The Lady and the Duke*, France, 2001) (support for distribution) and *Goodbye Lenin* (Wolfgang Becker, Germany/UK, 2003).

The MEDIA Plus programme, scheduled to end on 31 December 2005, was extended to the end of 2006 in order for a full evaluation to inform funding of MEDIA 2007. The MEDIA 2007 phase continues to target the pre- and post-production phases, but takes account of technological changes resulting from digitization and the need to bring professional practice in the ten new member states up to the level of the rest. A number of objectives are supported, including the training of professionals, funds for the development phase, the encouragement of a European perspective to facilitate the wider national exploitation of non-national European films (N-NEs), international exploitation (subtitling, festivals) and automatic funds for promotion packages including a subtitled copy, an international soundtrack of music and effects, and promotion materials. Distribution is perceived to be key to supporting European cultural diversity and a fundamental aim of MEDIA 2007 is the implementation of a European distribution strategy (*COM/2004/0470 final*: 5) to address the weaknesses highlighted in Figure 1.1. The aim is to put in place structures for coordinated marketing by distributors, sales agents, producers and exhibitors and includes funding for catalogues of works with high cultural but lower commercial potential. The MEDIA Plus and MEDIA training programmes are subsumed within MEDIA 2007, strengthening the centralization of the programme. The initial budget is €1,055 million for the period 1 January 2007 to 31 December 2013.

Besides giving a useful overview of the size and functioning of the audio-visual industries to those of us outside them, the statistics gathered by the European Audiovisual Observatory provide valuable information to industry professionals on the size of national markets and the types of films which are popular within them. The collection of figures on the market share of non-national films in each national market, the number of co-productions and details of the countries involved allow the Commission to assess the effectiveness and relevance of its financial interventions, and the MEDIA desks networks provide information about national support and its interaction with EU support.

Co-production agreements and Eurimages

In addition to the European Commission's MEDIA programmes, the European Union's Council of Europe set up Eurimages in 1988 as a support fund to encourage 'the co-production, distribution, broadcasting and exploitation of creative cinematographic and audio-visual works', in particular European multilateral co-productions (ECC 1988). It did this via interest-free but conditionally repayable loans (advance on receipts) to a maximum of 20% of the film's budget from funds made up predominantly from the contributions of its members and the repayment of other loans. Its initial budget of FrF55 million (£6.5 million) rapidly increased, as did applications for funding and the number of members. By the mid-1990s, Eurimages supported about one-fifth of all co-productions (whether bi- or tri-lateral) made in Europe (*Screen Digest* 1995: 134). Eurimages provided assistance in three areas – co-production (a minimum of three partners for feature films), distribution and exhibition. The annual number of feature film co-productions supported varied from 71 to 63 between 1994 and 1999, the total amount awarded decreased, but the number of applications for distribution support increased from 31 to 161 in this period. Between the statistical lines, the impact of changes in the film industry can be discerned, that is, the increase in the costs of production and the impact of increasing American domination of the distribution sector. The increase in membership has come from the smaller European countries, for whom there are clear advantages in gaining access to additional markets via co-production. The UK joined Eurimages in 1993 but withdrew in 1997 in spite of the general view that membership had been financially advantageous (Jäckel 2003: 77).

Eurimages support mechanisms were reformed in 2000 into a two-scheme system, the first of which dealt with films with 'international circulation potential' and the second with 'films of artistic value', and further reformed in 2003, resulting in a single support mechanism. There is a 19-point system for assessing a film project as European and rules on the maximum participation of the majority co-producer (not more than 80%) and minority co-producer (not lower than 10%) (Lange and Westcott 2004: 132). All applications are now judged on the selection criteria of artistic merit, the track record of the director, producers, artistic and creative teams, the circulation and commercial potential of the project, and the levels of confirmed finance, artistic and/or technical cooperation between the producers. The new system should go some way to countering claims of critics such as Martin Dale that European directors are caught in a 'subsidy trap' whereby 'most film-makers have to prove that their project isn't "commercial" in order to secure funding' (1997: 225–6).

Eurimages' support for distributors aims to complement that of the MEDIA programme by targeting distributors from its member states which are not able to benefit from MEDIA support, i.e. Croatia, Romania, Switzerland and Turkey. Similarly, its assistance to cinemas has been entrusted to Europa-Cinemas to complement MEDIA support, its network numbering 34 cinemas in five countries. Eurimages funds are small, but it can be argued that the consistency and persistence of its aims, and the interventions described above, have increased industry awareness of Eurimages and have had the secondary effect of encouraging film-makers to think in terms of co-production from the development phase onwards.

Playing the local and global cards

The plethora of regional, national and pan-national funding mechanisms, the difficulties of obtaining bank loans and of navigating the European support funds mean that European film-makers have to demonstrate enormous energy, commitment and tenacity to get their films made and exhibited. One example is the period drama *Villa des roses* (Frank van Passel, Belgium/UK/Netherlands/Luxembourg, 2002), whose gestation started in 1995 when the producer, Dirk Impens, and director team of one of Belgium's most successful films (*Mannekin Pis*, 1995) took options on Willem Elsschot's Flemish novel for $2,000. *Villa des roses* had been translated into English, influencing the decision to make the film in English, with a budget of $4.5million (Johnson 2000: 22). The first, extremely complex co-production package collapsed after German film fund Nordrhein-Westfalen rejected the project (which had the support of Belgium's Flemish Film Fund, Canal Plus and a French production company, the Dutch private investment Bank Labouchere and Wim Wenders' Road Movies Filmproduktion) on the basis of it not being commercial enough. NRW's participation would have secured 82% of the budget. In 1998–99 a second package was stitched together comprising Isabella Films (the Netherlands) bringing in the Dutch Film Fund and COBO Fonds ($523,000), Canal Plus Belgium ($110,000), Flemish broadcaster VRT ($88,000); Dan Films (UK) securing $750,000 from British Screen Finance and pay-TV broadcaster BSkyB; Samsa Films (Luxembourg) contributed $450,000 via a tax shelter scheme. Other funds derived from state funds from Belgium's Flemish and French communities, the UK National Lottery, Thuiscopie Fonds, NPS Television Fund Luxembourg, the European Co-Production Fund and Eurimages.

With so much effort going into the production package, the film went into production with less attention to a distribution deal and the film achieved poor results in Belgium, the UK and the Netherlands, but has reached larger audiences on satellite provider Sky TV. The film's form reflects these complex production packages. IMDb users seemed to either love the film or hate it. Set in 1913, the film opens with widow Louise Créteur (Julie Delpy) leaving her family in Honfleur to travel to Paris to work as a maid in a guest house run by an English couple. It closes with shots of Louise's deceitful German lover, Richard Grünewald (Shaun Dingwall), going into battle near Honfleur. Their love story, its decline, her abortion and his abandonment of her is set between these movements to and from Paris, focusing on the Villa des roses and its inhabitants. The *mise-en-scène* of the villa and its surrounding streets is dark and claustrophobic, the lack of detail reflecting the film's low budget, and the soundtrack contains rumbling and thundering noises which are attributed to the building of the Paris metro but which also, with stylistic economy, presage the coming First World War. The occupants of the villa are under constant surveillance by the cook, Ella (Shirley Henderson), via a series of tubes and spy holes and her acerbic and cynical presence is at the heart of the film. Claire Monk considered that the themes of the film would have been better served by the conventions of the heritage film (2000: 10, 60) but the gothic edge to van Passel's film is more in tune with its historical setting even if some of the allusions are unclear. Ella's panopticon[4] serves as an attempt by the lower class to retain some sort of control in a dark and chaotic world by amassing information on her English employers and the multinational guests. Interesting though the film is, the effect of the low budget in choice of actors and *mise-en-scène*, and what must have been agonizing efforts to secure the transnational production funding, was to dilute its focus and appeal. *A Very Long Engagement* (*Un long dimanche de fiançailles*, Jean-Pierre Jeunet, USA/France, 2003), also set in the First World War, did not make this mistake.

Another example of complex funding is Ken Loach's *My Name is Joe* (UK/Germany/France/Italy/Spain, 1998), produced by Loach's Parallax Pictures, FilmFour and made in Glasgow with finance from the Scottish Arts Council National Lottery Fund, film fund Nordrhein-Westfalen, Road Movies and two large Spanish companies, Tornesol and Alta Film. Several major television companies were involved – the very active German company WDR (West Deutscher Rundfunk), ARTE, the Franco–German company which makes prestige art productions for satellite, La Sept Cinéma and Germany's ARD. Loach's films are known to make more money in Europe than in the domestic market, but his track record means that distribution deals (distributors putting up minimum guarantees on the basis of a calculation of a similar level of revenue) are included. Like the other production partners, distributors Degeto (Germany) and Bim (Italy) had worked with Loach before. At the heart of the film is the love story between Joe (Peter Mullan, winner of Best Actor at the Cannes Film Festival), a recovering alcoholic, and Sarah (Louise Goodall), a health visitor, but Loach's care in fleshing out or holding back the context of his characters' lives gives them complexity, allowing the film-maker to comment on the marginalization of working-class populations in cities such as Glasgow where their physical strength and skills are no longer needed. Characters are framed in long shot to show them moving in their environment, clichés of Scottishness are avoided and the authenticity of accent in the dialogues resulted in subtitling for the British as well as foreign markets. As one of the DVD interviews suggested, the film works against any 'cosy consensus' that Britain is doing well while one-third of the population of a great city is forgotten and seen as 'irrelevant'. The consequences of the global flows of capital are made visual and have a relevance for many other European countries.

The general pattern for making authorial films in small European countries is to put together a co-production package. As the actor/director Baltasar Kormákur pointed out, in Iceland with its small population of 207,000 people there is no other choice (Seguin 2000: 9). His first feature, *101 Reykjavik* (2000), was an Iceland/Denmark/UK co-production, made with the support of the Icelandic Film Fund, Icelandair, Eurimages and BBC Films. Even in the large German film industry, film-makers wishing to make big-budget films must show their potential by first achieving local success. The German box-office receipts of Oliver Hirschbiegel's first feature, *Das Experiment* (Germany, 2001), put him in line for the internationally acclaimed *Downfall* (*Der Untergang*, Germany/Italy/Austria, 2004). The organisations managing and disbursing national and pan-European funds for cinema have to fight for their budgets in competition with other sectors of the economy. These funds ultimately derive from European tax payers, which means that disbursements have to be justified by references to the competence of the recipient(s) and the cultural importance of the project, and accounted for. These were new experiences for many sectors of the European film industries in the 1980s. The result of all these programmes may have been a valuable increase in professionalism, but at the expense of enormous bureaucratization.

Conclusion

Why did the European Union consider it necessary to expend comparatively large sums of money to intervene in the media arena? One partial explanation lies in the myth of the dominance of the English language and its link to global domination, resulting in French initiatives to enshrine the preservation of national cultures and linguistic autonomy in institutional objectives. From the financial point of view, European media professionals are also well aware of the opportunities of the digital revolution and, if the sums of money channelled through the MEDIA programme are not huge in comparison with the budgets of major American films, they have at least had the positive outcome of getting industry professionals used to thinking and working with the European context in mind. The measures described in this chapter attempt to hold on to exhibition spaces where ordinary people can see European films outside the festival circuits. In 1990, 451 films were produced in the 15 countries of the EU, 853 films in a total of 33 European countries

(EAO 1997: 72). Apart from a noticeable downturn in 1992 and 1993, EU production steadily increased to 634 films in 2002 and 686 in 2004 (EAO 2005/3: 12–13). Although the number of co-productions in the 15 original EU member countries has been prone to swing up and down, numbers have increased overall, as have the number of non-domestic European films released in each domestic market. The continued volatility, however, means that one or two European mini-blockbusters in the space left by American domination of the European box office effectively robs too many European films of their opportunities to make money. The spaces in which they are marginalized offer political metaphors for struggles over cultural power. In contemporary European cinema, producers and directors, writers and cinematographers and all involved in the industry have to take account of the integrating initiatives of the European Union.

The possibilities for European film-makers to cover their production costs and make a profit still appear extremely limited. Those film-makers wishing to develop beyond the confines of national, low-budget film have a few choices open to them, of which the low- to mid-budget, so-called, art film is one solution. Usually sold on the name of its director, this aims to cover its costs through institutional grants and subventions, pre-sales to television and satellite exhibitors, and through playing the film festival circuits in the hope of attracting prizes and some international distribution. This can take the form of foreign television and satellite, video and DVD sales. Once a film has achieved its main theatrical distribution, however, it may enter a limbo outside the statistical ken. The growth of internet access has led to a plethora of specialist sales opportunities, where films enter an afterlife of commercial exploitation for whoever owns the rights. The next chapter will consider the tension between what is still perceived to be the most typical form of European film-making – the art film sector – and the desire to reflect local concerns.

Notes

1. The MPAA and its predecessors were self-regulating bodies of Hollywood producers and distributors. The MPAA looks after American cinema interests abroad and set up a ratings system for cinema exhibition in 1968.
2. The Hollywood majors originally consisted of the 'big five' (Paramount, Warner Brothers, MGM, Twentieth Century Fox and RKO) and the 'little three' (Columbia, Universal and United Artists) vertically integrated companies. They operated as an effective cartel controlling the industry (Maltby 1995: 60–6). They imposed regulation of the American film industry through the MPAA. From the 1960s the spate of mergers and takeovers resulted in the original companies becoming parts of larger, multinational corporations, but the term 'majors' is still used as a shorthand for the powerful companies of the American film and media industries.
3. The abbreviation EAO (European Audiovisual Observatory Yearbook) will be used from this point on, followed by a figure denoting the volume referred to. From 2002 the EAO Yearbook was produced in five volumes yearly.
4. The panopticon was a term discussed by Michel Foucault (1977: 206–7) in his explorations of how societies managed and controlled their populations. Nineteenth-century prisons were designed as wings radiating out from a hub, so

that the prison population could be under surveillance at every moment. Countless twentieth-century European films use the trope of the panopticon to demonstrate social control, often to indicate the presence of conspiracies, representing a narrative attempt to give order to chaotic events.

Art cinema/auteurist films by admissions

Notes

(a) All data are taken from European Audiovisual Observatory Yearbooks, 1998–2005; (b) EU7 relates to information on the major cinema markets; (c) EU15 relates to members of the EU prior to 1 May 2004; (d) EU25 relates to expanded membership including Eastern European states post 1 May 2004; (e) EU29+ relates to the 25 states of the EU, plus Switzerland, Iceland, Norway, Romania and Turkey.
The European Audiovisual Observatory has changed its methodology slightly from year to year, for example initially giving dollar earnings of European films in the US market, then reverting to figures for cinema admissions. Although a few successful films appear to have had no release in the EU, the global, EU29 figures indicate that these gained their success in Eastern European accession states.

The ranking is based on figures for the top 50 films of any nationality by admissions in Europe. Where the letters 'EU' follow the ranking, this denotes the film's placing in the top 50 **European** films by admissions in Europe.

Film	Date	Country of prod	US earn $/ admissions	Ranking/year	Released in no of EU countries	Total admissions (millions) EU7	EU15	EU25	EU29+
8 femmes	2002	F	0.5m adm/02	30 2002	14				6.6
Todo sobre mi madre	1999	ES/F	1.1m adm/00	25 1999	14		6.3		
				29 2000 EU	11		1.2		
Hable con ella	2002	ES	1.1m adm/03	36 2002	14				6.0
Der Untergang	2004	DE/IT		43 2004	3				5.5
Pinocchio	2002	IT/F/DE		48 2002	1				4.6
Les rivières pourpres	2000	F		43 2000	4		4.5		
The Pianist	2002	F/UK/DE/PL	5.2m adm/03	45 2002	9				4.9
Two brothers	2004	F/UK		46 2004	10				4.9
Un long dimanche de fiançailles	2004	F/US	0.4m adm/04	49 2004	2				4.6
La mala educación	2004	ES		50 2004	14				4.5
Mar adentro	2004	ES/F/IT		11 2004 EU	3				4.1
Le goût des autres	2000	F		49 2000	7		4.1		
La neuvième porte	1999	F/ES		50 1999	10		3.5		
			3.4m adm/00	47 2000 EU	9		0.7		

Film	Date	Country of prod	US earn $/ admissions	Ranking/year	Released in no of EU countries	Total admissions (millions) EU7	EU15	EU25	EU29+
Secrets and Lies	1996	UK	5.9m/1996	44 1996	14		3.3		
La stanza del figlio	2001	IT/F		21 2001 EU	10			2.4	
Dancer in the Dark	2000	DK/F/DE/NL	0.7adm/2000	11 2000 EU	13		2.7		
La finestra di fronte	2003	IT/PT/TR		15 2003 EU	2				2.7
Lola rennt	1998	DE	7.2m/1999	12 1998	3		2.2		
Comme une image	2004	F		22 2004 EU	12				2.2
Stealing Beauty	1996	IT/F/UK	4.7m/1996	13 1996 EU	15		2.1	2.2	
Beaumarchais, l'insolent	1996	F	0.4m	14 1996 EU	6		2.0		
Harry, un ami qui vous veut du bien	2000	F		17 2000 EU	6		2.0		
Breaking the Waves	1996	DK/NL/SE/F	1.1m/1996	15 1996 EU	14		1.9	2.0	
				48 1997 EU	13		0.8		
Zemsta	2002	PL		22 2002 EU					1.9
Swimming Pool	2003	F/UK	1.7m adm/03	24 2003 EU	13				1.9
Dogville	2003	DK/F/SE/NL		25 2003 EU	11				1.8
		DE/NO/UK							
The Million Dollar Hotel	2000	DE/US		19 2000 EU	10		1.8		
La pianiste	2001	AT/F	0.3m adm/02	31 2001 EU	10		1.8		
Carne trémula	1997	ES/F	1.7m/1998	22 1997 EU	3				1.78
				49 1998 EU	14		0.6		
Das Experiment	2001	DE		34 2001 EU	4		1.76		
Lucie Aubrac	1997	F		23 1997 EU	3		1.74		
Le bossu	1997	F/IT/DE		24 1997 EU	3		1.72		
Italiensk for begyndere	2000	DK	0.8m adm/02	24 2002 EU	13				1.7
Amen	2002	F/DE/RO/US		26 2002 EU	8				1.6
18 ans après	2003	F		29 2003 EU	2				1.6
Gegen die Wand	2004	DE/TR		36 2004 EU	10				1.6

Film	Date	Country of prod	US earn $/ admissions	Ranking/year	Released in no of EU countries	Total admissions (millions) EU7	EU15	EU25	EU29+
La vie revée des anges	1998	F	1.9m/1999	14 1998 EU	9		1.6		
Le fate ignoranti	2001	IT/F		43 2001 EU	2		1.5		
Nirvana	1997	IT/F		28 1997 EU	5		1.5		
Être et avoir	2002	F		29 2002 EU	2				1.5
				40 2003 EU	6				1.2
La fleur du mal	2003	F		32 2003 EU	6				1.4
Kolya	1996	CZ/F/UK/US	5.8m/1997	30 1997 EU	14		1.4		
The End of the Affair	1999	UK/US		23 2000 EU	11		1.4		
Antonia's Line	1996	NL/UK/BE	4.2m/1996	23 1996 EU	11		1.3	1.4	
Abre los ojos	1998	ES		20 1998 EU	3		1.3		
Chaos	2001	F		47 2001 EU	3			1.37	
The Boxer	1998	IE/US	5.9m/1998	22 1998 EU	9		1.2		
La niña de tus ojos	1998	ES		23 1998 EU	1		1.2		
				24 1999 EU	3		1.2		
Chat noir, chat blanc	1998	F/DE		24 1998 EU	5		1.2		
				36 1999 EU	11		0.9		
Ça commence aujourd'hui	1999	F		23 1999 EU	10		1.29		
The Dreamers	2003	F/UK/IT	0.4m adm/04	41 2003 EU	4				1.1
Respiro	2002	IT/F							1.1
Une chance sur deux	1998	F		25 1998 EU	4		1.1		
My Name is Joe	1998	UK/F/DE/ES/IT		28 1998 EU	9		1.0		
Mies vailla menneisyyttä	2002	FI/DE/F		40 2002 EU	8				1.1
Irréversible	2002	F		41 2002 EU	6				1.0
Nakt	2002	DE		46 2002 EU	2				1.0
Nelly et Monsieur Annaud	1995	F/DE/IT	1.2m/1996	28 1996 EU	6		0.98		
Michael Collins	1997	US/UK	10.9m/1996	38 1997 EU	8		0.97		
Tillsammens	2000	SE/DK/IT	0.2m adm/01	34 2000	2		0.86		

Film	Date	Country of prod	US earn $/ admissions	Ranking/year	Released in no of EU countries	Total admissions (millions) EU7	EU15	EU25	EU29+
Den eneste ene	1999	DK		45 1999 EU	1		0.84		
Mifunes sidste Sang	1999	DK/SE		46 1999 EU	11		0.83		
Au cœur du mensonge	1998	F		47 1999 EU	7		0.83		
Aprile	1998	IT		33 1998 EU	10		0.8		
Bin ich schön	1998	DE		34 1998 EU	2		0.8		
Conte d'automne	1998	F	2.2m/1999	37 1998 EU	7		0.76		
The legend of 1900	1997	IT		42 1998 EU	1		0.69		
Malèna	2000	IT/US	0.5m adm/01	49 2000	2		0.69		
Lovers of the Arctic Circle	1998	ES		44 1998 EU	1		0.64		
Festen	1998	DK	1.1m/1998	45 1998 EU	8		0.63		
				19 1999 EU	15		1.57		

chapter two

Art cinema, a cinema of *auteurs*? Low- to mid-budget authorial film-making

Among the clichés about European cinema is that it is dominated by *auteurs*, that is, directors with the status of artists and authors, aiming to make films which reflect their own visions and concerns and with not enough regard for their commercial destination. Contemporary Europe still produces directors with *auteur* status, but the majority no longer fit the 'great white male' template of directors whose films were greeted as cultural events with relevance to the state of their nation. It is difficult for contemporary directors to stand out in all their originality in a media terrain where the output of many decades is available on video/DVD and cinema itself has lost its centrality to cultural experience with the proliferation of other media. This chapter will explore the current state of authorial film-making in a situation where the majority of national production is treated like art cinema in its own market and is marginalized when it crosses borders. The careers of Eric Rohmer and Jean-Luc Godard will be traced to show the evolution of authorial cinema and tested against Neale and Bordwell's explanations of it. These two French directors will also be contrasted to younger directors from Italy, Denmark and Britain who have also attempted to carve out for themselves a sphere of personal expression.

The common perception among media commentators is that Europe's 'strongly developed *auteur* culture, where film directors have enjoyed most of the power in the film-making process' is a problem, leading to eclectic and not easily publicizable films which fail to make a financial return for their investors (Finney 1996b: 5). The myth of the unworldly, uncompetitive and uncommercial European *auteur* cinema is an old one which has gained ground since the 1980s, resulting in a plethora of privately (rather than institutionally) offered workshops on 'good' commercial practice. As Marjorie Ferguson suggested, it pays to examine 'not only what is being hawked by whom, but who stands to lose or gain materially, politically' by rejecting the European film-making style in favour of thinking in terms of film as a homogenised product on the American model (1992: 73). The film industry's overt dislike of *auteur* cinema smacks of blaming the victim for the perpetrator's rapacity. It also diverts attention from the fact of American domination of the distribution and exhibition sectors.

Blaming *auteur* cinema for failing to generate a return on investment conceals the difficulties of carving out an exploitation window in the exhibition sector, in terrestrial and satellite broadcasting schedules, and in the racks of videos and now DVDs, but also the fact that this type of cinema has been international for a long time. It is important to reiterate at this stage that only a very few European films are made with direct competition with Hollywood in mind and, as Figure 2.1 demonstrates, the majority are low- to mid-budget productions, typically between $3 million and $10 million.

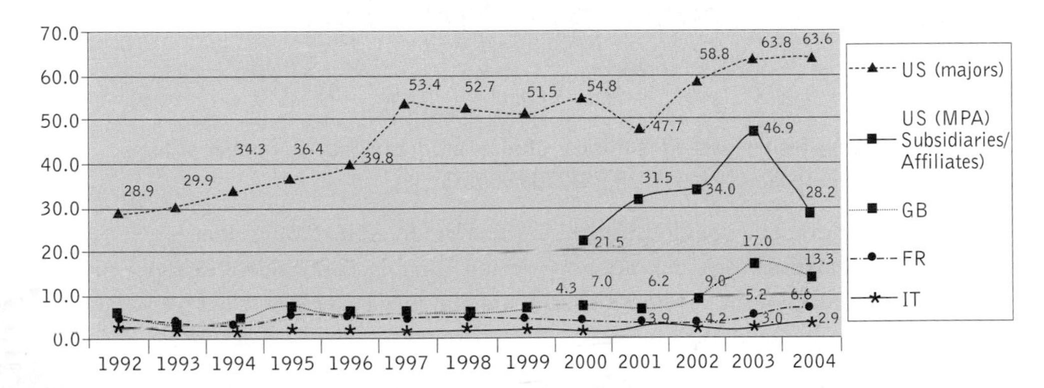

Figure 2.1 Average cost of production of feature films: 1992–2004 (in US$ millions)
Source: European Audiovisual Observatory Yearbook 2005/3

This chapter examines the contemporary irrelevance of the distinction between auteurist film-making practice, which privileges the director as source of meanings within the text and marketing tool, and art cinema, which is a disputed commercial category in a situation of decreasing independent exhibition circuits.

Examining the conundrum of how it is possible to exert authorial control over the film-making process in the complex context of interlinking media markets reveals that there are many types of *auteur*, but that they have in common the imperative to establish a recognizable creative profile and to find a constituency, that is, an audience. The gloss on Figure 2.2 attempts to explain the fact that about 100 of the films produced in 2003 appeared not to be in distribution.

However, 60% of 2002 UK film production remained unreleased by June 2004 and only 6.66% had a 300-plus screen release (Dyja 2004: 33). In the situation illustrated by Figures 2.1 and 2.2 it is difficult to create and maintain a constituency. The number of first-time directors who do not make another film and the number of European films which never achieve a theatrical release indicate the risk involved, and the waste of talent.

Yet there are ranks of film-makers who have achieved lucrative careers in the film and media industries, boasting prolific filmographies, but who either do not achieve the fit with earlier definitions of *auteurs*, or whose critical acclaim is limited to the marginal critical apparatus of the cult film. What both the 'great directors' (usually white and male) of the

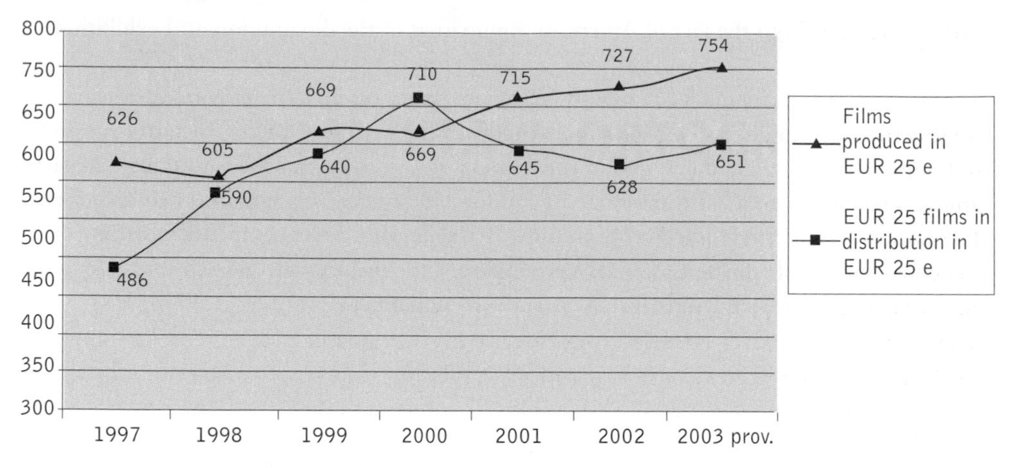

Figure 2.2 Comparison between the number of films produced and the number of films released in the European Union (EUR 25): 1997-2003

Superiority of the number of films released to those produced in 2000 is probably due to the diversity of methodologies for measuring production on a national level, and notably to the differences between the year in which a production may be registered and the year of completion/distribution of the film.

Source: European Audiovisual Observatory Yearbook 2005/3

European modernist tradition (Dyer and Vincendeau 1992: 17) and cult film directors have in common is the cultural capital of their audiences, and a study of audiences reveals the class basis of the art and auteurist sectors of the film industry.

Bourdieu's exploration of the class use of cultural artefacts included the insight that taste was key to the formation of a *habitus*, that is, the site of constitution of social identity (1993). Within a *habitus*, its members make 'classificatory judgements' about their own and others' cultural practices and act in ways which classify them as members of that *habitus* themselves (Bourdieu 1986: 169). The establishment of art cinema practice goes hand in hand with the development of middle-class notions of cultural power, as expressed in ideas of cultural taste. Knowledge of film history and the ability to understand and classify different forms of cinema practice differentiate a person as a member of a discerning, educated audience. The cultural importance of cinema can be gauged by the fact that any one *habitus* may use particular types of films to define their own cultural capital, middle-class audiences using historical films to indicate their knowledge of classic literature (even if they have not actually read the books), younger, educated audiences using their knowledge of film history to either identify 'canonical' films or valorize their ability to 'read' and decipher meanings in 'difficult' texts. Yet another audience refuses to differentiate high and low cultural texts, but displays knowledge of eclectic, sub-cultural information, or even refuses the tenets of high culture by celebrating the excessive and marginal borders of cinema production, thereby signalling their own independence of taste. Assigning a film to the category of art cinema, or auteurist cinema, is an act of cultural politics and by no means neutral.

What is an *auteur*?

As Stephen Crofts has explored, there have been several attempts to define authorship, ranging from postwar French critics to later media theory, and the notion itself has gone in and out of theoretical fashion (1998: 310–22). Most are problematic in the contemporary situation primarily because of their inability to account for changes in the production, distribution and exhibition of films. The *politique des auteurs* was developed by 1950s' French critics to raise the cultural status of cinema and to validate the superiority of European cinema over that of the USA. Assigning the status of author to a film-maker allowed the work of a director to be considered over time, individual films to be examined for the presence of recurrent themes and motifs, and for an individual corpus of work to be examined in relation to a national cinema or film movement. Critical consideration generally concentrated on the director's ideas and events in his/her life to explain text events in the films. This model ignored the commercial context of film production and the relationship of film-makers to their national cinema of origin is problematic now when directors like Neil Jordan and Jean-Pierre Jeunet alternate between Europe and Hollywood.

Subsequent attempts to come to terms with text, author and context include Steve Neale's historical approach, defining it as an attempt by Europeans to counter US domination of the film industry in the immediate postwar period (1981). He described how 'art cinema' evolved its own industrial and institutional forms, such as art-house circuits of distribution and exhibition, and how critics were essential to the process of defining quality. 'Quality' and 'art' came to be associated with a stress on visual style, the suppression of action in the Hollywood sense, the emphasis on character rather than plot, and the interiorization of dramatic conflict. The author, while existing outside the fiction, still had a role inside the textual space as an element of performance, ambiguity or excess. Although generally hostile to the idea of authorial intention marking the text, David Bordwell also explored the industrial codes of art cinema production, stressing the importance of the art-house cinema circuits, film festivals and state validation in defining this area of the industry (1979). He characterized art cinema as dominated by codes of realism, authorship and ambiguity. For Bordwell the presence of the author was signalled by style, which the critical industry helpfully identified for the spectator.

European art cinema has changed considerably since Bordwell and Neale examined it more than 20 years ago. Then, art cinema was considered as a separate form of film-making, with its own modes of production, distribution and exhibition. However, even when those articles were being written, the art film sector had already changed, so that it no longer looked so different from certain types of American independent cinema. The traditional division of film into three spheres of activity had also already become more complex. The media were becoming more interlaced and interdependent in what are now recognized as globalizing tendencies.

Art cinema practice has polarized. Many small independent cinemas which formed part of *cinéma d'art et d'essai* circuits have closed in the last 20 years, mainly due to the increased domination of American distribution and exhibition chains and suburbanization. As a result, art cinema in Europe has utilized mainstream, first-run cinema exhibition, or has been limited to marginal festival circuits, film societies or television. In this respect, art cinema shares its marginalization with the games industry in which the big franchises dominate the Christmas period and anything quirky or unusual is released in February (Gillen 2006: 3). Defining art cinema as 'usually produced with an appeal to a cultural rather than a commercial imperative' (Petrie 2000: 149) is too wide to take account of the complexities of contemporary film funding and exhibition. Film festivals too have proliferated since 1980 and now cater for a variety of mainstream and niche interests.

The entity of the film director survives as a legal requirement for attributing creative ownership of the film text and for the inclusion in national categories which will qualify for financial subsidy. The MEDIA programme's encouragement of a pan-European identity through subsidies to co-productions has also ensured the survival of directorial status. As Thomas Elsaesser suggested, when a film is a multicountry co-production, with American finance and an international cast, the paying public may not care about its provenance; in that case, 'the director as auteur is still a relevant production category' (2005: 491). *A Very Long Engagement* (*Une longue dimanche di fiançailles*, Jean-Pierre Jeunet, France/USA, 2004) was refused as French nomination for the Academy Awards because of its American financing, but is demonstrably French by its European subject matter, style and director. Some directors even attain the status of national treasures – such as Manoel De Oliveira in Portugal, Theo Anghelopoulos in Greece, Ingmar Bergman in Sweden – and are subsidized to continue their idiosyncratic style into revered age. In critical terms, the name of the director is still useful as an explanatory tool, in spite of – or perhaps because of – the postmodern aesthetics of disruption which draws attention to the author in the text as enunciative presence.

State organizations as well as the MEDIA programme have recognized the necessity of lively cultural spaces for the exhibition of alternatives to mainstream American films, whether produced with pretensions to serious purpose or not. Portuguese cinema demonstrates the difficulty of achieving this.

Portugal

For Portuguese cinema, it is not so much production finance which is hard to find as promotion and distribution assistance (Evans 2000: 30). Portugal produces around ten films a year, the majority of each budget being provided by the Portuguese Film Institute, ICAM, in co-production arrangements with Portuguese television, RTP, and other institutions. Evans suggests that Portugal's marginality, geographically and culturally, accounts for the artisanal and authorial character of its films which fit the low-budget, art cinema template. But even with low budgets, Portuguese films attain only 1.25% of their own market (EAO 2005/3: 49). Serge de Jésus Carreira suggested there are only three types of Portuguese film-maker. Firstly Manoel De Oliveira, who alone commands international stars and can achieve 30,000 admissions in France, and whose slow and melancholy style has influenced younger generations (1999). Secondly João César Monteiro, whose *Trilogy of John of God* (*Recordações da casa amarela*, Portugal, 1989; *A comédia de Deus*, Portugal/France/Italy/Denmark, 1995; *As bodas de Deus*, France/Portugal, 1998) brought him international notoriety on the festival circuit for the total freedom with which he expressed his erotic obsessions (Nagib 2005: 190). Monteiro died in 2003 and his regular producer, Paolo Branco, who has had a pre-eminent position in this small market, has had to find new directors. The third category comprises 'the rest', both those whose subsidized films have achieved festival recognition, such as Maria De Madeiros, Margarida Cardoso and Teresa Villaverde, and a new generation whose extremely low-budget genre films have been produced outside the traditional subsidy circuit with box-office success (Dale 2006: 230). Portuguese conditions have favoured the continuation of a hermetic art cinema, aided by the distribution possibilities of the enormous Portuguese-speaking populations of Brazil and Africa. The beleaguered art cinema category has been able to explore Portugal's postcolonial traumas, social change and political and gender issues without the compromises, or advantages, of its neighbours.

By contrast, French cinema is prolific and the opportunities for authorial recognition greater. Nonetheless, the survival techniques of French directors starting their careers in the heyday of the *politique des auteurs*, Eric Rohmer, Jean-Luc Godard and Agnès Varda, illustrate continuities and changes within the *auteur* profile and accommodation to this polarization within the European film industries.

Eric Rohmer and the middle-class audience

Eric Rohmer's career started in the late 1950s. He was one of the older members of the group of young critics writing for *Cahiers du Cinéma* which comprised Godard, Truffaut, Chabrol, Rivette and Doniol-Valcroze and, in different directions, Resnais, Marker, Varda, Malle, Demy and Vadim, who all became identified with the *Nouvelle Vague*. Like many 'new' movements, what they represented was a bid for cultural power by a young group, whose first films were works in progress, making a virtue of low budgets and youthful, unknown actors and their own sense that European society was changing. Rohmer made a dozen short films in the 1950s, contributed influential critical articles to film magazines, and wrote books on Murnau and Hitchcock. His identification with the *Nouvelle Vague* gave him recognition and a profile but not enough success from his short films, two of which he had conceived of as part of a series of six, to give up the day job. By selling the television rights of two of the short films, Barbet Schroeder and Rohmer gathered enough cash to film *La collectionneuse* (France, 1966), shot in colour on a shoestring with the cast and crew working for percentages. Its journey around the festival circuit ensured that it was reviewed and achieved an international distribution. Proclaiming his credentials as an *auteur* (personal vision and a series in which to explore it), critics knew what to look for and what to make of the film; and distributors knew how to market it. Rohmer's strategy was 'to make films in total freedom, and I thought that it would be easier to get my own way – and to get people to accept my conception – if I presented an ensemble rather than isolated films' (Barron 1971: 4). Announcing that your work is part of a series is a creative and marketing ploy which other auteurist film-makers, such as Kieslovski and Lucas Belvaux, have adopted subsequently.

The *Six Contes Moraux* (*Six moral tales*) had run their course by the early 1970s and Rohmer experimented with two films, *Die Marquise von O* (W. Germany/France, 1976) and

Perceval (France/Italy/W. Germany, 1978), both expensive literary adaptations which were unsuccessful. Rohmer would achieve a more constant success in the 1980s by rebadging his series as *Comédies et proverbes* (*Comedies and proverbs*) so that his films could focus on the choices, self-awareness and self-delusions of young women. In this respect his preoccupations cannot be divorced from the increasing influence of feminism in the Western cultural context in this period.

In common with other European countries, the 1970s was a period of crisis in the French film industry, precipitated by increasing US competition. As a result, independent exhibitors banded together in order to be effective, forming the UGC distribution chain, the industry became more conservative in its subject matter, moving towards historical epics and nostalgic dramas, cinemas renovated or closed, the suburban exhibition sector disappeared, producers found it difficult to finance enough prints, and the large players, Pathé and Gaumont, diversified. Pathé kept its cinema circuit, moved into TV mini series and exploited its library; Gaumont kept its cinemas, developed its video arm and moved into large-budget production of 'quality', international cinema. By the end of the 1970s various responses had developed – that of vertical integration in the case of Claude Berri and Marin Karmitz, and diversification. Several directors formed their own production companies, including Besson, Berri, Godard, Varda, Belasko and Rohmer. State intervention and subvention became crucial. Rohmer's choice was to remain in low-budget, art film production, using Les Films du Losange, the production company he and Barbet Schroeder had founded in 1962, to maintain his independence by ensuring that profits went back into the company. He developed his audience and found themes of international interest – the difficulties of forming a loving partnership as an autonomous woman in a socially mobile society; the difficulties of developing a satisfactory male mode of behaviour in a society in flux; and the consequences, self-deception, social fragmentation and loneliness. He achieved success in the American market in 1984 with *Pauline at the Beach* (*Pauline à la plage*, France, 1983) and his international recognition came with *The Green Ray*'s (*Le rayon vert*, France, 1986) award of the Golden Lion at the 1986 Venice film festival.

The *Contes moraux* and the *Comédies et proverbes* were succeeded in the 1990s by the *Contes des quatres saisons* (*Tales of the four seasons*). The main character in each film is what Wayne Booth calls an 'unreliable narrator', 'both self-deceived and deceiving' (1961: 343). Rohmer has used this device in all of his films, resulting in an ironic distance between the narration and the action of the film and providing a space for his educated audience to judge what the characters say about themselves, life, the universe, against what they do and how they react. The trope of irony is a source of considerable pleasure in generating a feeling of superiority at the characters' capacity for self-delusion. Philosophical discussions of choice and chance have now been superseded by ethical dilemmas. Rohmer's evocation of place, atmosphere and time is a considerable source of pleasure. His cinematic language is not adventurous and is expository in the sense that it situates his characters and their actions in a plausible and recognizable social space. The young actors of *A Summer's Tale* (*Conte d'été*, France, 1996) are rarely seen together in the same frame, reflecting their differences, while the mature characters of *A Tale of Autumn* (*Conte d'automne*, France, 1998) are invariably in two-shot and close social interaction. Questions of freedom and duty, sin and desire are also rehearsed in *The Lady and the Duke* (*L'anglaise et le Duc*, France/Germany, 2001), while *Triple Agent* (France/Greece/Italy/Spain, 2004) reintroduces the grand metanarratives in dinner-table discussion of communism.

A very short article in *Le film français* indicates the lessons that Rohmer, and his producer from the mid-1970s onwards, Margaret Ménégoz, learned. When asked how much attention they paid to international distribution, Rohmer replied that he left it to Les Films du Losange. Ménégoz understood the economic implications:

> Extremely close attention. The receipts of Eric Rohmer's films are divided approximately between 60–70% from foreign box office, 30–40% for France. A large part of distribution income comes from abroad, and provides finance for the next film.
>
> (Renouard 1996: 18)

When asked how they explained their faithful, international public, Rohmer had no explanation, while Ménégoz gave her view:

> Rohmer entertains them. His public is neither very old nor very young. Let's say 30–40 years old. Urban, cultured, graduate, student, it's a solid public. It's a question of taste and involvement. His films now appeal to a second generation audience. [...] The children of the generation of 1968 like Rohmer's films as much as their parents. We're even reaching the third generation!
>
> (Renouard 1996: 18)

'Rohmer' now is a commercial strategy for organizing audience reception and an element in distribution and marketing (Corrigan 1991: 103). This is not to say that Rohmer has rested on his laurels. *The Lady and the Duke* excited attention because of its formal innovation of using digital technology to situate its actors in a background generated from mattes of eighteenth-century line drawings of Paris. This was a very postmodern departure for a director renowned for the careful realism of his locations and sets.[1] The dialogue of the main protagonist, Grace Elliott (Lucy Russell), a royalist Englishwoman living in France during the Revolution due to her relationship with Philippe, Duke of Orleans (Jean-Claude Dreyfus), sparked controversy for its negative view of a sacred moment in French history.[2] Grace attempts to save a fugitive by hiding him in her apartment, thereby bringing herself and those around her into danger. It was an expensive film for Rohmer (around £4 million), necessitating the support of Pathé and the MEDIA programme, and provoked Etchegaray's comment that Rohmer's films were now so expensive that they could not cover their costs with their traditional audience (Anon 2004: 8).

Triple Agent was a low-budget co-production, subsidized by €600,000 from Eurimages and achieving only 93,000 admissions. It is a chamber piece centred around the suspicions of the wife (Katerina Didaskalou) of a White Russian general living in 1930s' Paris. The period setting allows debates about communism, art and politics but at the same time their artificiality fails to engage or indicate a contemporary relevance. These two films recall the unsuccessful 1970s' films which precipitated a new direction.

In his exploration of the middle-class way of life, Rohmer has occupied a defined niche in the cinematic market which, in an increasingly globalized media economy, has become international. He has exploited his films' potential in publishing spin-offs, in video and DVD releases, sales to terrestrial and satellite television, and a two-part documentary (*Eric Rohmer: Preuves à l'appui*, André S. Labarthe/Jean Douchet, France, 1994) on his work for the Franco–German cultural satellite channel, ARTE. Trading on his decision to foreground his films as parts of a series helps critics interpret his work for an increasingly international audience, which its lack of sex and violence favours. His style, mode of film-making and the scope of his plots have settled into simple patterns, but his films invite his audience to reflect on the complexity of their contemporary choices. The world of Rohmer's films is an idealized one where instability and change are introduced but not entirely overcome. He was awarded a Venice Golden Lion in 2001 for his life's work.

How has Godard survived?

The career of Jean-Luc Godard has been extraordinarily prolific, the IMDb database listing 89 films which he has directed between *Opération béton* (Switzerland, 1954) and the '11th arrondissement' section of *Paris, je t'aime* (2006), apart from his interventions as screenwriter, actor, producer, cinematographer. By the end of the 1960s he had achieved the status of *auteur*, each of his films attracting national and international attention for their freshness, ideas, cinematic innovations, refusal of realism and areas of ambiguity. In the 1970s his films engaged with Maoist politics, Brecht and Althusser. His oppositional 16mm film and video work, marked by his own voice-over, influenced independent and political film-makers, but was less able to cross into theatrical release than *Weekend* (Italy/France, 1967) and *Pierrot le fou* (France/Italy, 1967) had done. Godard has been considered the only director of the modern period to achieve truly iconic *auteur* status (Temple and Witt 2004: 191) and has also been cordially loathed as a director whose films have not been worth queuing to see for 40 years.[3] Yet even those industry critics who dismissed Godard's hostility to the rapaciousness of Hollywood at the 2001 Cannes film festival as 'the peevish ravings of a quaint old intellectual whose relevance has been overtaken by a world that has come to accept, even embrace, the compromises that come with the commodification of popular culture' came to appreciate the prescience of his sense of how Hollywood had changed.[4]

Godard's career raises many questions about the status of the European *auteur*, about the role of the intellectual and the possibility of her/his independence within late-capitalist modes of production. How has someone whose work has, since the 1970s, been so difficult or inaccessible managed to survive and make films to a revered old age? One answer has to be that Godard has consistently maintained contact with his constituency – an intellectual, educated, international audience, interested in his ideas about cinema and how he has expressed them on film. Like Rohmer, Godard's constituency now includes several generations, assisted by the growth of film studies courses and the videothèque phenomenon whereby enthusiasts collect off-air recordings and commercial video/DVD releases. Godard's continued career depends on the expansion and 'transformation of the roles of the traditional intelligentsia' (Frow 1995: 120–1) to include those whose employment and social standing depend on their possession of cultural capital.

Godard is, of course, a member of this class. Not only do his films and other works foreground his own mastery (a word which links him to the masculinist culture of the artist and aesthete) of European high culture of literature and philosophy, and of a century of film culture, but his work is also characterized by the indirectness of its 'insertion into the relations of production' (Frow 1995: 127). His authorial stance masks the commercial realities of low-budget, independent production. Godard owns his own means of production. His studio, Sonimage, was set up in 1973 after his Maoist phase, in realization that the only realistic alternative to the exploitation of pleasure represented by the global media industries was low-budget films (Reader 2004: 91). Sonimage moved to Switzerland with him and Anne-Marie Miéville and has provided the claim to autonomy which is a mark of the artist and cultural worker. However, since then, 'Godard' the film-making entity has consisted of the work of two people; his collaboration with Miéville has lasted since 1974 and he credits her with a 50% contribution to his work (Pajaczkowska 1990: 241). Critics have concluded that it is fruitless to attempt to tease out who does/did what (Grant 2004: 100–1), but his prior fame has imposed his name predominantly on their work. Colin MacCabe has described the astute commercial instincts shown by Godard in accepting commissions and deciding exactly how much time and money to devote to a project, on occasion morphing the theme into a subject of greater interest to them (2004: 96). Godard also works consistently with the same producers, Alain Sarde among others, and puts together co-production arrangements with French and Swiss television. Such is his 'name' and the interest of his constituency that he achieves good distribution in the USA, can cover his costs and invest in his next project.

This investment has taken the form of the embrace of successive new technologies, another factor which has kept him at the forefront of the development of cinema. Working in the more intimate media of video and digital technology has had an effect on the form of his work. Temple and Witt view Godard more as a multimedia artist, essayist and critic than a film director, as he has produced critical articles, 'features, shorts, sketches, essays, poems and collages in a variety of formats' (2004: 191). The video work for television of the 1980s was seen only intermittently after its initial broadcast, perhaps accounting for the fact that Godard went in and out of fashion in the period.

The continuation of Godard's career was assisted by developments in the French media in the 1970s, particularly by the French Television Act of 1974 which abolished the state monopoly, replacing it with seven institutional bodies. One of these was the Institut National de l'Audiovisuel (INA), which developed a policy of co-producing and commissioning films for television. Godard achieved a fortunate collaboration with INA, resulting in the acclaimed 12-part series, *France/tour/détour/deux/enfants* (co-director Anne-Marie Miéville, France, 1977–78) and the eight-part series, *Histoire(s) du cinema*, the last six parts being also supported by Gaumont (France, 1988–98). The latter has excited admiration for its scope, inventiveness and the sheer density of the ideas being explored. Godard aimed to:

> ... show that all histories are intertwined with the history of the twentieth century. Film history is the only visible part of the history, and from this point of view it is the history of the world that belongs to film history.[5]

Godard's perception that, in media-saturated societies, a sense of personal and national identity is created, nurtured and maintained by the types of media which people use and from which they attribute coherence to their lives and their world, is now widely accepted. But attempting to work through this idea by juxtaposing images and cultural references, sounds and voice-overs results in an incredibly ambitious work which continues to fascinate film scholars. What he tries to achieve by the juxtaposition of images is a third sense, 'a living image of the unfolding of History and the tempo of History' (Godard and Ishaghpour 2005: 33, 50). This preoccupation is picked up again in *JLG/JLG* (*JLG/JLG: autoportrait de décembre*, France, 1995), which starts with a flickering image of a childhood photograph of himself and explores movement and change.

Nouvelle vague (France/Switzerland, 1990), whose similar aim was to 'rediscover and describe in a romantic way the very source of love, through the audio and visual means which characterize cinema', was more problematic.[6] The slabs of inadequately subtitled dialogue in French and Italian are uncompromising. The film's co-production arrangements included Vega Films (which produced Godard's recent films), Canal Plus, the film arm of Swiss Télévision Romande, the CNC, and the Sofica investment bodies. *Notre Musique* (France/Switzerland, 2004) is divided into three parts, hell, purgatory and paradise, with the figure of the film-maker himself as a Dante-esque guide visiting Sarajevo. The film starts with the scratched celluloid recalling his Brechtian phase when black frames and scratches were inserted to emphasize that what was on the screen was a construction. Found footage of war films and the recognizable presence of Godard himself on screen interpellates the expert audience (Maule 1998: 117–23).

Godard has survived as a film-maker through a consistent profile of experimentation and exploration of the potentialities and histories of the moving image and by achieving a remarkable degree of artistic control over his production arrangements, whether with television or with powerful distributors like Gaumont and Canal Plus. The medium used has varied from work to work, but the integrating metadiscourse of Godard's personal countering of received meanings has imposed consistency. Although, across his work, Godard makes clear that his cultural politics are his alone, the prevalent discourse of cultural distinction functions to control the meanings and value to be assigned to his work in a way which does not escape the universalizing impulse of masculinist and Eurocentric traditions.

Agnès Varda

In order to exert some form of control, and not least financial reward, over a film, the artisanal character of much European production has privileged the multiple roles of successful directors. Agnès Varda's company, Ciné Tamaris, produces and distributes her films. One of the original *Nouvelle Vague* group, with scores of short films and features to her name, she is unashamedly authorial, the portability of new digital equipment assisting her stylistic choices in *The Gleaners and I* (*Les glaneurs et la glaneuse*, France, 2000). Varda is present in the film in body and voice-over, gleaning images both of the waste of resources in late-capitalist production (such as the pile of slightly malformed but perfectly edible potatoes dumped on the margin of a field to make it difficult for the poor and/or hungry to find them) and of the socially marginalized sectors of the population who take advantage of throw-away culture by gleaning from urban rubbish and the edges of society. The international success of this film prompted a sequel, *The Gleaners and I, Two Years Later* (*Les glaneurs et la glaneuse, deux ans après,* France, 2002), co-produced with the CNC and Canal Plus.

Varda's choice to stay in the artisanal sector of the film industry gives a higher profile to the fact that, with low-cost digital cameras, authorial status is no longer the purview of educated and articulate males but lies within anyone's grasp.

Dogme and the Danish bid for power

The example of the careers of the film-makers of the *Nouvelle Vague* has not escaped the notice of subsequent generations, but few revolts have been as effective as that of the Danish Dogme95 group. Like the *Nouvelle Vague*, Dogme95 did not come out of the blue but was the product of a long educational process for a small group of Danish Film School graduates, Thomas Vinterberg, Lars von Trier, Søren Kragh-Jacobsen and Kristian Levring. Von Trier launched the Dogme95 manifesto at a 1995 Paris conference. The groups' Vow of Chastity was a clear reaction to the American 'high concept' film-making style which was dominating European cinemas with what were regarded as flimsy narratives, cardboard cut-out characters, fast editing and dominant special effects. The manifesto set out ten rules for a renewal of film-making, rejecting auteurism by a refusal of the name of the director and the illusions offered by contemporary film-making practice.[7] From the start the precepts were difficult to obey, particularly that of using the Academy 35mm format when exciting developments in digital film-making were providing greater freedom to record how the world looked and sounded (Gaut 2003: 90).

The initial impetus was collectivist rather than authorial, although directors' names were rapidly assigned to films. Mette Hjort (2003: 31) in particular considers the Dogme rules a response to the inequities of globalizing processes where enormous American marketing budgets of $40 million plus represented the production budgets of almost 100 European films. For Hjort, Dogme95 is best thought of as 'a form of cinematic expression that comes to us from, and as a defence of, the margins of cinematic production that small nations and minor cinemas inevitably are'. In effect, the constraints imposed by low budgets and limited technical resources were elevated into self-imposed rules, intended to stimulate creativity, 'level the playing field' (Hjort 2003: 35) and address the vulnerabilities of minor cinemas. This explains their appeal to film-makers outside Denmark also wrestling with low budgets and a desire to reflect their own reality.

Although von Trier was the better-known director – his *Breaking the Waves* (Denmark/France/Sweden, 1996) had successfully grossed $4 million in the USA – it was the success of *The Celebration* (*Festen*, Thomas Vinterberg, Denmark, 1998) which cemented interest in Scandinavian cinema. *Festen* won a Cannes special jury prize and a US distribution deal. It was innovative in making a virtue of its use of digital video and in bridging the gap between the avant-garde and art cinema and in reaching the multiplex. *Festen* conforms to its self-imposed rules by limiting its story of a fraught family birthday party to 24 hours and using natural light, and it shares its use of location shooting and lack of genre identity with low-budget art films in general. In *Festen*'s case, the use of digital video gives the action the intimacy necessary to Christian's (Ulrich Thomsen) revelations that he and his dead twin sister had been sexually abused by their father, Helge (Henning Moritzen). Accusations gain increasing resonance by Helene (Paprika Steen) following clues leading to her finding the suicide note, and the misogynistic behaviour of their brother, Michael (Thomas Bo Larsen), towards his wife. However, Vinterberg's cinematography does not always conform to the rules, his jump cuts and occasionally swooping camera movements revealing the film school graduate's delight in the possibilities of the medium. *Festen* and von Trier's *The Idiots* (*Idioterne*, Denmark, 1998) were presented together at Cannes, with an announcement that other Dogme films were in preparation.

Although critics suspected that Dogme95 was a scam to obtain distribution deals (Matthews 1999: 39), the movement represented the consequences of the Nordic countries' response to globalization (Nestingen and Elkington 2005; Hjort and Bondebjerg 2001). From the 1980s the number of channels for subsidizing film production increased with the awareness that the cultures of the Nordic countries needed a protected space to develop and reflect the lives of their inhabitants. The internationalization of the cinemas of Denmark, Sweden, Norway, Finland and Iceland was assisted by the founding of Eurimages in 1988 and the Nordic Film and TV Fund in 1990. Arrangements with immediate Scandinavian neighbours made sense, none of whose populations could support a large-scale, commercial film industry. Co-financing drawn from transnational distribution agreements was considered a better way for films to reach international audiences than co-production (Brandstrup and Redvall 2005: 159–63). Consequently subventions available have evolved from the narrowly national (rigidly specifying national funding criteria) to a plethora of schemes to facilitate new entrants into the industry, and a variety of co-financing realities.

Lars von Trier's solution to the complexities of institutional funding was to form the Zentropa production company with Peter Aalbæck Jensen, which included his regular producer until 2005, Vibeke Windeløv, in the team. Although he has claimed that Zentropa allowed him the freedom to experiment without constraint (Addonizio et al 2000: 11), his production arrangements enable him to control his career to a degree which the next chapter will explore. Moreover, the oscillation between control and disruption is visible in all his films, but particularly in *Breaking the Waves* in the precepts of the Scottish religious community and in Bess's (Emily Watson) individual trajectory from marrying outside her community to prostituting herself as a pact with God to keep Jan (Stellan Skarsgård) alive.

The Dogme95 film-makers have now moved on, but their legacy is still very immediate. It matters not that von Trier has moved into big-budget international projects, or that some of the lesser known film-makers, such as Susanne Bier and Lone Scherfig, have moved into genre cinema (proscribed by the original manifesto). The shadow of the Dogme95 manifesto still resonates in situations where directors seek to make themselves noticed and where they need to make a virtue of necessity in terms of technical resources. Dogme shows the energy and possibilities offered by auteurist practice.

Other models of authorial control: Italy

The names of many successful European directors have imposed themselves through control not only of their directorial sphere but also of other areas of the industry. In Italy, Nanni Moretti is an actor/producer/director who also owns a cinema, the Sacher in Rome. He produces other director's films as well as his own and his cinema holds a short film festival. His films might appear autobiographical, in that he often acts in them, but Moretti performs the identity of someone of his generation, demonstrating the process of evolving a *habitus* (Wood 2005a: 174). Moretti is obsessed with language, particularly the sloppy imprecision of political and media language, and his 'characters' frequently use slogans to indicate their social and temporal positioning, or to contest the marginalization of the educated classes. His railing, both within and outside his films, against the mediocrity of the Italian political process, represented by Berlusconi's rise to power, has cemented his intellectual authority, assisted by Moretti's exploration in his films of the raw power of the human trajectory from life to death. *Dear Diary* (*Caro diario*, Italy/France, 1993) contains footage of Moretti's chemotherapy, *Aprile* (Italy/France, 1998) the birth of his son, and *The Son's Room* (*La stanza del figlio*, Italy/France, 2001) the grief-filled personal stocktaking of the fictional psychiatrist. His most bitterly satirical engagement with the Italian political process occurs in *Il Caimano* (Italy/France, 2006), which uses a fictional plot to make plain the Berlusconi exercise of power through the infantilization of the electorate and won Italy's equivalent of the Oscars, the David di Donatello. Moretti's constituency is a youthful, educated, left-leaning one and he has managed to establish himself with this audience niche internationally, while maintaining his intellectual authority in Italy through extending his film persona into that of political and cultural critic by personal interventions in political demonstrations and debates.

Gabriele Salvatores took the route of the mini-vertically integrated enterprise in the 1980s by establishing Colorado Films with the producer Maurizio Totti, the actor Diego Abatantuono, and Paolo Rossi. In 1991 *Mediterraneo* (Italy, 1991) won the Best Foreign Language Film Oscar and its good international distribution guaranteed commercial success. Salvatores' budgets progressively increased in the 1990s and his sci-fi film, *Nirvana* (Italy/France/UK, 1997), which cost $12 million, was sold in over 35 territories (Bizio 2002: 136). He also founded an independent agency, Moviement, for actors, directors, writers and musicians, in which the members are also shareholders. Salvatores' films are both local and global in that their narratives are grounded in Italian culture, but their generic hybridity and spectacular visual flair enable them to reach international audiences who may not understand all the cultural connotations (such as the Italian role in the Second World War in *Mediterraneo*, the southern poverty behind the 1970s' kidnappings in *I'm not afraid* (*Io non ho paura*, Italy/Spain/UK, 2002), or the yellow tones in his *noir* thriller, *Quo vadis baby?* (Italy, 2005).

Through its film laws and institutional bodies, the Italian government offers generous production financing which enables films to get off the ground. Subventions have, however, to be repaid out of box-office receipts and the director of a film which makes no money is denied access to subsequent grants. In addition, there are further payments, based on box-office receipts, to films which are retrospectively designated as quality films. This is defined as 'of national interest, or on serious themes, or with a script or cinematography which has won prizes'. Italian film-makers therefore have to concentrate their minds on their intended audience and have an interest in putting together creative teams which will produce films of the visual flair which is so typical of Italian production and which is often present in films with quite low budgets. Moretti and Salvatores have constructed authorial profiles enabling them to access national subventions, while protecting their careers by controlling distribution as well as production of their films.

Authorial control: the UK

The look of value on the screen, the name of the director and control over direction and production have also characterized Kenneth Branagh's films, although his profile is far from the elitist authorial image of Godard. The global/local interplay is visible in Branagh's exploitation of his place in the British theatrical tradition and his work in Hollywood. In both cases he uses his name to cross over into the mass audience by projecting an ordinary 'blokishness' which British critics have loved to hate, especially when he published his memoirs at the age of 23. Taking control of his artistic career entailed forming the Renaissance theatre company in 1987, winding it up in 1995. Branagh has cornered a market in filmed Shakespeare adaptations which have drawn on his aims to make the Bard understandable to new audiences and on his contact book of well-known actors. The results display an energetic and anti-intellectual path to appreciating Shakespeare which has earned him the critics' sneers of being a middle-brow 'luvvie'.[8] Anti-Branagh criticism signals his work as the site of class wars in the arena of national identity in the 1990s when the Thatcherite conservative ethos of entrepreneurialism clashed with the desire for stasis offered by conservative and upper-class high culture. Branagh's energy and working-class, Belfast background was perceived as an affront to notions of the reserved and revering thespian tradition.

Branagh's move into film-making in the early 1990s was initially very successful. His *Henry V* (UK, 1989) both draws on the iconography of *Star Wars* and its greyness and dirt recall photographs of the First World War. *Peter's Friends* (UK, 1992), made between *Dead Again* (USA, 1991) and *Much Ado About Nothing* (UK/USA, 1993), is a chamber piece, put together at great speed and clearly aimed at the American market of thirty-somethings receptive to British television comedies, the 'Woody Allen audience'. This niche audience dictated the low budget of $2.3 million, put together by Renaissance Films, UK's Channel 4 television, Goldwyn and Entertainment Film, with the actors working for 2 per cent shares of the producer's net. The film has limited locations and props, the camera work organized to foreground the actors' performances in a story of commonplaces and betrayals in a reunion of university friends. The film returned over 120% of its production costs. His energetic *Much Ado* starts with a touristic long-shot of the beautiful Tuscan countryside, drawing the viewer in to a hermetic world in which the talents of his Anglo-American cast, Denzel Washington, Keanu Reeves, Michael Keaton, Branagh himself, Emma Thompson and Richard Briers, are displayed. With an estimated budget of $18 million, the film grossed over $30 million in the USA and UK alone, paving the way for *Mary Shelley's Frankenstein* (UK/Japan/USA, 1994), which again generated over $30 million gross, but on a budget of $45 million. Branagh's literary and theatrical adaptations are postmodern in their display and love of gothic emotional and visual excess and penchant for the foregrounding of instability and conflict.

Branagh reverted to low-budget Shakespeare adaptations in the late 1990s. These have the advantage of well-known texts, such as *Hamlet* (UK/USA, 1996), which are frequently the subject of school examination syllabuses, and the prestige of established actors. Branagh's budgets have once again slowly increased to the $27 million for his first opera film, *The Magic Flute*, co-financed by the Peter Moores Foundation with the aim of expanding the audience for opera in English and scheduled for 2007 release. Like Shakespeare, opera is a genre with legs, not going out of fashion and with an infinite shelf life among opera fans (Wood 2005b: 191). Branagh epitomizes the director as star, his anti-elitist profile overcoming critics' snobbish dislike of his combination of 'ordinariness' and entreprencurialism as his audience responds to his use of popular media references and the deliberate playing down of grand actorly gestures characterized by his upping the career profile of the accomplished UK television actor, Richard Briers. His films cross over from high culture into the multiplex.

Michael Winterbottom

The contemporary difficulties of the concept of the director as *auteur* are epitomized by Michael Winterbottom. His films are marketed under his name, but he escapes the authorial badge, mainly because his output defies easy classification. Whereas critics can type François Ozon's films by their queer sensibility and rejection of the patriarchal family, Winterbottom is a chameleon *auteur* whose films make the commercial and ideological context of film production visible. While admitting that financiers are often puzzled by the diversity of his output, Winterbottom maintains that 'films are so hard to get financed that if I'm interested in an idea, I'll just do it, whatever the genre' (Maher 2005: 15). He has his own production company, Revolution Films, but no consistent profile for critics to explain. He has directed adaptations of classic books, *Jude* (UK, 1996), *The Claim* (UK/France/Canada, 2000) and *A Cock and Bull Story* (UK, 2005); dramas of contemporary issues such as people smuggling, *In This World* (UK, 2002), which won the Berlin Golden Bear and BAFTA awards, and the civil wars in the Balkans, *Welcome to Sarajevo* (UK, 1997); a lesbian road movie, *Butterfly Kiss* (UK, 1995); an acclaimed television drama-documentary made for Britain's Channel 4 with a budget of £1.5 million, *The Road to Guantánamo* (UK, 2006); the sexually explicit, low-budget (£1 million) *Nine Songs* (UK, 2004), which won the best cinematography prize at the 2004 San Sebastián film festival and had a wide international distribution; and science fiction with *Code 46* (UK, 2003, co-produced with the BBC with a budget of around $7.5 million). His cult classic, *24 Hour Party People* (UK, 2002), centred on Tony

Wilson's (Steve Coogan) contribution to the Manchester club scene in the 1970s and 1980s, the chaotic history of Factory records and the Hacienda club.

Winterbottom's film-making is visually assured, particularly in exploiting the pictorial elements of the lowering skies and bleak countryside in *Jude*, the claustrophobic and chaotic in *Welcome to Sarajevo*, *24 Hour Party People* and *A Cock and Bull Story*. The latter film is a multi-layered interpretation of Sterne's *The Life and Opinions of Tristram Shandy, Gentleman* through the device of a film crew attempting to film an adaptation of the book. The multi-generic result has events in the present both in the film crew's and in the actors' personal lives interact with the text they are trying to adapt. Shandy's (Steve Coogan) inability to get his story to the moment of his birth resonates with the film director Mark's (Jeremy Northam) efforts to control his relentlessly competitive actors in order to tell the story. Coogan's extra-marital dalliances and his inability to empathize with his pregnant partner rhyme with Shandy's egocentrism. Critics worried that audiences unfamiliar with Coogan's earlier media personae would not appreciate the film, but it functions well as a comedy about film-making – Mark lures Gillian Anderson (Widow Wadman) to the set, the finance coming with her enables them to shoot the battle scene in which Shandy's uncle (Rob Brydon) is wounded in an unnameable part of his anatomy. With enjoyable postmodern wit and irony, Widow Wadman and battles are then left on the cutting-room floor of the fictional film within a film, while Winterbottom has allowed the viewer to see the process of their creation. Winterbottom's cinema is inconsistent, his hopping from genre to genre preventing formation of a neat authorial profile.

Conclusion

In a territory as vast as Europe, the sheer numbers of talented people mean that young and old jostle for attention for their ideas and projects, and for financing. Ways into the film industry include film school training, experience in making adverts, music videos and short films. Peter Cattaneo, Lyn Ramsay and Shane Meadows all entered the film industry by the short film route. Festivals showcasing short films have mushroomed alongside the huge increase in short film production generated by the financial accessibility of digital film-making equipment and the internet's potential to introduce films and names to a wide audience.[9] Those who take the short films route to recognition start with a high level of control over their production and can take advantage of the many training schemes for new film-makers offered by the MEDIA programme. The necessity to retain some control over output and career in a fiercely competitive market explains why so many young film-makers have multiple roles, commonly as director/screenwriter and often as actor/director. Directors whose film(s) have gained critical, festival or web attention then have the task of building themselves a profile and constituency. The myth that authorial film-making takes no account of a film's audience is revealed as a total fallacy by the difficulties of breaking into the industry and by the fact that those who have made their mark by achieving mainstream box-office success are often courted and lured into the US, international film industry which, like any capitalist enterprise, needs a constant stream of different products in order to tempt the jaded palette of the consumer.

Authorial cinema survives as a category because it is enshrined in institutional practice and in public discourse. *Auteurs* have a cultural and commercial function, licensed by virtue of their skills and aims to explore areas outside the mainstream and existing as a commercial performance of 'the business of being an auteur' (Corrigan 1991: 104). However, whereas the marketing of European authorial cinema openly fetishizes the director's name and identifies markers of authorial enunciation in their films, the real business of negotiating production finance and distribution deals is largely concealed. As Rod Stoneman suggests, the contemporary *auteur* must be market responsive:

> European cinema will fail only if it tries to imitate industrial models. The intensity and clarity and formal motivation that enable an auteur to have something to say that is distinct and interesting have to be maintained, but in tension with a responsivity to the market. The traditional self-expression of the artist is inadequate in an expensive cultural industry.
>
> (Quoted in Sheehy 2001: 8)

The polarization of auteurist film-making results in the low- to mid-budget style of production described above and its alternative, the European big-budget ($11 million plus) quality cinema explored in the next chapter.

Notes

1. Rohmer claimed that he spent three years working on the digital backdrops and that the stylized look was born out of necessity as there was not enough money to construct the sets (Dalton 2002: 23).
2. His character's pro-monarchist views had led French historians to accuse him of right-wing revisionism and treachery in his portrayal of revolutionaries as cruel and sadistic. Rohmer uses the events of the Revolution to open up debate about responsibility and justice. In interviews he rejected the idea of the sovereignty of the people excusing violence (Henley 2001: 20), a view rejected by French critics, but with a resonance for other European civil wars at the end of the twentieth century.
3. Philip French describes *Notre Musique* as coming to his long-suffering fans 'like a bobbing bottle with a piece of blank paper inside' (2005: 9).
4. Particularly how Hollywood cannibalizes others' histories and memories and how the distribution sector has come to be more important than production (Brown 2001).
5. 1990 Berlin Film Festival notes (translated by Waltraud Loges), quoted in 35th London Film Festival Programme, 1991: 262.
6. Production notes quoted in 34th London Film Festival Programme, 1990: 157.
7. http://www.dogme95.dk/the_vow/vow.html – accessed 18 January 2000. The vow refuses mainstream cinematic artifice. Shooting must be done on location with existing props. Sound must be linked to image, the camera must be hand-held and special lighting and filters are not allowed. Genre films are not acceptable and the format must be academy 35mm.

8. 'Luvvie' is a term derived from British actors' habit of addressing colleagues as 'love' and has developed pejorative connotations of a rather precious group of insiders.
9. The online and offline distributor Atom Films claimed to have received 40,000 short films in the two years before 2000. The talent revealed by the digital short film explosion forced the UK Film Council to rethink its policy (Cole 2000: 16).

chapter three

The evolution of the 'quality' film

The previous chapter gave some examples of the development of the art cinema sector of European film production and of evolutions in the figure of the director/*auteur*. Several well-known figures were notably absent, predominantly because they do not fit the Neale and Bordwell explanations of the European art film. This chapter will explore a form of cinema which started to develop out of art cinema practice in the mid-1970s, quality cinema, and will examine how global and local trends have impacted on it. Quality cinema occupies the top end of the authorial and art cinema market and is characterized by big budgets, stars, international distribution and visually, by spectacle. There have been several creative solutions to the problem of developing a career profile and reaching an audience, of which the international, quality film represents the most expensive. The careers of some Italian directors will be used to demonstrate the move into this sector and the difficulties of leaving it. Recent films by Lars von Trier show the perils of Americanization in adopting international, big-budget style. The possibilities of the French *cinema du look* to combine spectacle with serious purpose will be examined, as will Pedro Almodóvar's exploitation of Spanishness for an international audience.

Quality cinema represents one solution to the problems which have become more acute since 2000. The number of cinema tickets sold in 2004 amounted to 1,006 million (EU25), but only 27.4% of admissions related to European films, slightly up on 2003. On average, 70.5% of the European market went to American films, but 11.2% of the EU admissions total was contributed by international co-productions involving a US producer and one or more European partners. The international European film aims at a production quality to compete with US films worldwide. The increase in co-productions with the USA shows an ambition to benefit from American distribution networks, but the profits generated from distribution go back to the USA. This type of cinema implies an acceptance of the economic imperatives of global media competition which, as Tim Bergfelder has suggested, are viewed with suspicion by left-wing and conservative critics and politicians alike, the former suspecting acceptance of American capitalist agendas and the latter identifying a loss of national cultural distinctiveness (2000: 139). There is some truth in both views, but this chapter will also explore the distinctly European themes and appearance of quality cinema which, by its nature, engages with the experience of having plural identities in the contemporary world.

The evolution of the quality film

How does a film-maker enter quality film production and what are the advantages and drawbacks? As Chapter Two argued, the mid-1970s provided the pivotal moment when European film industry practice and the consequences of the proliferation of television stations collided to produce new film-making strategies to hedge the risk of film production. The adage that 'you're only as good as your last film' indicated the calculation of a director's next budget, based on her/his last success. A director would be offered similar budgets to those of successful films, but a major success could result in a quantifiable budget leap. The postwar development of systems of grants, tax breaks and subventions for films deemed to have cultural importance was crucial as the emphasis on prestige and 'quality' was effective in encouraging producers to identify certain directors and creative workers who would be likely to deliver the product necessary to qualify for these attractive financial incentives. Financial pressures could not be ignored. Many art film directors used their cultural background and the structures of their national (and then international) film industries in order to indicate their position as the controlling force behind the films. In doing this they were supported by, and took advantage of, wider developments in the media industries, such as the expansion of television, cable, satellite and video. From the 1980s onwards the development of big-budget films, made largely with co-production deals, directed by well-known directors (often associated with art cinema practice), but firmly directed at a mainstream, mass audience, is visible.

Critics have neglected to explore this category, or to discuss the changes in narrative style and techniques that aiming at a mass audience have entailed in the work of individual directors. Quality cinema is similar to *auteur* cinema in its validation of the director as guarantor of originality in conceiving the project and of technical mastery of cinematic techniques, but differs in having high production values, large budgets and wide distribution.

Miramax

From the early 1990s onwards the achievement of a Miramax distribution deal meant the potential to achieve good profits on worldwide in-depth distribution and the history of the company's success illuminates the changes in film marketing and the films themselves since the end of the 1980s. Miramax, headed by Bob and Harvey Weinstein, was an independent US distributor, set up in 1979, specializing in co-production and distribution arrangements for independent and foreign-language films. In 1993 the Disney organization bought Miramax for an estimated $75 million, but prudently allowed the Weinsteins to retain the company's separate identity. The advantage for Miramax was access to sectors of the parent company's vertically integrated structure, particularly the marketing and publicity expertise of Buena Vista, and the financial wherewithal to supply hundreds of viewing copies of the films. Miramax went from a relatively small company in the mid-1990s to a global distributor in ten years by putting in place rigorous tracking systems to monitor international box office daily (Brown 2000: 25). The cost of TV and video rights, currency fluctuations, company information in individual countries and territories were all monitored and factored into any release pattern. Gone are the days when an Italian company had enough time between the rumour of an American blockbuster's production and its release in Italy to produce and rush out their cheap film with a similar title to take advantage of the well-funded American advertising campaign. By the end of the 1990s the company had also capitalized on the increased speed of information flows and the need to combat piracy by planning simultaneous global releases for event films, a category which includes big-budget quality cinema.

For quality cinema, festivals are still important as marketing and sales opportunities. The Cannes film festival, which takes place at the end of May, tended to be regarded by American producers and distributors as an auteurist (and expensive) event at the wrong time of year when adverse criticism could kill a blockbuster's successful release (Turan 2002: 28–29). However, European release patterns have become year-round and the summer months, which in Southern Europe were regarded as a dead season, are now prime release periods since cinemas all have air-conditioning. By 2000 Miramax switched much of its efforts to Cannes, rather than relying on Venice to launch its films' European campaigns (Brown 2000: 26).

The list of films co-produced and/or distributed by Miramax shows not only the hedging of risk in a very varied annual slate but also that film-makers whose work has performed well attract subsequent Miramax distribution, particularly those such as Neil Jordan, Jean-Pierre Jeunet, Gabriele Salvatores, Quentin Tarantino and Léos Carax, taken up by the Weinsteins at the beginning of the 1990s when Hollywood production went through a phase of tiring the audience. The Miramax slate included American genre and cult films (marketed under the Dimension label), small, low-budget films with local content, and big-budget quality films. Budgets were tightly controlled and although event films such as *Shakespeare in Love* (John Madden, USA/UK, 1998) had a budget estimated at between $30–40 million (generating over $100 million at the North American box office), the company's average budget was around $14 million. The company also purchased libraries of old French films for distribution and reined back on buying distribution rights in 1999 to prepare for entry into the DVD market. *Écran-noir*'s study of Oscar wins and nominations had Miramax topping the US companies league in nominations for Best Director and Best Screenplay, reflecting the quality niche the company had developed (Anon. 2000). Their success led to imitations and competition from New Line/Fine Line, Universal's October Films, Fox Searchlight and Sony Classics.

The Weinsteins parted company with Disney in 2004, forming a new company. The split was attributed to the Weinsteins' frustration at Disney's refusal to invest in lucrative projects such as *The Lord of the Rings* and TV franchises, and Disney's refusal to distribute *Fahrenheit 9/11* on the grounds of Michael Eisner's disagreement with the film's politics (Hopkins 2004: 37). The films which The Weinstein Company has distributed since then have been predominantly American popular genre products. It remains to be seen whether the Weinsteins will be able to persuade their financiers to invest in the sorts of European quality production which so enhanced Miramax's reputation and whether their new company will have the money to develop the business intelligence to replicate their worldwide success.

The Italian case

The Italian case provides some answers to the questions posed earlier. Francesco Rosi is one of the second wave of postwar 'great directors' who had a long apprenticeship in the popular and art sectors of the Italian film industry before making his first film in 1956. His authorial breakthrough came with *Salvatore Giuliano* (Italy, 1961), a hard-hitting exploration of the reasons behind the death of a Sicilian bandit, which won the 1962 Berlin Silver Bear and came tenth in Italian box office lists that year. This success, like Fellini's with *La dolce vita* (Italy, 1961), showed producers and distributors that it was possible to make money from 'difficult' subjects (Wood 2005a). By the mid-1970s, Rosi had established his reputation as a political film-maker; his films won prizes at major festivals and his co-production arrangements and increasing use of foreign stars cemented his international profile.

When the deregulation of Italian television impacted on cinema-going from 1976 onwards, Rosi's films were already commanding big budgets and international releases. *Carmen* (Italy/France, 1984) initially seems untypical for a director with a reputation as a political film-maker, but Gaumont's choice of Rosi to direct the film appears logical on closer inspection. Rosi's political films had been investigative narratives exploring mysteries in Italian civic life. He therefore had experience of managing complex stories and of communicating his political ideas clearly. His films have the look of quality with carefully composed and spectacular architectural shots, foregrounding his enunciative presence within the films and his skills in constructing set pieces involving hundreds of extras, foreign stars and complex camera movements. His ability to engage his audience emotionally in his political analyses was also an advantage in moving into mainstream international film-making. So, too, was the cultural strategy of his production/distribution company, Gaumont, which was signing up older, established European directors who would provide the event films which would fill their first-run city-centre cinemas at premium prices.

Rosi's cinema foregrounds disruption and excess, expressed narratively by events (such as deaths or accidents) which initiate investigations, and visually through stressed camera angles, wide-angle long-shots and the use of contrasting architectural paradigms. Both are associated with the neo-baroque, a typical form of Italian postmodernism which does not imply a return to the baroque but to contemporary culture's preference for open narratives, chaos and catastrophe (Calabrese 1992: xii). In Rosi's films, visual excess aims to draw attention to the social use of space and to the complexity of situations which the powerful prefer to represent as open to simple explanations.

A director with a reputation for competence in the sphere of big-budget art or quality cinema needs projects which are internationally exportable, because such films do not amortize their costs on the home market. Projects must find recognition with international audiences, hence the consistent use by all European (and increasingly the American) film industries of the books of well-known or cult authors. Industrial constraints – the need to maximize selling opportunities of a variety of products besides the film itself, and the mass-appeal imperatives of commercial broadcasting – have resulted in the increased homogenization of prestige productions from both sides of the Atlantic. As Rossi suggested, commercial concerns have an effect on form:

> Berlusconi recently enunciated the iron principles of production as: 'filmed in English, with the needs of the international market in mind and with no sequence lasting more than 7 minutes, in order to facilitate the harmonious placing of adverts when the film is broadcast'.
>
> (Rossi 1988: 4)

In the case of Rosi's García Màrquez adaptation, *Chronicle of a Death Foretold* (*Cronaca di una morte annunciata*, Italy/France/Colombia, 1987), the needs of the international market involved the suppression of dialogue and a release with different language tracks for different territories. The presence of Gaumont and terrestrial and satellite television interests ensured its financial success, but it was disliked as an adaptation. *To Forget Palermo* (*Dimenticare Palermo*, France/Italy, 1990) was co-produced by the Cecchi Gori company, Berlusconi's Reteitalia television channel and Gaumont. Using the device of an Italo-American politician's (Jim Belushi) honeymoon visit to Sicily to discover his roots, the film explored mafia control of international drug trafficking. An established director wishing to explore contemporary issues has a choice between working in mid-budget television films or big-budget, international, complex projects where polemical debate and incisive critiques of society are inappropriate, but where serious ideas, spectacle and the director's name guarantee quality. Rosi's last film, an adaptation of Primo Levi's internationally acclaimed book, *La tregua*, is an example of the latter, inviting comparison between the holocaust and the Balkan genocide. Where films do not succeed in having an enormous international distribution, they may still manage to make their mark by hedging their bets through production deals with television and satellite. Made with the collaboration of Italian state television, RAI, and Canal Plus, *The Truce* (*La tregua*, Italy/France/Switzerland/Germany, 1996) is a picaresque narrative which follows the journey home of a mixed group of holocaust survivors. Starting with the icy tones of the liberation of Auschwitz by the Red Army, the film gradually takes on the verdant greens and warm colours of spring and summer as Primo (John Turturro) and his fellow Italians return to the enjoyment of life and living. The pace is slow, prompting reflection not only on the sense of the precariousness of life which has been lost at the end of the century but also on the positive contribution of the Soviet Union to ideas of the just state and its citizens. It was successful in Italy, had wide satellite exposure and appeared both as a sell-through video and as an Italian newsstand video title. The film's marketing stressed the prestige of the film-maker, Rosi, as much as the author, Levi. However, it had the misfortune to have Miramax buy the distribution rights when the company had also bought the rights to Roberto Benigni's *Life is Beautiful* (*La vita è bella*, Italy, 1996). Miramax gave the latter film saturation marketing, achieving enormous financial success.

Rosi's move into quality film shows that this sector tends to reinforce a director's existing profile and to militate against creative changes. Directors rapidly become associated with a particular genre or type of film and, like the fine art market, an artist is not seen as 'serious' if she/he displays too radical a shift in style. Critics can explain stylistic development in time, but not inconsistencies in form or subject. Rosi's recent work is typified by a very postmodern nostalgia, by less critical success and by difficulties in maintaining a convincing political agenda. All three are bound up in the crisis of metanarratives identified by Lyotard (1984).

The actor/director Roberto Benigni represents another response to globalization, having started in alternative television where his popularity launched him into films in which he starred. He came to international attention through appearances in independent, cult English-language films such as Jim Jarmusch's *Down By Law* (USA, 1986) and set up his own production company, Melampo Cinematografica, to control his career. His comedies tapped into the irreverent attitude towards institutions unleashed by the corruption scandals of the early 1990s and his appearance in Fellini's *The voice of the moon* (*La voce della luna*, Italy, 1996) cemented his profile as the thinking person's comic. Avoiding the sexism, parochialism and regional accents of most Italian comics, Benigni's success with both intellectuals and children has disassociated him from his television past and moved him into the quality sector (Repetto and Tagliabue 2000: 20). Only a comic actor of his reputation could have succeeded in putting together the *La vita è bella* holocaust comedy which won three Oscars and much notoriety for Guido's (Benigni) fantasy explanations of life in the concentration camp for his son, Giosuè. Cleverly constructed in two parts, the early scenes of the beautiful Tuscan town, bathed in golden light, both appeal to the touristic gaze of the international spectator and suggest the fundamental goodness of Italy, in contrast to the darkness and violence of the concentration camp sequences.

No such controversy attaches to the films of Franco Zeffirelli who, like Rosi, started as an assistant to the great *auteur*, Luchino Visconti. Successful quality films invariably draw on strong generic elements, national stereotypes and touristic impressions of a national identity. Zeffirelli's right-wing views have made him critically unfashionable, but he has had a prolific career making literary adaptations, biblical epics and opera films with international stars for terrestrial and satellite television, and occasional cinema release. Like his contemporaries, he makes the most of the spectacular potential of the characteristic spaces of Italian towns and countryside. His films are characterized by showy visuals and appeal to the cultural capital of an international, educated audience. *Tea with Mussolini* (*Un tè con Mussolini*, Italy/UK, 2000) is a simple story of a young Italian boy brought up by a group of eccentric English women in 1930s' Florence. The opening tracking shots introduce the characters of well-known actors while the long shots foreground recognizable Florentine landmarks. Fine performances, a simple story and abundant use of cliché also mark *Callas Forever* (Italy/UK/France/Spain/Romania, 2002). Jeremy Irons plays the gay impresario tempting Callas (Fanny Ardant) to one last performance in a story of a talented woman rising above personal heartbreak and tragedy, while wearing wonderful 1960s' costumes. The multi-country co-production qualified for Eurimages funding and Canal Plus's assistance guaranteed the satellite distribution which is Zeffirelli's usual sphere. Appeal to the opera-buff audience is guaranteed by the selected highlights of Callas's performances on the DVD.

Liliana Cavani, whose *Night Porter* (*Il portiere di notte*, Italy, 1974) gave her international notoriety, also makes quality films, but manages to communicate the dangers and allure of amoral materialism. *Ripley's Game* (*Il gioco di Ripley*, Italy/UK/USA, 2002) is an adaptation of Patricia Highsmith's psychological thriller, filmed in English and starring John Malkovich and Dougray Scott. It had a typical quality film budget of $30 million and Fine Line distribution. The film displays all the characteristics of *film noir*, with the Italian inflection of distorted camera angles, spectacular architectural shots and yellow tones.[1] The neo-baroque use of different architectural paradigms to suggest instability can be seen in the excessive postmodern pastiche of the interiors of Ripley's (John Malkovich) house and the asymmetry of the huge windows. In the final sequence where Ripley's partner performs her harpsichord solo in the baroque church, the obsessively repetitious music finds its visual counterpart in the circular soaring movements of the camera through the enormous space.

Bernardo Bertolucci is one of the few directors who managed to exit the quality sphere of production. He established his auteurist credentials early, dabbled in Godardian counter-cinema, then returned to the art cinema mainstream by taking advantage of RAI television's cultural agenda to reach wide audiences in the 1970s. His budget breakthrough came with the phenomenal financial success of *Last Tango in Paris* (*Ultimo tango a Parigi*, France/Italy/USA, 1972), which moved his worth several notches up the investors' league tables (Wood 2002: 45). From the mid-1980s Bertolucci's films questioned the values of European society, exploring other cultures and belief systems, and were granted large budgets to do this – $25 million for *The Last Emperor* (Italy/Hong Kong/UK, 1987, which won nine Oscars and grossed $93 million) and *The Sheltering Sky* (UK/Italy, 1990), and $33 million for *Little Buddha* (France/UK, 1993). These visually sumptuous films managed to explore ideas about gender and personal authenticity and the moral vacuum left by the discrediting of the grand metanarratives. With *Stealing Beauty* (*Io ballo da sola*, Italy/France/UK, 1996) Bertolucci returned to mid-budget production and his films since then – *Besieged* (*L'assedio*, Italy/UK, 1998) and *The Dreamers* (*I sognatori*, Italy/France/UK, 2003) – are quest dramas of the search for identity and history. All feature youthful characters living outside their country of origin, searching for meaning among the effects of globalization. *Stealing Beauty* cost $10 million. It was a financial and critical success for Fox Searchlight, the studio's prestige art-house division which produces and distributes what are regarded as risky films, using internationally known directors but aiming at a successful, worldwide distribution.

The Italian route into the quality film is dependent on a successful commercial and critical profile, experience of international actors, exceptional communication skills in skilful plotting and spectacular visual flair. The majority of Italian directors do not achieve this. One film-maker who has made his calling card to move into this sector is Paolo Sorrentino, whose *The Consequences of Love* (*Le conseguenze dell'amore*, Italy/Switzerland, 2004) won several prestigious David di Donatello prizes. This *film noir* follows the fate of a middle-aged accountant, Titta Di Girolamo (Toni Servillo), confined to a luxury hotel in Switzerland where he banks a suitcase of money for the mafia each week. Again, the oscillation between control and chaos is played out visually in the dichotomy between the cool, modernist interiors of the bank and hotel and the warm, curling decorations of the hotel bar where Titta falls in love with the young barmaid (Olivia Magnani). Love is the disruption which spurs him to steal from the mafia to buy her shoes and a car, for which he is called to account by his Boss. The complexity of the narrative and *mise-en-scène* is encapsulated in the sequence where Titta is driven by two hoods to the quarry where he will be lowered into a block of concrete. As the mafiosi sing along to Ornella Vanoni's *Rossetto e cioccolato*, the car enters a yellow-lit tunnel, Titta's gaze pans outside the car, motivating flashbacks to his theft of the money and murder of two gangsters, while the song's words obliquely explain his psychology. *The Consequences of Love* was one of the few films to break the £1 million barrier in UK box-office receipts, a signal that the market is getting used to non-national European films.

Lars von Trier

Lars von Trier's career also demonstrates the inexorable rise in budgets which goes with entry into the quality sector and a progressive abandonment of the precepts of Dogme95. *Breaking the Waves* (Denmark/France/Sweden, 1996) was critically and financially successful, unusual for a hand-held cinemascope production set in the ultra-conservative protestant communities of the north of Scotland and combining excessive melodrama with a generically different montage style.

Von Trier broke the Dogme95 precepts by choosing to make a musical with *Dancer in the Dark* (Denmark/Germany/Netherlands/USA/UK/France/Sweden/Finland/Norway, 2000), which follows the difficult choices of a Czech immigrant in the USA, Selma (Björk), who is progressively losing her sight. *Dancer in the Dark* combines psychological realism and emotional power with unsettling fantasy, ensuring critical interest. The Dogme-like hand-held camera work, moving from character to character so that they are always situated in their environment, and sudden moves to song and dance sequences in the factory where Selma works, foreground directorial artifice and break the spectatorial illusion. In its winning the Cannes *Palme d'or*, use of famous international actors, Björk, Catherine Deneuve, song and dance, and the much-publicized disagreements between Björk and von Trier, the film scored PR coups. *Dancer*'s festival success ensured a Fine Line distribution in the USA.[2] His publicity machine again worked overtime in preparations for the filming of *Dogville* (Denmark/Sweden/France/Norway/Netherlands/Finland/USA/UK, 2003), in which the will-she/won't-she saga of whether Nicole Kidman would sign up for the film was played out over several weeks. Like *Dancer in the Dark*, *Dogville*'s production was backed by the Franco–German satellite channel, ARTE, among a host of others. Both films are transnational, with extremely complex production packages of institutional and regional funding, television, satellite and distribution company finance. Both are set in the USA, but (as von Trier has a phobia about flying) filmed in Scandinavia (in the Trollhätten studios known familiarly as 'Trollywood'), prompting interesting reflection on the nature of globalized film. Both films have an American presence in the multinational production package but use their critical stance towards the American criminal justice system, capitalism and small-town social attitudes to also suggest contemporary parallels about humanity's capacity for evil. Moreover, both films are marketed on their director's name and are deliberately controversial so as to court maximum publicity.

Dogville is filmed on an open set in which streets and houses are marked out on the studio floor, concentrating attention on the actors' performances in the melodramatic events of Grace's (Nicole Kidman) visit to the town, fleeing from mafia pursuit. Grace is sheltered by the townspeople in return for services, initially as a servant, but degenerating into sexual servitude which has her chained up like a dog. *Dogville*'s dark themes are complemented by the *chiaroscuro*, high-contrast lighting and the monochrome brown tones of the costumes. Given *Dogville*'s subject, length (three hours plus), anti-realist aesthetic, notoriety, stars and cost (DKK 83 million, about €11.5 million), it needed wide international distribution to an international, first-run, art cinema audience. It was widely distributed in Europe, Australasia, North and South America and Hong Kong, prompting an answer to Trevor Elkington's question as to why global audiences would be interested in films from the Nordic region (2005: 32). Von Trier's films were high-concept crossovers from art cinema, marketed on his Dogme reputation, and they indicate that global flows do not always proceed from the United States to the rest of the world; American audiences have also been internationalized. Philip French was fairly typical of critics finding *Dogville* 'ludicrous, pretentious and naïve [but...] also boldly conceived, genuinely risky and disturbing' (2004a: 9), in a way that accountancy-driven Hollywood mainstream certainly is not. Von Trier's audiences are cosmopolitans in Hannerz's sense of taking a stance towards diversity, 'an orientation, a willingness to engage with the Other' (1990: 239). Competence in an esoteric field, such as the auteurist cinema of a small, Northern European country, 'entails a sense of mastery' (Hannerz 1990: 240), which contributes to a sense of existing in a global culture.

Manderlay (Denmark/France/Germany/Sweden/Netherlands, 2005) was equally controversial. In the company of her gangster father and his gang, Grace (Bryce Dallas Howard) asks to be left behind at the deep-South plantation they come across. Indignant at the casual brutality with which the plantation's white owners treat their slaves, Grace imprisons the owners and frees the slaves. The slaves are neither sufficiently grateful, nor equipped (and neither is Grace) to run the estate. Grace agrees to chopping down trees for fuel, only to realize too late that they provided shade for crops and cabins. She lusts after a black labourer and takes to sleeping in the slave huts. Like *Dogville*, *Manderlay*'s Brechtian distancing devices of stylized sets at chalk-marked locations in a dark studio stage at Trollhätten acquire their own reality and absorb the audience on its own terms. But *Manderlay* was too like von Trier's previous film, was equally long but lacked many stars, and it recouped only a fraction of its estimated $14.2 million budget from its theatrical release. The two films were originally conceived as a trilogy, but the third, *Washington*, was shelved indefinitely. In 2003 the Danish Ministry of Trade and Industry, responsible for administering the law on companies, accounts and business law, launched an investigation into the financial situation of several Zentropa companies (Zentropa established co-ownership of several production companies in the early 2000s). Zentropa's internet company, Tvropa, filed for insolvency, several large television projects failed to materialize and staff numbers were cut by 25% (Kibar 2003). Among the many 'statements' issuing from Zentropa was one suggesting that the company would take over the distribution of its films in order to get the best deals.[3] The net result of von Trier's long foray into the quality sector is that his name is known worldwide and while he has an enthusiastic international audience, his last two films were criticized for being anti-American. Von Trier clearly considered that a change of direction was called for.

In February 2006 von Trier announced that, in his fiftieth year, he would be 'narrowing down', and that 'over the last few years I have felt increasingly burdened by barren habits and expectations (my own and other people's) and I feel the urge to tidy up' (Macnab 2006a: 23). Von Trier's business partner, Peter Aalbæk Jensen, is an advocate of low-budget production, preferring to 'produce two films for $4.3 million' rather than just one (Neiiendam 2003: 18). Given the extremely complex financing of von Trier's big-budget films, and the risk involved, downsizing makes sense and avoids the stress and pressure associated with large-scale productions. As Bertolucci's career has shown, well-known directors can move back into low-budget, auteurist film-making where they can make more personal films and their name brings distribution deals which cover the film's costs. Other directors have gone down this route. The financial and critical success of Mike Leigh's 1990s films, particularly *Secrets and Lies* (UK, 1996), which won the Cannes *Palme d'or* and five Oscar nominations, led to a big budget for *Topsy Turvey* (UK, 2000). Set in the 15-month period between the first night of Gilbert and Sullivan's *Princess Ida* in January 1884 and the first night of *The Mikado* in March 1885, *Topsy Turvey* allows Leigh to range over the professional concerns of the actors and owners of the D'Oyly Carte Company, employing his usual strategy of working with an ensemble cast. It is different only in the sumptuous costumes and sets in which rich colours dominate. *Topsy Turvey* was not followed by other, high-budget films, but a return to low-budget contemporary social dramas in the auteurist mould. Costume drama resurfaced with *Vera Drake* (UK, 2005), set in 1950s' Islington, which won the 2004 Venice Golden Lion.

Some down-sizing is relative. Paul Verhoeven returned to his Dutch roots in 2005 after mixed results for his recent US films to shoot *Black Book* (*Zwartboek*, Netherlands/Belgium/UK/Germany, 2006). The central character Rachel (Carice van Houten), a beautiful Jewish cabaret artiste, survives membership of the wartime resistance and a love affair with an SS officer, her personal history opening up the political realities of Dutch collaboration with the occupying Nazi forces who paid seven guilders 50 for each Jew handed over (Macnab 2005: 6). *Black Book*, produced by key producer San Fu Maltha, was conceived as a quality, international production. In its violent set pieces of bombing raids and resistance attacks, Nazi kitsch gatherings, explicit sex scenes and a tightly scripted plot with many twists and turns, Verhoeven's American experience is visible, foregrounding the convergence between American high-concept and European quality cinema.

The *cinéma du look*

The French have always been ambivalent about quality cinema, the term *cinéma de qualité* being coined in the 1940s and 1950s to describe rather unadventurous, big-budget films with high production values and stars. The *cinema du look*, defined by Ginette Vincendeau as non-naturalistic, aestheticized and characterized by spectacular *mise-en-scène* (quoted in Powrie 2002: 37–8), fits within the quality cinema category as I have defined it and has had a profound influence on French cinema. Originally identified in the 1980s and early 1990s and associated with the films of Jean-Jacques Beineix, Luc Besson, Léos Carax and Jean-Pierre Jeunet, Powrie considers them as France's first postmodern film-makers, using the complex puzzles and excessive visuals characteristic of the neo-baroque, resulting in generically hybrid works which have become cult films. Guy Austin identifies the technical mastery resulting in self-conscious spectacle and cinephile quotation, which has laid it open to criticism of Americanism and superficiality, particularly by *Cahiers du Cinéma* critics (1996: 119–122). Sue Harris suggests that, with the hindsight of the twenty-first century, the *cinema du look* is a historically contained phenomenon, its death coinciding with the return of the right with Chirac's election in 1994, after which it lost its experimental edge (2004: 228–9). The two survivors of this group, Besson and Jeunet, have both diversified into other production roles, Besson into a prolific production career and Jeunet into screenwriting. Besson's 1990s' work, from *Nikita* (France/Italy, 1990) to *Léon* (France/USA, 1994), has been characterized by neo-baroque ultra violence and a cool visual style which foregrounds the surface aesthetics of the films. Nikita's (Anne Parillaud) physical shape and little black dress are pressed into static poses against the bleached-out surroundings in which she is called upon to kill her designated (by her male controller) targets. Stansfield's (Gary Oldman) stylized violence in *Léon*, and the conflicts of *The Messenger: Joan of Arc* (*Jeanne d'Arc*, France, 1999) and *The Fifth Element* (*Le cinquième élément*, France, 1998) combined with their stylish visuals and use of genre conventions, gave them instant box-office returns. The style derives from advertising aesthetics, comics and the speed of computer games (which *The Fifth Element* became). Besson has been a director/producer from his first feature film (*The Last combat*/*Le dernier combat*, France, 1983) and had a mutually advantageous co-production arrangement with Gaumont until *The Messenger*. At that stage he was able to equip his own studio and state-of-the-art digital post-production facilities at his Normandy château (Sojcher 2002: 144). His raft of companies has enabled him to become a prolific independent producer with a sure sense of popular taste, epitomized by the *Taxi* films.

Jeunet has also built on his cult 1990s' successes, *Délicatessen* (France, 1991) and *The City of Lost Children* (*La cité des enfants perdus*, France/Germany/Spain, 1995), whose spectacular and inventive style won awards. He achieved enormous success with *Amélie* (*Le fabuleux destin d'Amélie Poulain*, France/Germany, 2001), which was criticized for its failure to show the realities of multi-cultural France. *Amélie* is a romantic comedy, justifying its use of heightened realism in the warm tones of its evocation of Paris. Characters are frequently framed to include the digitally constructed shape of the cathedral of Notre Dame de Montmartre in the background (France has achieved a well-founded dominance in CGI) and the dominant colour tones change from red to green to express Amélie's (Audrey Tautou) emotional state. Jeunet's budget for *A Very Long Engagement* (*Un long dimanche de fiançailles*, France/Germany, 2004) was $55 million, reflecting the number of locations and the cost of the battlefield scenes, but it too is marked by an aestheticized *mise-en-scène* and a neo-baroque oscillation between the golden-filter shots of Brittany and the cool, blue tones of the battlefield scenes.

The films of the *cinema du look* may appear limited to a visually spectacular display and inventiveness, but, as in many other quality films, style is the objective correlative of the social instability underlying the surface romanticism, which explains why it has moved into mainstream French cinema. There are other factors at work and the French company UGC's move into cinema exhibition in Britain ensures that French films like *Amélie* have a chance of distribution in one of the larger EU markets.

Pedro Almodóvar

Almodóvar's cinema has provided a gift to international art cinema distribution and to film studies courses. He provides an exemplar of the adroit utilization of the political and cultural context of the cinema market, and its global realities in his move into quality cinema. Under the Spanish dictator Francisco Franco, Spanish cinema concentrated mainly on genre films which avoided offending the regime, or very cerebral films which avoided censorship. Franco died in 1975, a significant period for European cinema as it coincided with the proliferation of private TV stations for which cheap films provided fodder. Pedro Almodóvar, who stems from Andalucia, made several short, Super 8 films between 1974 and 1978 and took a crucial part in the wave of self-examination, particularly about the Civil War which took place in Spanish culture after the death of Franco. At the very end of the 1970s a wave of youthful, vibrant work coincided with a crisis in the Spanish film industry which was parochial, traditional and unpopular with paying cinema-goers and young people wishing to enter the industry. Almodóvar epitomizes the volcanic forces unleashed by the death of Franco's fascist regime. Within the constraints of this chapter, it will not be possible to examine the complexity of Almodóvar's work, but examination of his journey towards a cultural myth reveals much about the evolution of the European film industry and the preoccupations of Europeans at the start of the new millennium.

Almodóvar started with small feature film productions which established his reputation, and his notoriety. *Pepi, Luci, Bom and Other Girls on the Heap* (*Pepi, Luci, Bom y otras chicas del montón*, Spain, 1980) is interesting because of its elements of kitsch and parody. The presence within the film of the external context of the *movida* (the urban Madrid sub-culture which expressed all those counter-cultural elements suppressed under Franco (Smith 1994: 16–8) can be seen in transgressive female relationships (the punk, Bom, urinates on the masochistic stereotypical housewife, Luci). Competition from television decimated the national mass market for films, but Almodóvar's understanding of the changed nature of film distribution convinced him of the importance of the marginal, niche audience. Whereas *Pepi, Luci, Bom* was a no-budget production with its actors unpaid, Almodóvar's second feature, *Labyrinth of Passion* (*Laberinto de pasiones*, Spain, 1982), had a modest budget of $175,000 which included a contribution from Madrid's Alphaville cinemas where it developed a cult reputation for its depiction of the marginality of its youthful actors. At the time these films were seen by few people, but their enthusiastic proliferation of previously taboo themes of incest, male and female homosexuality, debunking of traditional Spanish stereotypes and the precepts of church and state meant that those who did see them were representative of the currents of the new Spain, and they played a crucial part in cementing Almodóvar's reputation.

Paul Julian Smith considers that *What Have I Done to Deserve This* (*¿Qué he hecho yo para merecer esto?*, Spain, 1984) was Almodóvar's crossover film, leaving behind the alternative and the *movida* and entering a new, auteurist phase with a substantial budget (around Pts70 million), a wider public and an international release (1994: 61). Like all of his films, *What Have I Done* has complex storylines, being an early example of his penchant for fragmented and interlacing stories, which Barry suggests are a positive feature of postmodern narratives, 'symptomatic of our escape from the claustrophobic embrace of fixed systems of belief' (1995: 84). Ditching the grand metanarratives which, in the Spanish context, consist of conformity to ideologies of state, patriarchy and conservatism results in micro-narratives which 'mimic the uncertainties and extreme relativism of postmodernity' (Branston and Stafford 1999: 61). In *What Have I Done*, these micro-narratives are cumulative as Gloria (Carmen Maura) interacts with her abusive husband, Antonio (Angel de Andrés López) and her sons, Toni the drug dealer, epitomizing capitalist New Spain (Juan Martínez), and Miguel the homosexual prostitute (Miguel Angel Herranz), whom Gloria 'places' with her dentist. Almodóvar's skill is to ground his film firmly in the realities of post-Francoist Spain and to suggest, through narrative excess, the traumas of contemporary Europe, deprived of the comforts of patriarchy as a source of information on appropriate conduct, which has to negotiate anew a sense of the proper ordering of society.

Since 1984, Almodóvar's films have all explored just what that proper ordering of contemporary society might be, opting for a pluralistic approach to social relations, sexuality and relationships which has found an increasing audience in Europe and worldwide. As has been explored, cultural capital is a marketable commodity, in his case depending on awareness of feminist principles, queer politics and the role of the media. In the 1980s Almodóvar developed a loyal audience, capable of recognizing and enjoying his use of saturated red colour to symbolize freedom and his playing with sexual and gender stereotypes. Almodóvar's depiction of heterosexual relationships lays bare the unequal and unrewarding nature of the marriage bargain, usually in the 1980s by juxtaposing it to the rewards of prostitution. He also explores the role of media discourse in perpetuating patriarchal social structures by having his female characters voice clichés which contribute to their disempowerment. His box-office success gained additional prominence in the Spanish context when domestic production and audiences shrank to an all-time low in the 1980s in the face of competition from television and new media. Whereas other film-makers found it difficult to make films and to deal with the system of funding for quality film which came to be known as the Mirò Law,[4] Almodóvar managed to consolidate his audience and, significantly, formed his own production company, El Deseo, with his brother Agustín. In common with other film-makers, control of production has been seen as a prerequisite for control of one's career. *Women on the Verge of a Nervous Breakdown* (*Mujeres al borde de un ataque de nervios*, Spain, 1988) won a prestigious Goya prize, an Italian Nastro d'Argento, a Félix and an appearance at Venice. Almodóvar gained another measure of notoriety with *¡Atame!* (*Tie Me Up! Tie Me Down*, Spain, 1989) which excited controversy by its female protagonist, Marina's (Victoria Abril), acceptance of rape and imprisonment by her abductor, Ricki (Antonio Banderas).

Controversy over sexual and gender roles also followed *High Heels* (*Tacones lejanos*, Spain/France, 1991), defined by Ilott as a 'carefully and cleverly packaged commercial film that never forgets its audience' (1996: 43). Through the mother-daughter relationship between Rebeca (Victoria Abril) and her mother, the former pop-star, Becky (Marisa Paredes), and their relationships (and murder of) the former's husband and latter's lover, Manuel (Feodor Atkine), the film touches obliquely on the socialization of the female sex and the complexities of female identity formation. *High Heels* is an enjoyable comedy, pitting the would-be achieving middle-class couple of Rebeca and Manuel against the vibrant and colourfully transgressive world of Femme Letal (Miguel Bosé), a judge who has a career sideline as a drag artist, whose performance is a pastiche of Becky's 1960s' singing style, repeated in a very postmodern way by his loyal club audience. Drag, as Judith Butler has suggested, introduces complexity to the binary opposition male/female by playing with the distinction between 'the anatomy of the performer, and the gender that is being performed', thereby foregrounding the 'regulatory fiction of heterosexual coherence' (1990: 137). Although Paul Julian Smith (1994: 133) considers that by representing the judge as a literal travesty of justice (he has the responsibility of interrogating Rebeca after her confession that she has killed her husband, chooses to believe Becky's confession and absolves Rebeca) the women's freedom and achievement is undervalued, in fact judge Domínguez/Letal functions as the narrative disruption which throws into relief the problematic mother-daughter relationship and the two women's complete ignoring of heterosexist ideology. Rebeca's rather bland, middle-class home interiors are contrasted to the colourful and womb-like environments of Femme Letal, in which he seduces Rebeca.

High Heels had a budget of $3.87 million, 20% of which was put up by Ciby 2000, a new division of French construction company Bouygues, in exchange for distribution rights; Ciby acted as guarantor of Almodóvar's company, El Deseo's, loan of the other 80% of the budget (Ilott 1996: 44). The film came in below budget because, as Agustín Almodóvar explained, the script (on which budgets are usually estimated) is finalized only just before shooting one of Almodóvar's films, at which stage the budget is an actual rather than a notional one. El Deseo also took good care to build on each film's market audience for the next film (Ilott 1996: 50). Ilott concluded that a strong *auteur* delivers an audience which can be developed and that the brothers' avoidance of pre-sales enabled them to concentrate on their audience rather than on the needs of distributors (1996: 51). *Kika* (Spain/France, 1993) reverted to earlier patterns, but subsequent Almodóvar films followed this careful pattern of domestic and international appeal, convincing a new generation of Hispanic film-makers that Spanish films could be successful outside Spain. Inside Spain, El Deseo has had a galvanizing effect on the domestic film industry, resulting in a flow of new directors, such as Julio Medem, Alejandro Amenábar and Mariano Barroso. In the 1990s, Spanish films reversed the decline and attained 12% of Spanish box office, audiences returned, investors were attracted and international sales agents were lured into the domestic market. By 2000 the success of the new generation of Spanish films led to a measure of vertical integration in the industry as distributors and exhibitors moved into production, producers (for example, Lola Films) moved into specialist distribution, and foreign distributors, UGC, Buena Vista, and Le Studio Canal Plus, sought out big-name *auteurs* and successful genre films. As a result Spanish companies achieved links with international partners to get pre-sales production finance, one result of which was the successful, up-market Spanish horror film, *The Others* (*Los Otros*, Alejandro Amenábar, Spain/France/USA, 2001).

Almodóvar provides a variation on the quality profile, which he fully achieved by 1997 with his international success, while retaining his Spanishness. Mark Allinson has identified Madrid as a constant presence in Almodóvar's cinema, not as a site of recognizable landmarks but as a 'city of possibilities' (2001: 112). Madrid is a 'world city' in Hannerz's sense of a centre of creativity which encapsulates the global flows of postmodern society by providing a space for cultural diversity and the meeting of diverse peoples (1996: 136–7). In Almodóvar's cinema the city is a complex postmodern spectacle, both the site of the activities of people 'specializing in expressive activities' (Hannerz 1996: 130), such as television presenters, performers, advertisers, fashion designers, musicians, and therefore the site where the media shaping of personal, national and global identity is demonstrated. Almodóvar's appeal to his international audience lies in the fact that his films deliver both the expected and the unexpected, and these are commented on and explained in advance by the critical apparatus of interviews and articles. Audiences expect the participation of his *chicas*, the group of female actors through whom contemporary problems of gender and identity are richly rehearsed and who bring the intertextual presence of their previous roles to subsequent films. Interlacing micro-narratives introduce transgressive and extraordinary elements, flashing backwards and forwards in time to serve as a 'slap in the face' for the audience who are not allowed to become too immersed in one promising plot line (Smith 2002: 26). High and low cultural forms mix with camp and kitsch, introduce the *frisson* of dangerous forays into the worlds of fetishism and transgression, but contain them within genres recognizable to art cinema. In *Live Flesh* (*Carne trémula*, France/Spain, 1997), visual and narrative motifs of circles abound, from the initial sequences in which Victor's (Liberto Rabal) prostitute mother (Penélope Cruz) gives birth to him on a circular bus route, to the former drug addict, Elena (Francesca Neri), giving birth to Victor's son in a Madrid taxi at the end. In *Talk to Her* (*Hable con ella*, Spain, 2002), the stories of Marco (Darío Grandinetti) and Benigno (Javier Cámara) intersect when Benigno observes Marco moved to tears at a Pina Bausch dance performance, and the relationship deepens in the hospital where the women they love are both in a coma after accidents. All the characters express the loneliness of fragmented modern lives. Marco is an Argentinian whose marriage has broken up; Lydia (Rosario Flores) is a bullfighter immersing herself in her profession to recover from a broken relationship; Benigno is a nurse, on his own after caring for his mother, who develops an obsession with Alicia (Leonor Watling), a dancer whose body he cares for. Other performances divert the narratives and slow them down. They also complement the micro-narratives. The plot of 'The Shrinking Man' pastiche silent film which Benigno recounts to Alicia gains resonance when it is discovered that Benigno has raped the unconscious Alicia and that she is pregnant. Benigno tries to teach Marco to communicate with Lydia but the impossibility of full communication with another person is indicated during Marco's visit to Benigno in prison at the end of the film, in which they are separated by glass. The complexity of Almodóvar's films is a considerable source of pleasure.

The experience of the past four years reveals that the big-budget, quality film is an increasingly risky business, and Pedro Almodóvar is one of the few successes. His films make 81% of their income outside Spain and are a gift to critics in providing plenty of material for interpretation. Local films, such as *Torrente 2: Misión en Marbella* (Santiago Segura, Spain, 2001), Spain's fourth highest grosser ever, are still popular, but the market is polarized between small films which are amortized locally, or international, quality productions of which Almodóvar's films are an exceptional example. El Deseo increasingly seeks television and regional domestic support in its production packages as Almodóvar has conquered the US and Latin-American markets, but he steadfastly resists making an English-language film, in spite of winning the Best Foreign Language Oscar for *All About My Mother* (*Todo sobre mi madre*, Spain/France, 1999). Although Almodóvar's film language and themes have moved from the alternative to the auteurist mainstream from the early 1980s to the present, he demonstrates how individual artistic control of the creative aspects of a film, commercial control of production and the attention to the audience results in a quality profile, without any loss of his Spanish identity.

Conclusion

The difficulties inherent in the quality film sector are encapsulated in Bille August's *Smilla's Sense of Snow* (*Frøken Smillas fornemmelse for sne*, Germany/Denmark/Sweden, 1996). Produced by Constantin Film, which is vertically integrated and active in film distribution, it was a widescreen, Dolby digital production with an international cast, but also profited from subventions from the Eurimages programme, the Nordic Film and TV Fund, the Danish Film Institute and Bavarian FilmFernsehFonds. An adaptation of a book by a widely translated cult author, it featured as number one in Denmark's overall top ten films for 1997 and was distributed in depth in Germany and Scandinavia. The film was criticized for its difficulty in dealing with an intelligent heroine, lapsing into stereotype and, as MacNab suggests most tellingly:

> Such films look spectacular, feature high-profile stars, and sometimes rake in returns at the box office ... but they're always likely to lack the conviction that film-makers can bring to more modest projects, made in their own language and rooted in their own culture.
>
> (1997: 52–3)

However, such criticism ignores both the complete insertion of American culture in contemporary Europe and flexibility offered by national stereotypes in the hands of an accomplished director. The careers of the authorial film-makers examined in this chapter show that financial and critical success is necessary for a move into the quality sector and that its satisfactions include the international recognition which complex, big-budget productions offer. While some film-makers become trapped in this form of film-making, others use their enhanced commercial profile to return to modestly financed production, but with the international distribution which their status has earned. Clear narratives, comprehensible to an international audience, do not preclude explorations of the contradictions and chaos of contemporary life. Polemical debate may have no place in the quality template, but all the more interesting then are the manifestations of neo-baroque disorder in spectacle, ultra-violence, obsessive repetition and heightened realism which the technical expertise of film-makers working in this sector can marshal to express complexity behind their ostensibly simple stories.

The *European Cinema Yearbook*'s material on vertical integration between distribution and exhibition and the analysis of the trend towards multi-screen cinemas, usually owned and programmed by a US company, would indicate a continued polarization in the European film industry. The international, quality cinema is one solution to the problem of maintaining European cultural presence in a period of rapid globalization.

Notes

1. The yellow tones derive from the fact that *noir* thrillers were originally published by Mondadori in the late 1920s in yellow covers, hence the use of the word *giallo* (yellow) as a shorthand term for any mystery story or detective fiction.
2. Fine Line is a division of New Line and part of AOL/Time Warner. Its policy is to seek commercial *auteur* films with box-office potential.
3. The Zentropa Company would join with the distributor, Nimbus, to distribute Danish films initially, the reason given being the increase in national films to 25 a year and the competition for distribution in a crowded market (Jensen 2006: 30).
4. The Minister responsible, Pilar Mirò, proposed a system of subsidies for quality films through advance credits, similar to the French *avances sur recettes* and the Italian *minimi garantiti*. In the Spanish case, artistic quality was judged by a committee of experts and had a deleterious effect on the art cinema sector.

Box-office hits

Notes

(a) All data are taken from European Audiovisual Observatory Yearbooks, 1998–2005; (b) EU7 relates to information on the major cinema markets; (c) EU15 relates to members of the EU prior to 1 May 2004; (d) EU25 relates to expanded membership including Eastern European states post 1 May 2004; (e) EU29+ relates to the 25 states of the EU, plus Switzerland, Iceland, Norway, Romania and Turkey.
The European Audiovisual Observatory has changed its methodology slightly from year to year, for example initially giving dollar earnings of European films in the US market, then reverting to figures for cinema admissions. Although a few successful films appear to have had no release in the EU, the global, EU29 figures indicate that these gained their success in Eastern European accession states.

The ranking is based on figures for the top 50 films of any nationality by admissions in Europe. Where the letters 'EU' follow the ranking, this denotes the film's placing in the top 50 **European** films by admissions in Europe.

Film	Date	Country of prod	US earn $/ admissions	Ranking/year		Released in no of EU countries	Total admissions (millions)			
							EU7	EU15	EU25	EU29+
Harry Potter and the Chamber of Secrets	2002	US/UK		1	2002	13				42.7
				24	2003	12				9.1
Harry Potter and the Prisoner of Azkaban	2004	US/UK		2	2004	14				40.5
Troy	2004	US/UK/MT		3	2004	14				27.7
The Lord of the Rings: The Return of The King	2003	US/NZ/DE		5	2003	9				27.6
				4	2004	14				27.1
Bridget Jones's Diary	2001	UK/US	13.2m adm/01	2	2001	13		26.2		29.9
Notting Hill	1998	UK	116m/1999	2	1999	14		27.4		
Astérix et Obélix contre César	1998	F/DE/IT	1.3m	7	1999	14		23.8		
Astérix et Obélix: Mission Cléopâtre	2002	F/DE	0.4m adm/02	10	2002	14				22.0
Bean	1997	US/UK	45m/1997	3	1997	15		21.4		
Die Another Day	2002	UK/US	25.8m adm/02	11	2002	10				20.4
			1.2m adm/03	32	2003	12				6.5

Film	Date	Country of prod	US earn $/ admissions	Ranking/year		Released in no of EU countries	Total admissions (millions) EU7	EU15	EU25	EU29+
Le cinquième element	1997	F	63.8m/1997	4	1997	17		18.7		
The Full Monty	1996	UK	44.8m/1997	31	1997	11		18.1		
			10.9m/1998	45	1998	6		3.4		
Terminator 3: Rise of the Machines	2003	US/DE/UK		8	2003	14				17.0
Shakespeare in Love	1998	UK/US	6.2m/1998	8	1999	14		17.3		
James Bond: The World is Not	1998	UK/US	117.8m/1999	9	1999			17.32		
Enough			1.6m adm/00	28	2000	11		7.4		
Bridget Jones: The Edge of Reason	2004	UK/US/F/DE IE	6.4m adm/04	10	2004	13			16.3	
Le fabuleux destin d'Amélie	2001	F/DE	3m adm/2001	12	2001	12		15.0		16.2
Poulain			3m adm/02	38	2002	13				5.5
The English Patient	1996	US/UK	55m/1997	7	1997	12		14.7		
Johnny English	2003	UK/US	4.6m adm/03	10	2003	14				14.6
Lara Croft, Tomb Raider	2001	US/UK/JP/DE		14	2001	12		12.6		14.5
American Wedding	2003	US/DE		11	2003	14				14.2
Chicken Run	2000	UK/US	19.4m adm/00	13	2000	11		13.1		
Van Helsing	2004	US/CZ		14	2004	14			12.9	
Love Actually	2003	UK/US	9.5m adm/03	14	2003	14				12.7
				13	2004 EU	12				3.9
Der Schuh der Manitou	2000	DE		15	2001	3		12.5		12.8
				34	2002 EU	3				1.3
Taxi 2	2000	F		14	2000	13		11.7		
				45	2001 EU	8				1.5
The Others	2001	ES	17.9m adm/01	18	2001	6		11.2		
				12	2002 EU	11				3.5
Red Dragon	2002	US/DE/UK		18	2002	10				11.0

Film	Date	Country of prod	US earn $/ admissions	Ranking/year	Released in no of EU countries	Total admissions (millions) EU7	EU15	EU25	EU29+
About a Boy	2002	UK/US/F/DE	7m adm/02	19 2002	12				10.97
King Arthur	2004	US/UK/IE		18 2004	14				10.9
Chocolat	2000	UK/US	12.5m adm/01	20 2001	13				10.8
(T)Raumschiff Surprise – Periode 1	2004	DE		19 2004	1				10.7
Les choristes	2004	F/CH/DE		20 2004	12				10.4
Traffic	2000	US/DE		22 2001	11				10.4
Gangs of New York	2002	US/DE/IT/UK		19 2003	14				10.1
Goodbye Lenin	2003	DE	0.6m adm/04	22 2003	13				9.6
Tomorrow Never Dies	1997	UK/US	73m/1997	13 1997	11		9.6		
			52m/1998	40 1998	9		3.7		
2 fast 2 furious	2003	US/DE		23 2003	14				9.5
Sense and Sensibility	1995	US/UK	39m	10 1996	13		9.4		
Le dîner de cons	1998	F		17 1998	4		9.03		
The League of Extraordinary Gentlemen	2003	US/DE/CZ/UK		25 2003	14				8.9
Les couloirs du temps	1997	F		10 1998	4	8.7			
Le pacte des loups	2001	F	1.9m adm/02	29 2001	11				8.5
				44 2002 EU	8				1.0
Trainspotting	1996	UK	16.5m/1996	15 1996	15		8.2		
40 days and 40 nights	2002	US/UK/F		25 2002	12				8.2
The Bourne Supremacy	2004	US/DE		28 2004	13				7.9
The Bourne Identity	2002	US/DE/CZ		27 2002	11				7.8
La vérité si je mens	2001	F		32 2001	2			7.6	
Taxi 3	2003	F		29 2003	8				7.5
Sieben Zwerge – Männer allein	2004	DE		34 2004	2				7.3
The Hours	2002	US/UK		30 2003	14				6.7
Le placard	2000	F	1.2m adm/01	37 2001	7			6.7	

Film	Date	Country of prod	US earn $/ admissions	Ranking/year		Released in no of EU countries	Total admissions (millions) EU7	EU15	EU25	EU29+
Gosford Park	2001	UK/US/DE/IT	7m adm/02	29	2002	13				6.7
La vita è bella	1997	IT	10.3m/1998	26	1998	7		6.7		
			47.5m/1999	16	1999	13		10.0		
8 femmes	2002	F		30	2002	14				6.6
Todo sobre mi madre	1999	ES/F	1.1m adm/00	25	1999	14		6.3		
				12	2000	12		2.1		
Taxi	1997	F		25	1998	9		6.7		
Sliding Doors	1997	US/UK	11.9m/1998	27	1998	10		6.6		
Cold Mountain	2003	UK/US/RO/IT	8.4m adm/04	38	2004	14				6.7
Goldeneye	1995	UK/US	13.9	18	1996	9		5.7		
AVP: Alien vs Predator	2004	US/UK/CZ/ DE/CA		41	2004	14				5.7
Evita	1996	US/UK	0.4m/1996 49.6m/1997	29	1997	7		6.1		
Hable con ella	2002	ES	1.1m adm/03	36	2002	14				6.0
Lara Croft Tomb Raider: The Cradle	2003	US/UK/DE/NL		34	2003	14				6.0
How to Lose a Guy in 10 Days	2003	US/DE		36	2003	14				5.9
Fuochi d'artificio	1997	IT		32	1997	1		5.4		
Der Untergang	2004	DE/IT		43	2004	3				5.5
Calendar Girls	2003	UK/US	1.1m adm/03	39	2003	14				5.2
The Italian Job	2003	US/F/UK		40	2003	14				5.2
Spy Game	2001	US/UK		40	2002	11				5.2
Resident Evil	2002	DE/UK/F	6.8m adm/02	41	2002	12				5.2
Torrente 2: Misión en Marbella	2001	ES		45	2001	2			5.3	
Werner, das muß kesseln!	1996	DE		21	1996	2		5.2		

Film	Date	Country of prod	US earn $/ admissions	Ranking/year	Released in no of EU countries	Total admissions (millions) EU7	EU15	EU25	EU29+
Billy Elliot	2000	UK	3.8m adm/00	39 2000	7		5.0		
			0.9m adm/01	34 2001	11			7.5	
La gran aventura de Mortadelo y Filemon	2003	ES		43 2003	3				5.0
La vérité si je mens	1997	F		36 1997	3		4.9		
Les trois frères	1995	F		26 1996	3		4.9		
Two brothers	2004	F/UK	3m adm/04	46 2004	10				4.9
The Pianist	2002	F/UK/DE/PL		45 2002	9				4.9
				9 2003 EU	14				3.6
The Talented Mr Ripley	1999	US/UK		40 2000	12		4.8		
Le huitième jour	1996	F/BE/UK	0.4m/1996	27 1996	10		4.7		
Pinocchio	2002	IT/F/DE	0.4m adm/02	48 2002	1				4.6
Un long dimanche de fiançailles	2004	F/US		49 2004	2				4.6
Les rivières pourpres	2000	F		43 2000	4		4.5		
				32 2001 EU	9			1.8	
La mala educación	2004	ES		50 2004	14				4.5
Pédale douce	1996	F		30 1996	5		4.3		
Quo vadis	2001	PL		47 2001	1			4.3	
Snatch	2000	UK/US	3.0m adm	48 2000	7		4.2		
				48 2001 EU	5			1.35	
G.O.R.A	2004	TR		12 2004 EU	5				4.2
Enemy at the Gates	2001	UK/DE/US/IE	9.5m adm/01	48 2001	11			4.2	
Black Hawk Down	2001	US/UK		49 2002	9				4.2
Bend It Like Beckham	2002	UK/DE		50 2002	11				4.1
Mar adentro	2004	ES/F/IT		11 2004 EU	3				4.1
Le goût des autres	2000	F		49 2000	7		4.1		
Le pari	1997	F		39 1997	3			4.0	

Film	Date	Country of prod	US earn $/ admissions	Ranking/year	Released in no of EU countries	Total admissions (millions) EU7	EU15	EU25	EU29+
O Brother, Where Art Thou?	2000	US/F/UK		50 2000	12		4.0		
Captain Corelli's Mandolin	2001	UK/F/US		13 2001 EU	11			3.9	
Chouchou	2003	F		50 2003	3			3.9	
Yamakasi	2000	F		14 2001 EU	6			3.8	
Girl with a Pearl Earring	2003	US/LU		15 2004 EU	14				3.7
La neuvième porte	1999	F/ES		50 1999	10		3.5		
				47 2000 EU	9		0.7		
Knockin' On Heaven's Door	1997	DE		45 1997	1		3.5		
Rossini	1997	DE		47 1997	2		3.3		
Le bonheur est dans le pré	1995	F		40 1996	7		3.4		
Spice World – The Movie	1997	UK	29.3m/1998	39 1998	3	3.4			
L'auberge espagnole	2001	F/ES	0.6m adm/03	13 2002 EU	5				3.4
Tais-toi	2003	F/IT		10 2003 EU	3				3.4
Das Wunder von Bern	2003	DE		11 2003 EU	1				3.3
Le boulet	2002	F/UK		14 2002 EU	4				3.3
Ali G Indahouse	2002	UK		15 2002 EU	6				3.3
La leggenda di Al, John e Jack	2002	IT		16 2002 EU	1				3.3
Kleines Arschloch	1997	DE		49 1997	2		3.3		
Männerpension	1996	DE		43 1996	2		3.3		
Secrets and Lies	1996	UK	5.9m/1996	44 1996	14		3.3		
				31 1997 EU	13		1.3		
Vizontele	2000	TR		15 2001 EU	2		3.3		
The Adventures of Pinocchio	1996	UK/US/F/ DE/CZ	15.3m	45 1996	5		3.1		
Natale sul Nilo	2002	IT/ES/UK		17 2002 EU	1				3.1
Fierce Creatures	1997	US/UK		14 1997 EU	8		3.1		

Film	Date	Country of prod	US earn $/ admissions	Ranking/year	Released in no of EU countries	Total admissions (millions) EU7	EU15	EU25	EU29+
Lock, Stock & Two Smoking Barrels	1998	UK/US		7 1998 EU	4		3.1		
Angela's Ashes	1999	IE/US		9 2000 EU	12		3.1		
Kiss of the Dragon	2001	F	6.8m adm/01	18 2001 EU	11		3.1		
Il postino	1994	IT/F	12.7m	47 1996	10		3.0		
Chiedimi se sono felice	2000	IT		10 2000 EU	1		3.1		
Tanguy	2001	F		17 2001 EU	3		3.1		
				21 2002 EU	8				2.0
Jeanne d'Arc	1998	F	14.1m	7 1999 EU	3		3.0		
				27 2000	10		1.3		
Le peuple migrateur	2001	F/DE/IT	1.6m adm/03	18 2002 EU	9				2.9
Torrente, el brazo tonto de la ley	1997	ES		8 1998 EU	1		2.8		
Dancer in the Dark	2000	DK/F/DE/NL		11 2000 EU	13		2.7		
El otro lado de la cama	2002	ES		19 2002 EU	1		2.7		
La stanza del figlio	2001	IT/F		21 2001 EU	10		2.4		
Lola rennt	1998	DE	7.2m/1999	12 1998 EU	3		2.2		
Harry, un ami qui vous veut du bien	2000	F	0.7m adm/01	17 2000 EU	6		2.03		

chapter four

Outclassing Hollywood at the box office?

In her review of *Rob Roy* (Michael Caton-Jones, USA, 1995), Liz Lochhead quotes a Quentin Tarantino character railing against Merchant Ivory films for not being movies – for being films for people who don't like movies (1995: 15). This chapter is about movies. Some of them started out with pretensions to be mere films, engaging with the realities of life in end-of-century Europe in all its contradictions, but, for reasons which this chapter will explore, became movies and made a lot of money. Making money, is, of course, an honourable aim which motivates investors, directors, producers, actors, sales agents, distributors, exhibitors, video, DVD and book publishers and many others. As the statistics at the head of this chapter show, the films which have appealed at the box office are many and varied. Films conceived of as potential blockbuster movies feature prominently in the statistics. Apart from finding and entertaining an audience, financially successful films have had an impact on the careers of the creative teams and stars and, like comets, produce a shining tail behind them in terms of copies, new subjects and themes. How they became movies, and their success in national or international terms, are sources of endless fascination for those who follow them. This chapter will identify the characteristics of this elusive category, primarily by examining the production arrangements and narratives of big-budget British and French films. Their use of European craft expertise in the fields of cinematography, production, costume and set design, as well as CGI, and their skilful manipulation of stereotypes will shed light on the evolution of the template and the dangers of getting it wrong.

The difficulty of identifying the template for big box-office success for European films lies in the fact that, for certain types of film, this is no longer achieved in the face of competition from Hollywood blockbusters, but as an adjunct to US production. Just as auteurist European films can be packaged by semi-autonomous divisions of the American studio conglomerates such as New Line and the pre-2004 Miramax, films aimed at a mass, international market and co-financed and produced with the USA become effectively a division of the US media industries. They may look local but have been carefully packaged and put together with financially tried and tested components (Wyatt 1994: 78). The process has, of course, been going on for some time and is by no means a one-way traffic. Andrew Higson has claimed that there are five responses to American domination of national cinema – collusion, direct competition, product differentiation, state regulation and international cooperation (1995: 4–9). In this big-budget sector of the European film industry the first three predominate. Collusion involves the appropriation of American movie conventions, finance and industry structures but, as this chapter will explore, this type of film-making is complex and not easy to categorize in neat boxes. Just as the Franco–Italian co-production treaties of the 1960s aimed at ensuring access to two national markets and continuity in the creative infrastructure, behind current USA/Europe co-productions lies the necessity to share the risk deriving from the increase in the costs of film-making and the blockbuster phenomenon. Direct competition draws on local skills, expertise and finance in a determined mobilization of local elements in product differentiation. International co-operation takes advantage of MEDIA and Eurimages funds for European co-productions. Indeed, more than ten years ago John Hill questioned the enthusiasm in some film industry quarters for big-budget, pan-European cinema designed to compete with Hollywood movies (1994: 68). The Europudding, and the difficulties of assessing market appeal, represent the dangers of competition with Hollywood. Moreover, this chapter will show that the American market itself is not the greatest objective, but the conquering of lucrative worldwide markets is.

Co-productions with the USA

At the top of the list are those films conceived of as event movies and co-produced with various European countries. Co-productions with the USA have increased steadily since 1995. Apart from the impact of postmodern business practices identified earlier, another reason for US co-productions is the fluctuation in the market share of US films in the European market. Admissions to US films in the European Union increased by around 100 million between 1996 and 2004, mainly attributable to countries of Eastern Europe whose film industries suffered a collapse and consequent painful attempts to adapt to the new capitalist realities in the wake of the break-up of the empire of the former Soviet Union (EAO 2005/3: 50). There has been a reduction in the US share of the cinema box office in the largest European markets and a slight rise in national share. What the statistics also suggest is that this has been at the expense of non-European, non-US films. In business terms, the American move into co-productions with Europe has the logic of remedying poor business returns by annexing successful elements of rivals.

A feature from 1996 to 2002 was the presence of USA/German co-productions, taking advantage of generous public and private financial support for production. The German share of a co-production is able to draw on automatic public support (the FFA, Filmförderungsanstalt) and other public schemes such as those of the regions (the *Länder*, whose aid decreased from 37% to 27% of production costs in this period) and government funds for culture and media (the BKM) (EAO 2003/3: 103). FFA funds were generated by a levy on cinema tickets, contributions from TV broadcasters, tax on the home video industry and loan repayments (Lange and Westcott 2004: 74). Funds were generated by German taxpayers and one of the conditions of entitlement to German state aid was that studio filming had to take place in Germany. However, a loophole in the 1998 Federal law on film funding stated that if the film's subject required shooting outdoor scenes in a foreign country, up to 30% of indoor scenes could be shot in a studio in that country (Lange and Westcott 2004: 83). The resulting outflow of German tax payers' money was stemmed in the revised law which came into force on 1 January 2004, which stipulated that technical production companies and production companies had to be located in Germany or in an EU member country.

Tax incentive schemes also fuelled a US feeding frenzy on German funds. Germany also had large private investment funds which raised around $1.5 billion (€1.5 billion) in 2002 from private investors to finance film and television production. Although tighter legislation of film funds reduced investment from 2002 onwards, these private funds were 'an important source of production cash for both Hollywood studios and international producers' (Blaney 2002b: 6). Clearly the German public and private funds were regarded as an additional bank for Hollywood production, providing lines of credit without the necessity to spend the money in Germany.[1] This explains the presence of a German national co-production attribution to films such as *The Lord of the Rings: Return of the King* (Peter Jackson, USA/New Zealand/Germany, 2003) and *Terminator 3: Rise of the Machines* (Jonathan Mostow, USA/Germany/UK, 2003). It was estimated that prior to 2002, 10–15% of US production was being financed by German film funds and that 'little more than 10% of the money raised by the funds was staying in the country' (Blaney 2006: 5). For American media companies Germany provided a constant source of projects for which (in the case of television series) US networks had to assume only 60–70% of the overall costs. In the words of Petra Klein, director of private banking and real value investments, Vereinsund Westbank, for German private investors the lure is to 'participate in the revenues of Hollywood-style productions' (Blaney 2002a: 8). In effect, European private investors are seeking to play the Americans at their own game, their investments being their entry ticket to a share in the profits generated by US domination of the high-concept end of the film industry.

High-concept co-productions

Justin Wyatt defines high-concept films as distinguished by their style and a marketable concept in their premise or stars (1994: 23). The concept must be easily visualized for advertising purposes (high production values, spectacle, stars, music, character and genre). As previous chapters have explored, the characteristics of European cinema fit most of these criteria through the quality of its creative teams, producing films which have a 'look' way in excess of their actual budgets. Although American co-production arrangements favour established European directors and genres popular with the Home Box Office (HBO) audience, such as the heritage film, romantic comedies, children's films and epics, for the big-event films such as *Harry Potter* and *Bridget Jones*, what is important is the director's track record in big-budget productions rather than her/his name.

These big-budget movies are franchise films where the source material (usually popular books and comics) comes in series so that studio executives can see a continuity of exploitation possibilities. In the case of *Harry Potter*, there are currently seven volumes, six of which are completed movies, in production or pre-production. The producer, David

Heyman, brought the idea to Warner Brothers at a moment when J. K. Rowling's book, *Harry Potter and the Philosopher's Stone,* had already sold hundreds of thousands of copies, but before it had moved into global dimensions of tens of millions. There were therefore indications that, even though the production budget for *Harry Potter and the Philosopher's Stone* (Chris Columbus, USA/UK, 2001) was around $130 million, the book sales showed that the movie was always going to be a hit (Harding 2001: 8). Released with around 1,500 prints, the movie made over $318 million at its box-office first run and billions of dollars in peripheral merchandising. It broke records when released on video and DVD and in games formats and generated the incongruous sight of stacks of Harry Potter figurines and t-shirts in Italian motorway service stations. Commuters making their way to the suburban train platforms ten and eleven at King's Cross station in London have to shoulder aside crowds of tourists posing alongside a baggage trolley impaled in the wall below a sign reading 'platform nine and three-quarters'. The series allows there to be permanent sets for the dining hall of Hogwarts School of Witchcraft and Wizardry, the Gryffindor common room, Privet Drive (home of the horrible Dursley family of non-wizard Muggles) and Gringotts Bank at the old Leavesden studios in England (conveniently near the Watford exit on the M25 motorway, which links the airports of London Heathrow and Gatwick). A return to book reading by young boys was attributed to the *Potter* books and worries that the movie franchise would run its course have been shown to be unfounded. Clearly there is something else at work besides the publicity behemoth of Warner Brothers.

What, then, are the ingredients which power the success of the *Harry Potter* franchise worldwide? The films stick quite closely to the source books which, as Alison Lurie reveals, are deeply subversive in their revelations of the pretensions and failings of adults and their suggestion that children 'are braver, smarter, and more interesting than grown-ups, and that grown-up rules are made to be broken' (1999). In her exploration of the sources tapped by the author, J. K. Rowling, Wendy Doniger identifies myths widespread in many cultures of the deprived child who is at the mercy of cruel adults, but who is revealed as special and a potential hero (2000: 26). She also suggests that this scenario is present in the traditional British boarding school story and the *bricolage* of 'new stories crafted out of recycled pieces of old stories' is a factor in the books' success. Both books and films can be appreciated at many levels and have a wider appeal than children's fiction. The conflict between social conformity and its opposite, the strange and exuberant world of witches and wizards, appeals to adults and children alike and crosses geographical boundaries, justifying release in over 3,000 prints (Hunter 2002: 22). Following the flight of the owls delivering letters to Harry reveals that Privet Drive consists of identical, semi-detached houses, and the swirly-patterned carpet, furniture and clothing of the Dursleys indicates that they are lower middle class and conventional, the only thing signalling their difference from their neighbours being the fact that they hate their nephew, Harry, and make him sleep in the cupboard under the stairs. There is satisfying comedy in the first film in Harry's revenge on his cousin Dudley by vanishing the glass surrounding the snake pit at the zoo so that Dudley falls in, and the snake and Harry commiserate with each other over their hard lives. Hogwarts School is situated in an immense, many-turreted castle whose warmth, splendour and interesting magical elements are in complete contrast to the restricted life of the Dursleys and evoke an upper-class lifestyle lived by exceptional individuals – even if some of them look as ordinary as Harry's friend, Ron (Rupert Grint). Like the books, the films create and sustain a well fleshed-out world, which is the stuff of all successful cult artefacts. Mention of Muggles, Defence against the Dark Arts, Quidditch and Dementors allows Potter fans to communicate their enthusiasms to each other. In a neat twist, Harry is literally marked out as exceptional by the z-shaped scar on his forehead, discovers his prowess at the sport of Quidditch, but is only average at his lessons in wizardry. The franchise relies on recognition of the concept of the young boy who discovers he is a wizard and the promise of spectacular sets and conflicts rather than well-known stars. The choice of producer (Heyman) and directors – Chris Columbus (American), Alfonso Cuarón (Mexican) and Mike Newell (British) – ensure that the films are within the Hollywood high-concept tradition but sufficiently different to ensure an international success. Indeed, this combination of familiar story models, comedy and the exotic (as represented by magic lore, British characters and settings), together with the distribution power of Warner Brothers, has enabled the films to conquer the North American market usually denied to European films.

The combination of Britishness and universal archetypes is also visible in *Bridget Jones's Diary* (Sharon Maguire, UK/France, 2001) and *Bridget Jones: The Edge of Reason* (Beeban Kidron, UK/France/Germany/Ireland/USA, 2004). Based on Helen Fielding's best-selling books, the writing team includes Richard Curtis, whom Philip French describes as the British master of the 'event comedy', created with American and international audiences in mind (2004b: 9). Many explanations for the popularity of the character of Bridget Jones have been offered – the ubiquity of the experience of the single state by thirty-something women, the difficulty of finding a suitable male sexual partner when work invades one's life, the experience of being overweight, self-doubting and lonely, despite having good friends, or because the character is 'every woman's worst personal nightmare … yet she still turns out all right' (Lawrence 2004: 11). The latter comment encapsulates the Bridget character, who is incompetent and overweight, yet played by the American actress Renée Zellweger, who gained weight to play her. Here the secondary text of publicity and reviews intrudes into viewing of the film, adding the appeal of knowledge that, while we may all be overweight, the actress on the screen has demonstrated that becoming slim is attainable. The ludicrous nature of the Western obsession with female slimness is embodied in the figure of Bridget, who constantly bemoans her size but whose voluptuous figure is clearly attractive to the two men in her life.

While the first Bridget Jones film marshals its British setting, female stereotypes and the archetypal Cinderella plot, the second film directed by Beeban Kidron loosens its grip on reality by, literally, venturing into the global arena. Bridget goes to Thailand as assistant on the dastardly Daniel Cleaver's (Hugh Grant) tourist television programmes. He persuades her to carry a souvenir home for him and she is arrested at the airport when the sniffer dogs reveal that she is carrying drugs. The second half of the film descends into farce as Bridget is incarcerated in a Thai jail, makes friends with her fellow inmates and leads a rousing chorus of Madonna's *Like a Virgin* with sundry bar girls and prostitutes, before being rescued by Mark Darcy (Colin Firth). The film concludes with Bridget's parents renewing their wedding vows in matching mauve outfits in an improbably snowy churchyard. Part of the film's pleasure lies in the difficulty of gauging the level of irony in the plot. In Beeban Kidron's hands the spectacular kitsch elements of Daniel's trite travel documentaries, the prison singing and the Christmas card church sequence serve to allegorize a contemporary reality of globalization. Daniel literally embodies a cynical Western appropriation of the tourist elements of Eastern cultures, his predatory and exploitative nature written on his charming body. Western music, in the form of Madonna's incongruous song, bonds Bridget and her fellow prisoners. In their friendship, the Thai girls reveal stories of personal betrayal and cruelty by their pimps, forcing Bridget to acknowledge her own stupidity in neurotically rejecting Darcy and her own distance from the exploitation they reveal. The kitsch colours and clothing of the 'second wedding' sequence allegorize the impossibility of the Western romantic dream, even as Bridget and Mark are reconciled. In its excessive, kitsch elements, this film stretches the genre of the romantic comedy to the limit in a way which Omar Calabrese defines as neo-baroque (1992: 50).

These USA/Europe co-produced franchise films have drawn on their source books' success to justify both the incorporation of an exotic Englishness into the blockbuster formula and the series format. Faced with the weaker role played by American blockbuster films on the international market since 2002, the US majors have hedged their bets with co-productions which appear non-American, but which have at the same time influenced the form of the resulting film.

Event films and national stereotypes

British films have been particularly susceptible to these stereotypical representations of Europeanness being marshalled with varying degrees of kitsch and irony. *Notting Hill* (Roger Michell, UK, 1999) followed on the success of *Four Weddings and a Funeral* (Mike Newell, UK, 1994) and, in spite of its low budget (around $6 million), was conceived as a high-concept film with a recognizable formula (British boy meets and wins American girl) and stars. The stereotype of the shy and inarticulate Englishman is augmented by his circle of friends who fall into the 'lovable eccentric' category, including his flatmate Spike (Rhys Ifans), sister Honey (Emma Chambers), assistant Martin (James Dreyfus) and friends who have created the perfect restaurant which nobody visits. *Notting Hill* follows the mainstream formula of equilibrium, disruption, complication, climax and resolution in a new equilibrium. Resolution is attained through William's (Hugh Grant) action of publicly confessing his love for film star Anna (Julia Roberts) at a huge press conference, and the film's final sequence shows William and a heavily pregnant Anna sitting companionably on a park bench. The final confession of the inarticulate Englishman has become a stereotypical plot element in other films aiming at international box-office success. In *Wimbledon* (Richard Loncraine, UK/France, 2004), the sliding career rankings of a British tennis player, Peter Colt (Paul Bettany), pick up after he meets a young American tennis prodigy, Lizzie Bradbury (Kirsten Dunst). Overcoming his low self-esteem, the opposition of Lizzie's father (Sam Neill), misunderstandings, a noxious rival and his warring parents' poor role model for wedded bliss, Peter wins the Wimbledon Men's Final, uniting the entire country and his parents in supporting him. In explaining his win to the press, Peter makes a public declaration of love for Lizzie and the film closes in a wintry USA with Peter and Lizzie teaching their two children to play tennis. Although the character of Lizzie is not well fleshed out, and the pattern of tennis setbacks followed by triumphs becomes repetitive, Darius Khondji's cinematography gives *Wimbledon* a quality look, and the factors of the producers' (Working Title and Studio Canal Plus) links with American distributors and European satellite and theatrical distribution ensured wide exposure.

Love Actually (Richard Curtis, UK/USA, 2003) provides a variation on the formula when one of the eight stories closes with the inarticulate English writer, Jamie Bennett (Colin Firth), taking himself in hand to confound the English stereotypes by learning Portuguese and travelling to Portugal to make a Christmas declaration of love to his cleaner, Aurelia (Lúcia Moniz), before her large extended family. Clearly a winning formula was reached by the production company, Working Title, which capitalized on the $258 million worldwide box-office success of *Four Weddings and a Funeral.* Working Title's co-production arrangements with Universal Studios and others have increased the budgets of the films discussed above to $20–30 million, and the box-office gross to around $244 million worldwide, but most of the money goes back to Universal. Mass tourism from the UK may have eroded the appeal of the British accent, but the stereotype has clearly been constructed to signal the superior competitive competence of American characters, while allowing British, middle-class male characters to be saved from their emotional incompetence by New World women charmed by their exoticism. The fact that a confession of love is wrung out of British male characters with difficulty also signals the sincerity of the commitment expressed, redeeming the former failures by the quality of the relationship they promise. Charlotte O'Sullivan expressed a more cynical view of the formula in suggesting that, unlike *Four Weddings* where 'vulgar' America was represented as 'in thrall to cultured, wealthy Britain', in these later films the USA has to be represented as superior in order for the British middle-class rich to appear as the underdogs, thereby concealing the fact of cultural similarity (1999: 50). Another plausible reason for the narrative differentiation of American and British characters lies in the complex world of contemporary film distribution, in which certain films make more money from their non-US than their US theatrical release (Gubbins 2005). British elements appeal in countries where the ideology of overtly American blockbusters would not.

The stereotype of British incompetence has also been exploited to great financial effect in films starring Rowan Atkinson. *Bean: The Ultimate Disaster Movie* (Mel Smith, UK/USA, 1997), produced by PolyGram Filmed Entertainment, Working Title and Tiger Aspect, was based on the highly successful *Mr Bean* television comedy series which ran from 1990 to 1995 and was sold to 245 countries and for airline in-flight entertainment (Balmforth 1995: 13). The film was inexpensive in star terms, but a large amount of its estimated $22 million budget went on prints and publicity. Bean (Atkinson) is a caretaker in London's Royal National Gallery, sent to America to retrieve a stolen painting in spite of his manifest inability to perform simple tasks. *Bean* reuses some of the most memorable TV gags (the airline sick-bag sequence is a classic) and employs an uncomplicated camera style and very little dialogue so that a minimal level of prior knowledge is required to appreciate it. At the time of writing it is still number three in the top 25 European films by admissions since 1996, with almost 26 million admissions in Europe alone (World Film Market Trends: European Audiovisual Observatory Focus 2006: 16). *Bean* is another film which grossed over $100 million before its US release, making $45 million in the USA and a total of $232 million worldwide. *Bean* has legs, in that it has had a long shelf life on video and DVD and video games. It, too, has been a staple of airline in-flight entertainment and English-language teaching schools. Whereas airlines are experimenting in the mid-2000s with films from the quality and art film sectors, such as *Downfall* (*Der Untergang*, Oliver Hirschbiegel, Germany/Italy/Austria, 2004) and *Pride and Prejudice* (Joe Wright, France/UK, 2005), comedies and children's films have long had access to this additional market. Rights are usually negotiated separately and what all airline films have in common is the ability to be cut to remove any material deemed potentially offensive to passengers, and an absence of sex and nudity. *Bean* may have fart and snot jokes, but no sex or violence.

Rowan Atkinson also has the leading role in the James Bond spoof, *Johnny English* (Peter Howitt, UK, 2003), also produced by Working Title, with Rogue Male Films. Summed up by the tagline 'He knows no fear. He knows no danger. He knows nothing', *Johnny English* is based on a series of 17 TV advertisements for Barclaycard in which the 'hero' bungles stunts which secret agents usually perform with ease (he shoots himself with a tranquillizer dart), having his subordinate Bough (Ben Miller) save the day with his Barclaycard. The 60-second adverts were shot with high production values and the mini-movie feel appealed to Working Title (Dawson 2003: 17). A flavour of the film's humour can be gauged from the scene where English, Bough and the commando-suited team have to scale a cliff and enter a fortress. English insists on taking the hard route up a concrete tunnel where he is regularly showered with excrement. His companions take another route, remaining immaculate and generating further jokes about bad smells. Camp elements also include John Malkovich as a sinister French billionaire plotting to take over the world by stealing the Crown Jewels. For all their farce and incompetence, Atkinson's English characters (as in the popular TV series, *Blackadder*) persevere, achieving their objectives by luck rather than design. Although mainly associated with the critically despised 'rom com' (romantic comedy), derided as glossy, eccentric examples of British whimsy (Solomons and Smith 2004: 3), Working Title has been successful with other genres, *Pride and Prejudice* (Joe Wright, UK/France, 2005) and *Nanny McPhee* (Kirk Jones, USA/UK/France, 2005) marking a lucrative change of direction in 2004.

The other facet of stereotypical Englishness, familiar through roles as Hollywood villains, is perfidy and the capacity for evil. In *Rob Roy* (Michael Caton-Jones, USA, 1995), Englishness is contrasted with Scottishness in a Manichean conflict of good and evil. *Rob Roy* illustrates the high-concept criteria perfectly. At first sight, a film about a mythic Scottish hero might seem too parochial and remote for an international film, but the narrative is carefully constructed as a battle between good (Scots) and evil (English), with pointers to the western in the emphasis on a man's honour and the importance of the land. *Rob Roy* opens with titles explaining who he was, where and when, but the film also uses the full resources of visuals and music to assist the audience in making sense of the multiple sub-plots. Rob Roy McGregor is associated with Scottish music, drawing on the Gaelic oral and instrumental traditions and well-known folk bands and, when he walks back to his croft by the loch, shots of the untamed natural world, green and gold colours evoke the colours and conventions of food advertising to suggest health and goodness. After his exertions stealing cattle, he bathes in the loch before entering his croft, kissing his two sons and amorously waking his wife, Mary (Jessica Lange). The skin colouring of northern peoples is notoriously luminously white, but McGregor is lean and tanned, and the whole sequence establishes his credentials as a fit and suitable hero who derives his authority from his links with the land and concern for his people.

The English, by contrast, are associated with the unnatural formality of the gardens of Montrose's (John Hurt) castle and with the cruelty and perfidy of those with English accents, Montrose and Cunningham (Tim Roth), and their men, Killearn (Brian Cox) and the Red Coats. Moreover, although sub-plots abound, they function to enhance the Manichean opposition of good and evil. McGregor loses the money loaned by the Duke of Argyll because he is too trusting and his uxorious nature renders his family vulnerable to attacks by Montrose, resulting in Mary's rape by Cunningham. Cunningham gets Betty, the servant girl, pregnant, and his callous treatment of her results in her suicide. The complexity of the mythic story is shorn of all its contradictions, leaving a tale made comprehensible by the combination of stars, geography, music and spectacle. The organized differentiation of the two factions, the rhythmic cutting between the spheres of action and the polycentrism of sub-plots around minor characters, are components of neo-baroque, postmodern taste (Calabrese 1992: 44) so that the film internalizes the tensions between stasis and movement represented by the bid for precedence of the Scottish version of history.

In the British case the increasingly complex situation of contemporary European film-making suggests that collusion with Hollywood and international cooperation are necessary for big-budget films' success, yet producers and directors appear to have turned Hollywood economic hegemony to their own account by cooperating on international projects to take advantage of the US majors' distribution networks. Although mega-successful co-productions bear the stamp of American styles of editing, camera movement and plot construction, the films are differentiated by their use of British settings, national characteristics and use of non-American stereotypes to reach the maximum international audience.

French cinema: style and spectacle

France shares with the UK a relatively limited domestic market, but differs in the consistent support given to the film and media industries by the French state. As Jäckel and Creton have detailed, France has a strong, regularly updated regulatory framework to support the French film industry and visual culture, and sophisticated models for the interaction of private companies and state bodies (2004: 201–20). Besides state institutes providing credit and investment for audio-visual products, tax shelter schemes, the SOFICAs (Sociétés de Financement de l'Industrie Cinématographique et Audiovisuelle), were set up in the 1980s as a conduit for private investment in film and television production. Their importance grew in the 1990s, especially following the 1993 GATT talks when the then Minister of

Culture, Jack Lang, encouraged the production of big-budget films designed for export. The emphasis was initially on the history or historical dramas which critics and politicians regard as reflecting the superiority of French culture and style. The rules have been relaxed to include English-language co-productions and the most successful have been in popular genres such as comedies, sci-fi fantasy and the family film. Production and marketing budgets have increased enormously and the international position of French cinema has been helped by the mergers and alliances which have made Pathé, Gaumont and UGC into powerful, vertically integrated media groups.

It was *The Fifth Element* (*Le cinquième element*, Luc Besson, France, 1997) which indicated that a French movie could beat a Hollywood blockbuster at the box office by disguising itself as an American movie and, predictably, critics hated it. Geoff Brown's review is fairly typical in bemoaning the lack of plot, 'Besson's incoherent English-language script and the less-than-special effects' (1997: 37). Besson refuted an allegation that his film was his calling card to Hollywood, giving his desire to make films reflecting contemporary tastes as his aim (Serenellini 2002: 49), and these include a predilection for spectacle, comic-book visuals and narratives and American genres. *The Fifth Element* confounds some science-fiction conventions by having a young, orange-haired woman, Leeloo (Milla Jovovich), as the supreme being, the fifth element who will save the world, and for his spectacular visuals Besson drew on the work of French graphic artists, Jean 'Mœbius' Giraud and Jean-Claude Mézières, whose strong verticals and diagonals allow the cartoon frame to be filled with detail. The sequence where Leeloo escapes her captors and crawls down a ventilation shaft to emerge on a narrow ledge of a high building overlooking vehicles teeming in the air above city streets is a spectacular start to the film (and the basis for the subsequent video game). Not only did it take a quarter of the $90 million budget, but her dive is reminiscent of *The Big Blue* (*Le grand bleu*, Luc Besson, France/USA/Italy, 1988), with the hovering, zooming cars resembling the creatures of the deep. Susan Hayward has identified a feature of Thierry Arbogast's work as director of photography in his reliance on natural light and favouring the medium shot, which creates visual tensions in the widescreen Cinemascope format (2002: 54–7). In this respect Besson's cinematography is the counterpoint of the visual excess of his use of colour and disturbing graphic asymmetry, which also finds a correlative in the references to surveillance and the deleterious consequences of technology. The film draws on elements which are both familiar (Bruce Willis, yellow taxis, mysterious sects, a threat to destroy the world, shoot-outs recalling western saloons) and new (Jean-Paul Gaultier's punk costumes, extraordinary cityscapes, Arab-influenced music). The film was entirely French-financed and filmed in great secrecy, reflected in the decision not to develop toys and other merchandise in advance of release which would give away the look of the film. Besson's vision was rewarded. Audiences loved it, responding to the film's spectacle and inventiveness and, Hayward suggests (2002: 55), to the fact that Besson's characters suffer from the loneliness and constraints of contemporary society, but seek solutions to their sense of isolation. *The Fifth Element*'s eight César nominations was the occasion for its theatrical re-release and the start of an aggressive video release aiming to ship 3 million copies (Meaux Saint Marc 1998: 17). It achieved almost 22 million admissions in Europe alone and set a pattern in making $122 million of its $186 million outside the USA on its first release.

More significant was the fact that one-fifth of *The Fifth Element*'s budget came from the US-based producer and distributor, Largo Entertainment (owned by JVC), with the Nippon TV network, in return for exclusive, all-media rights to the film in Japan, an example of JVC's alliances with European companies in order to extend its reach into the film industry (*Screen Digest* 1997: 100).

Alliances of effective French and foreign companies were behind both *Asterix and Obelix Take on Caesar* (*Astérix et Obélix contre César*, Claude Zidi, France/Germany/Italy, 1999) and *Asterix and Obelix: Mission Cleopatra* (*Astérix et Obélix: Mission Cléopâtre*, Alain Chabat, France/Germany, 2002). CNC, Claude Berri's Renn Productions (which had built on iconic successes of heritage films *Jean de Florette* (Claude Berri, France, 1986) and *Manon des Sources* (Claude Berri, France, 1987)), the satellite giant Canal Plus and Pathé were involved in the complex production budgets. Roberto Benigni, who starred in the 1999 film, brought his company, Melampo Cinematografica, into the package. With estimated budgets of $48 million and $47 million respectively, the two films were huge French successes, with over 21 million admissions in Europe alone. Significantly, both films were produced without American investment, taking advantage of Eurimages' co-production funds and finance from German *Land* Bavaria. With international French star Gérard Depardieu as the giant Obélix and popular French comic Christian Clavier as Astérix, and based on Goscinny and Uderzo's perennially popular comic books, the films, like the books, cross over well between the child and adult audience. The books have been translated into many languages, relying on the potential for puns and wordplay in the characters' names in different tongues. There is certainly no cultural cringe involved in these tales of resourceful Gauls battling the might of an evil Empire (Rome), which perhaps explains the latter film's box office of around $108 million in non-US territories and a mere $3 million in the USA.

The first *Astérix* film was also notable for its digital special effects, supervised by the CGI expert Pitof (Jean Christophe Comar), of the Duran-Duboi company, who also worked on *The Messenger: The Story of Joan of Arc* (*Jeanne d'Arc*, Luc Besson, France, 1999) and *The City of Lost Children* (*La cité des enfants perdus*, Jean-Pierre Jeunet/Marc Caro, France/Germany/Spain, 1995). This is another area in which France excels in the face of severe international competition. The leading companies MacGuff Ligne, Buf Compagnie, ExMachina, Duran-Duboi, Gribouille and Mikros Image maintain their position in the industry through a combination of technical quality, innovation and creativity (Jullier and Mazdon 2004: 227–9). Indeed, many of the creative sfx teams who have worked on big-budget productions like the *Astérix* films, *Brotherhood of the Wolf* (*Le pacte des loups*, Christophe Gans, France/Canada, 2001), *Amélie* (*Le fabuleux destin d'Amélie Poulain*, Jean-Pierre Jeunet, 2001) and *A Very Long Engagement* (*Un long dimanche de fiançailles*, Jean-Pierre Jeunet, France/USA, 2004) started out on the fabulous worlds of *The City of Lost Children*.

Brotherhood of the Wolf illustrates how European expertise can transform a genre – horror (the hunt for a murderous wild beast set in the late eighteenth century) – and achieve cult success. The digital sfx teams were not the only ones to win prizes. Dominique Borg won a 2002 César award for best costume design, the costumes being made by the world-famous Farani workshop in Rome.[2] Among other films, Borg was costume designer on *Artemisia*

(Agnès Merlet, France/Germany/Italy, 1997), for which she was nominated for César and Golden Globe awards, *Les Misérables* (Claude Lelouche, France, 1995) and *Camille Claudel* (Bruno Nuytten, France, 1998). Borg won a César for the latter film, which also scooped a raft of prizes and nominations and earned $205 million in the USA. The production designer/art director, Guy-Claude François, had also won prizes and nominations for his work. Keith Reader suggests that the role of set designer as part-*auteur* of a film has received little serious consideration of how it might be conceptualized (2000: 37), but suggests that notions of realism and space might provide ways of theorizing it. Scenographic space is constructed by a team whose task is, as Giuliana Bruno reminds us, to build a *habitus* in which clothes, architecture, interiors, cosmetics, the gestures and morphology of bodies 'define our way of living space' (2002: 322). Horror cinema is mainly discussed in terms of camera identification and the withholding and revelation of the object of the gaze (Clover 1992: 8–10), but in contemporary cinema Bruno's notions of the haptic are more useful. She considers the haptic to be a way of constructing cinematic space through camera and actors' movement within it, sound and *mise-en-scène* which creates meanings at a sensory and emotive level (2002: 6). While *Brotherhood* delivers plenty of violent fights, spectacle and suspense, the haptic elements enable the film to be read at a deeper level. The film's framing device, whereby the elderly Marquis Thomas d'Apcher (Jacques Perrin) writes down his recollections of the hunt for the murderous wolf which ravaged the countryside in his youth in 1768, while a revolutionary mob of 1789 howls for his blood outside his chateau, is conventional, but also structures a reading of the narrative. Young Thomas (Jérémie Renier) made friends with the scientist and explorer Grégoire de Fronsac (Samuel Le Bihan), who is sent from Paris by the king to investigate both the beast and rumours of sedition in the countryside. Grégoire and his Iriquois companion, Mani (Mark Dacascos), are the only male characters seen partially clothed, their muscular torsos objectified as they fight or make love to women, signalling their physical as well as intellectual superiority. However, it is their movements in space in the majority of the film, the kinaesthetic elements which enable societal structures to be perceived. From their arrival, fights are filmed at close quarters and their peasant attackers are undifferentiated bands dressed in dark, wet rags and using metal hooks as talons. There are many scenes in which the camera follows the two heroes as they gallop through trees or sunken lanes in which a wider view is unobtainable. Haptic contact with their movements brings contact with their emotions of fear, frustration and ignorance; they literally cannot see the wood for the trees. Visits to the brothel, where Grégoire meets the beautiful Sylvia (Monica Bellucci, later revealed to be a Papal agent), follow the men through doorways and up stairs peopled by suggestively posturing, half-naked girls, and the final location of the beast in a cage in a subterranean crypt guarded by the thugs with metal talons is similarly claustrophobic. The interior architecture of church and chateaux on the other hand is coercive, reinforced by the priest's exhortations to reject the king's liberal version of Christianity and the conversations of the aristocrats in richly decorated, formal spaces. Movement and space materialize the semiotics of power, expressing the rigidity of class and patriarchal control with the beast and his master, Jean-François de Morangias (Vincent Cassel), externalizing the violent reaction to the perceived threat to an established social order. The beast preys on peasants and especially women, de Morangias rapes his sister, Marianne (Émilie Dequenne), with whom Grégoire has fallen in love. The revolutionary mob's howls of anger become explicable.

Colour (and a Duboicolor technician is listed in the credits) is also used to enhance and express the tensions between order and disorder in the film. Peasants are dressed in dark, plain clothes, Grégoire, Mani and Thomas in light shades. Aristocrats and their surroundings are distinguished by the intrusion of saturated red colours in costume and architectural details, culminating in their masked red-cloaked conclave where their seditious views are expounded. Aristocratic sartorial extravagance as 'a mechanism for tyrannizing over rather than surrendering to the gaze of the (class) other' (Silverman 1994: 183) is here deconstructed through postmodern excess. As the older Thomas goes out to his death, Grégoire and Marianne are pictured on a sailing ship off the coast of Africa, the swirling high-angle camera movements and pervasive deep blue of sea and sky signalling their freedom and escape from social control. *Brotherhood* illustrates how European films become movies as recognition of creative excellence propels film-makers, cinematographers and other creative personnel towards increasingly large budgets and the international arena.

Amelie's director, Jean-Pierre Jeunet, had already made this journey, also demonstrating the logical development of the *cinema du look*'s playfulness, digressions, foregrounding the visual over discursive elements of narrative (Harris 2004: 224–5) and the presence of usually concealed elements of *mise-en-scène* to signal the presence of the film-maker in the text. *Amélie* is a romantic comedy and fairy story of a Parisian café waitress who wants to do good and who makes a journey towards her own love and commitment. Released after French press allegations of national collusion with the Nazi occupiers, and of scandals involving politicians, *Amélie* carefully avoids specific references to politics or time, which earned Jeunet accusations of fascism for ignoring the contemporary, multicultural reality of France (Johnston 2001: 40). Although aimed at the domestic youth market, *Amélie* crossed over into the international, adult market, largely due to being taken up by Miramax, building on the film's initial success in French-speaking territories. The film tapped into archetypal fairy tale formats, nostalgia for the perfect childhood, and used its Frenchness to differentiate itself from Hollywood movies. The use of saturated reds and greens has a function in the story, but also evokes brightly coloured childhood picture books, imagination, fantasy and innocence. Parisian landmarks such as the Cathedral of Sacré Cœur, the Rue St Vincent and the Canal St Martin, metro stations and roofscapes were digitally enhanced to emphasize their iconic nature, and close-ups of Amélie stressed her enormous eyes, gamine haircut and expressions, providing eye-catching images for the poster campaign. These elements worked in France and their success prompted foreign distributors to devote more resources to the film's publicity, stressing the film's romantic comedy, heart-warming qualities and good reviews. *Amélie* was conceived as a small film, but became an event movie, whose private view by French President, Jacques Chirac, was also fodder for its publicity campaign (Johnston 2001: 40). Publicity for Yann Tiersen's original soundtrack mentioned the mix of the traditionally Gallic – piano, guitar and accordion – and the unusual elements of carillon, vibraphone and harpsichord, the 'spirited' masking 'classical, minimalist undertones'. *Amélie* is typically postmodern in its evocation of a complete fantasy world peopled with eccentrics and the dichotomy in its musical influences mirrors the oscillation between stasis and a visual excess which signals the impossibility of Amélie's cosy world.

Like Hollywood films, French successes also indicate that, although a good financial return can be achieved from an American theatrical release, the majority of a film's income will derive from outside the USA if the film combines familiar cinematic and high-concept conventions. Collusion with American styles of narrative, genres and editing is therefore not strictly necessary, resulting in an increasing emphasis on the Frenchness of its international blockbusters.

Roberto Benigni and the dreadful case of *Pinocchio*

Life is Beautiful (*La vita è bella*, Roberto Benigni, Italy, 1997) is the only Italian film to achieve blockbuster status, with over 20 million admissions in Europe alone. Benigni exerts an unusual level of control over his career through his own production company, Melampo, and direction, but his subsequent film, *Pinocchio* (Italy/France/Germany, 2002), is a lesson on the pitfalls inherent in big-budget European production. Encouraged by the three Oscars won in 1998, Benigni and the independent producer Elda Ferri put together a package for the Cecchi Gori company (without which big-budget films do not get made in Italy), Berlusconi's Medusa distribution and Miramax. At €40 million ($40.2 million), *Pinocchio* was hyped as Italy's most expensive production ever and was Italy's Oscar candidate. A 940-print release in one-third of Italy's cinemas earned it $31 million by November 2002, but it was unpopular outside Italy. The Peerless Camera Company was involved in the special effects (also involved with *Gladiator* (Ridley Scott, UK/USA, 2000), *Enemy at the Gates* (Jean-Jacques Annaud, USA/Germany/UK/Ireland, 2001), *Harry Potter and the Prisoner of Azkaban* and *Kingdom of Heaven* (Ridley Scott, UK/Spain/USA/Germany, 2005)) and costumes were designed by Danilo Donati, who had worked with Fellini, guaranteeing a spectacular, quality look to the film. The Blue Fairy's (Nicoletta Braschi) coach, drawn by hundreds of white mice, is particularly successful. As an adaptation of a widely translated classic of children's literature, *Pinocchio* should have done better as it fulfilled Italian film industry perceptions of criteria for international success, quality and Italian stereotypes (F.F. 2002: 4). However, Benigni's *Pinocchio* returned to the Italian source text by Collodi, which is very Italian in its setting and cruel humour. Shorn of the saccharine elements of the Disney version, and with a manifestly middle-aged actor playing the wooden boy, audiences did not find it appealing.

European stars

Within the terms of the event films discussed in this chapter, which compete with American films for worldwide box-office returns, few contemporary European actors sell films on their instantly recognizable star persona. This is not to say that they do not have international profiles and appeal. As Ginette Vincendeau has observed, French stars (and, by extension, European stars in general) work across the *auteur*, popular and (if they are lucky) international film industry sectors (2000: 2). The lists at the head of this chapter were compiled on the basis of theatrical box-office earnings which, in this industry sector, depend on appeal to the multiplex cinema audience. Ilott identified the typical multiplex cinema-goer as mostly affluent young people looking for undemanding entertainment, which does not suit European cinema (1996: 12–13). The films at the top of the event films' list seem to support this argument and explain the presence of comedies and sagas based on well-known books which have a crossover appeal between children and adults. Others belong to the genres of romantic comedy or horror which appeal to the young adult audience in their 20s and early 30s. Actors who have achieved international recognition are mainly representatives of the more powerful European film industries of France and the UK, or Spanish actors who have emigrated to the USA. Hugh Grant, Gérard Depardieu, Kenneth Branagh, Penélope Cruz, Juliette Binoche, and Audrey Tautou are examples. There are, moreover, large numbers who work regularly in mainstream, Hollywood-style movies, but who perform generic functions of 'the effete European', 'the British villain', 'the monk/sage/being from another planet', 'the passionate foreign woman', 'the *diva*', 'the eccentric nanny'. Jeremy Irons, Alan Rickman, Gary Oldman, Ian Holm, Jeroen Krabbe, Emma Thompson, Fanny Ardant, Rutger Hauer and many others are in this position. Then there are those who have moved into the quality sphere of the art film sector, Bruno Ganz, Ralph Fiennes, Kate Winslet, Rachel Weisz, Javier Bardem, Monica Belucci, Dame Judi Dench, Dame Maggie Smith, Catherine Deneuve, Charlotte Rampling, Keira Knightley, Daniel Auteuil, Vincent Cassel and many up-and-coming young actors, all of whom may be considerable stars in the European arena but whose names would not open a film on their own.

Gérard Depardieu, Hugh Grant and Kenneth Branagh are exceptions. They have solid foundations in the theatre and TV, but Depardieu has managed to acquire identification with elements of Frenchness whose sound basis in his experiences in working-class comedies of the 1970s and 1980s melded sexual vigour, energy and an anti-conformist attitude. Vincendeau has shown how his persona has mutated over time so that he embodies a symbolic social national identity which can absorb changing contemporary anxieties about class and masculinity. Depardieu's imposing presence has been used predominantly in the 'cultural superproductions' which are the French equivalent of the heritage film (Vincendeau 2000: 231–2). Branagh's cultivation of an image of ordinariness has enabled his Shakespeare adaptations to reach a multiplex audience where the naturalism of his speech and performance has rendered the Bard more accessible. He embodies the ambiguity identified by Richard Dyer in the ordinariness of the persona and the 'specialness' of the star (1979: 49). In Branagh's case these elements have oscillated between his frequent forays into Hollywood and his Shakespeare adaptations (where his star status has been a factor in attracting Hollywood actors to his Shakespeare productions). Hugh Grant's persona has only recently acquired two notes as his Daniel Cleaver role in the *Bridget Jones* movies deliberately plays against type in creating a louche and negative character. The stereotypes discussed above relate to a 'right time' (Finney 1996a: 58) when the upper-class colonial conqueror English stereotype did not fit film industry economic necessities, and the role of the diffident, seemingly incompetent upper middle-class male (who nonetheless succeeds in his aims) took over. Grant's age now necessitates a younger replacement, hence the grooming of Paul Bettany for stardom.

Conclusion

The films discussed here have not sought to compete with Hollywood on its own territory but to conquer the international market which is also crucial for American films. These European films succeed by employing mainstream, Hollywood cinematic conventions of framing, pace and narrative, but building on their difference from American cinema. As event movies, they employ excess in their spectacular *mise-en-scène* and play on their non-Americanness by utilizing national stereotypes, stories, locations and characters. They go where American films do not go, and it is significant that the most successful of them eschew sex and violence, and evoke non-verbal comedy and slapstick, archetypal myths or common generic forms. Although subtexts may indicate a sophisticated engagement with contemporary politics and social realities, these are generally constructed at a deeper level only available to audiences with high levels of cultural competence.

As we have seen, producers and creative teams gradually access this movie sector by achieving recognition for excellence, winning prizes at festivals which propel their careers up an industry notch. European film personnel cannot rely on this sector for continuous income, but those who work in it achieve additional recognition in the quality sector of the industry, hence explaining the 'look' of contemporary European films being above budget expectations. The stylish and the unusual can capture mass audiences, nationally and internationally, with good scripts, stars, cinematographers, directorial teams and publicity. There are national films which cover their costs and even achieve huge returns on their home market alone, which will be enjoyed in Chapter Six. The ideal of modestly budgeted films which catch public interest internationally and cover their costs many times over is represented by *Trainspotting* (Danny Boyle, UK, 1996) and *Billy Elliot* (Stephen Daldry, UK/France, 2000). The determinedly local film can find a response in its own restricted market and (with good publicity) internationally. In the following chapters we will also explore the fact that theatrical box office is not the only gauge of a film's success and that older audiences and women can ensure that a European film finds an audience response.

Notes

1. In fact, as media lawyer Wolfgang Brehm of Brehm & Von Moers pointed out, a loophole in the Media Ruling allowed a producer to spend all the money in Hollywood by employing a production services company (Blaney 2002a, 8).
2. The Farani atelier has over 40 years' experience of making costumes for famous art film and international directors such as Federico Fellini, Franco Zeffirelli, Roger Vadim, Pier Paolo Pasolini, Ridley Scott, David Lynch and Roland Emmerich. They recently made the costumes for *Pirates of the Caribbean: Dead Man's Chest* (Gore Verbinski, USA, 2006). The atelier draws on wide knowledge of European culture and fashion history, and a high level of inventiveness and expertise in interpreting a film's design. In Giorgio Ferrara's *Tosca and the Women (Tosca e altre due*, Italy, 2003), Baron Scarpia's yellow velvet coat featured intricate, raised ribbon and flower designs incorporating various forms of pasta (Licastro Scardino, di Napoli Rampolla and Tosi Pamphili, 2004: 168). Key pieces are often exhibited like the works of art they are.

chapter five

Popular cinema and local stories

The European Union has invested several million euros in support of the continent's film industries and monitors the fate of films from member countries and associated states in order to justify its cultural policies. Yet underneath the high-profile successes of European cooperation lie vibrant and seething strata of popular cinema, most of which rarely make it outside national borders. What are the attractions of the low-budget, local production model for European film-makers? Firstly, local production enables young film-makers to make their debut and established film-makers to build a career in a local niche market. National production still flourishes, with annual ups and downs. One year Austrian or Danish film will record an increase in production, the next year a decrease. Low-budget, national productions, mostly in co-production with national television, are the solution for most film-makers and they make 90% of their revenue on their national market. These films are rarely exported, but occasionally a comedy, such as the German film *Goodbye Lenin* (Wolfgang Becker, Germany, 2003), will break through and have a limited release internationally. They are examples of the localizing tendency within global media financing – cheap, local productions, often in minority languages and financed by a combination of EU and national grants.

In this chapter I want to consider two types of popular European cinema. Firstly I will focus on genres which persist because individual examples continue to hit the desired national audience demographic and cinematic tastes which remain stubbornly local and national. Films appealing to the young male audience and the 24–34-year-old middle-class audience will be examined in the first two sections, and the varieties of national comedies in the third. Secondly, the final short sections will focus on two perennially popular, transnational genres, the horror and the porno film. I will also consider the constant cross-fertilization between the local and the mainstream.

Appealing to the young male audience

The films discussed in the previous chapter appear to suggest that mass public taste has become Americanized. Shorn of historical or contemporary complexity and controversy, the box-office statistics would indicate that 'the popular', in European terms, is synonymous with Americanized narrative forms and genre formats. This is a view often suggested

(Bondebjerg 2001; Dyja 2004) by those who interpret industry figures. Yet experiencing the viewing of a film in a cinema is not the only indication of a film's engagement with its public. British film industry statistics may suggest that popular taste is for the children's adventure or the romantic comedy, and 'top 25' lists of video and DVD sales that the 7–14 age group must be the biggest consumers of film, but there are other indicators that there are additional mass audiences out there, not least young men, the over-34s and older women. If producers are lucky and hit the audience spot, audiences join up like lumps of mercury to form Arnold Schwarzenegger's opponent in *Terminator 2*, or a recognizable niche market.

A coherent picture of possible niche markets was not visible to British producers at the end of the 1980s, a transitional situation in which American domination of film distribution and exhibition was impinging on the ability of European films to conquer their own markets. The situation was particularly difficult in the UK, whose industry had traditionally been subordinate to the better funded US industry, particularly because of the shared language. The combination of a slight global economic recession which generated aggressive mergers and multiplex developments, plus a Conservative government inimical to the idea of cultural subsidy, led to a noticeable reduction in the average budget of a UK film and recognition that the British film industry was incapable of financing big-budget movies (Ilott 1992: 20, 30). It has taken 15 years for average British film budgets to increase and there still exist significant numbers of micro-budget films. These are generally unsuccessful because they are unable to access distribution and/or exhibition, but tolerated and even encouraged because of the training ground they provide for creative talent. The explosion of multiplex development suggested to producers that the youth audience was one to target and the most successful low-budget British films since 1995–96 have aimed at this demographic but have achieved a crossover to older audiences. *Shallow Grave* (Danny Boyle, UK, 1994) and *Trainspotting* (Danny Boyle, UK, 1995) are the most successful examples financially. Both films are notable for the shifting of attitude towards crime identified by Claire Monk (1999a: 175) and indeed, the most successful, non-heritage recent British films have all displayed this characteristic of greater tolerance towards some forms of criminal activity, including drug-taking. In the 1980s and early 1990s, the combination of the Thatcher government's policies towards both businesses and the trades unions, and the emphasis on individual effort and materialism, resulted in a real class shake-up which, among other effects, necessitated the reconfiguring of advertising's traditional social categories. Categorizing the population by social class (ABC1 being upper, professional, salaried and C2DE being skilled and unskilled working class and the unemployed) did not reflect social change and could not encompass, for example, huge amounts being earned as City of London money brokers by those of working-class origin, or Princess Margaret's son being an upmarket carpenter. Lifestyle categories were introduced, illustrated in *Shallow Grave* by sets and locations emphasizing the middle-class consumerist lifestyle (the enormous bowl of fruit on the table in front of the trio interviewing potential flatmates), arty colours on the walls, and Scottishness.

The advertising industry fed the conspicuous consumption displayed in glossy men's and women's magazines, but it was the UK recession at the end of the 1980s which laid bare the illusions of class mobility. When redundancies came, high earners were just as much prisoners of the cash nexus. Not only the breakdown of traditional masculinist hierarchies (which had structured that mainstay of popular British cinema, the gangster film) but also the marginalizing of whole populations as a result of the decline of heavy industry meant that those whose region was considered expendable according to the tenets of global capitalism fought back in ways considered criminal 50 years previously. *The Full Monty* (Peter Cattaneo, UK, 1997) opens with a newsreel whose upper-class voice-over extols the former achievements of the steel town of Sheffield, which is promptly contrasted to the lives of the unemployed men whose reality is being forced to practise job applications for posts which do not exist. The reality of family breakdown under financial stress is illustrated through all of the characters, particularly Gaz (Robert Carlyle), whose wife has a new, financially secure partner, and Gerald (Tom Wilkinson), who cannot confess his job redundancy, leaving the house as usual each day but only to go to the JobCentre. For all of them the mirage of earning a large sum of money through a striptease performance (and going all the way to complete nudity) is a no-contest situation in spite of it being illegal to earn money while receiving state benefits. *The Full Monty* was hugely successful, making £46 million in its UK theatrical release from a budget of £3.5 million, clearly touching a national chord. The expression has re-entered the English language, charged with all the connotations of desperation engendered by the film. In a piece of cinematic intertextuality, a rural Welsh woman discovers a line of plump ten-year-olds practising the full Monty routine in her backyard (*Very Annie Mary*, Sara Sugarman, UK/France, 2001); just one of a number of small details which, like the importance of the talent contest, the house which does not sell and the old-fashioned knick-knacks in every home help to create an image of small communities in the Welsh valleys which stopped moving forward when traditional mass employment ceased. With finance from the British National Lottery, disbursed through the Arts Councils of England and Wales, and support from the French satellite giant Canal Plus, *Very Annie Mary* is a low-budget comedy which reaches its public through television, satellite and DVD, at one and the same time illustrating the fact that lottery funding was initially awarded only to films which would not otherwise be made, while refuting the suggestion that only commercially viable films should be worthy of support (Snoddy 2000: 12).

Another huge success, *Waking Ned* (Kirk Jones, UK/France/USA, 1998), made by the director of the Absolut vodka advertisements, features an entire Irish community involved in a conspiracy to cheat the National Lottery and claim the millions won by Ned, who has inconveniently just died. Distributed by Fox Searchlight and marketed as an Irish film (although filmed in the Isle of Man), *Waking Ned* made £7 million in the UK and $19.4 million worldwide by a studious combination of Irish stereotypes and playing to common aspirations to win large sums of money. The narrative predominantly concerns men, centred on two old men, Jackie O'Shea (Ian Bannen) and Michael O'Sullivan (David Kelly), in remote rural Ireland who perform Irish yokelry as an intelligent strategy to achieve their aims. It is an old-fashioned film but the combination of wish-fulfilment, drunkenness, rural craftiness and comedy had enough mass appeal outside the Irish diaspora for its director's next feature to be the Working Title/Universal big-budget production *Nanny McPhee* (Kirk Jones, USA/UK/France, 2005).

The gangster genre

The social realism of the British gangster genre was superseded for ever in the early 1990s, influenced by a slew of ultra-violent American films typified by *Reservoir Dogs* (Quentin Tarantino, USA, 1992). Boggs and Pollard suggest that the brutality of this Hobbesian cinema of mayhem in which social rules and conventions have been loosened says something about how American society works (2003: 164–7). Like their American counterparts, chaos, disorder and unpredictability characterize the new cycle of British gangster films in which greed and the lust for power are played out with no sense of morality, family or community. These films find a response in a population which senses that their needs are not being addressed, that the democratic process has been hijacked to attend to the interests of business and the upper classes, and that they are powerless to change the situation. Despised by critics, gangster films have only recently been accorded serious academic attention (Hill 1986; Chibnall and Murphy 1999; Leach 2004). *Lock, Stock & Two Smoking Barrels* (Guy Ritchie, UK, 1998) is set in the criminal underworld of the East End of London, its main characters pooling funds to enter a big-money card game, becoming involved in gangland violence when the cards go against them. PolyGram's astute marketing techniques (based on the attention to market segmentation typical of the record industry) earned it £11.9 million in the UK and $3.7 million in the USA, prompting American investment in the subsequent film, *Snatch* (Guy Ritchie, UK/USA, 2000). Both films reflect the moment of 'new laddism', representing an aggressive reaction to feminism, anxieties over male roles and the glorification of consumer culture where the right shoes and fashionable clothes indicated status. The 'cool' advertising influenced images, stop-motion photography and distorted camera angles identified by Emily Shaw (1998: 288–9) epitomize a postmodern style in which asymmetry, narrative and visual disorder are correlatives of chaotic masculine worlds in which the characters search for identity. However, despite the PR company's trawl for online journalists' marketable quotes and Luc Besson's writing credit, *Revolver*'s (Guy Ritchie, France/UK, 2005) philosophizing earned it critical (but not audience) displeasure (Silver 2005: 1–2). Ritchie's protagonists lack self-knowledge, so that the disorder represented by chaos and ultra-violence opens up an ironic space within which male behaviours can be rehearsed and judged.

Disruptive events are conventions of the genre, one of the most spectacular occurring in the opening sequences of *Sexy Beast* (Jonathan Glazer, UK/Spain, 2000), when retired criminal Gary Dove's (Ray Winstone) self-satisfied contemplation of the morning in his Spanish villa is shattered by a huge rock which bounces down the hillside and into his swimming pool. It heralds the arrival of Don Logan (Ben Kingsley), seeking to 'persuade' Gary to take part in one last heist. In common with another gangster film convention, there are two male protagonists, Gary's large, sleek, tanned, well-oiled figure contrasted to Don's small but monstrously bullying and foul-mouthed character, two ways of acquiring and exercising male power being written on their bodies. Greater awareness is expressed in two films directed by Mike Hodge (director and writer of the iconic *Get Carter*, UK, 1971), *Croupier* (France/UK/Germany/Ireland, 1998) and *I'll Sleep When I'm Dead* (UK/USA, 2003), both starring Clive Owen. In the former, Jack, an unsuccessful writer, is drawn into the criminal world associated with gambling when he takes a job in a casino. His writer's gift for observation and detail gives him some detachment from his milieu, but he is unable to prevent his slide into violence. In the latter, Will Graham, a feared gangster who had retired to the country when he had a nervous breakdown, returns to the city on the death of his brother, Davey (Jonathan Rhys Meyers). Will's elliptical conversations with his ex-girlfriend Helen (Charlotte Rampling) bring into the open explanations for the violence which erupts around him, but also describe emotions and feelings usually firmly marginalized in the genre. Altered circumstances are the disruptions which initiate investigations and also suggest perspectives on what is investigated. Will discovers that his brother committed suicide as a result of being raped by one of the enemies he had incurred by consciously emulating Will's former lifestyle and manners. Both films are imbued with a sense of melancholy, heightened by the neo-*noir* visuals and Owens' performance. As an actor, he is able to project the stillness of contained violence and the sadness that self-knowledge brings. Leach suggests that any possible social and psychological explanations for the gangster's behaviour are 'inadequate in the face of the enormity of the evil he represents' (2004: 181), but the *noir* elements offer a postmodern reading of instability when older social and gender models do not answer contemporary needs and behavioural boundaries have to be explored. These are films with budgets of £3–4 million which generate $6 million or so in a US theatrical release and have legs in video and DVD sell-through.

Boundaries of behaviour are also tested in a film which does not feature in the charts of European box-office success, *The Football Factory* (Nick Love, UK, 2004), which has nonetheless acquired a cult following. With a micro-budget of around £500,000 it demonstrated the value of word-of-mouth publicity as a pirate DVD was in great demand at the time of its release (Eimer 2004: 14). Love's updating of a popular novel follows a group of London football hooligans in their 20s and 30s as they live for weekends when their Chelsea Headhunters have opportunities to drink huge amounts of lager, snort cocaine and fight, preferably with their arch-enemies, Millwall supporters. It was criticized for the wisdom of releasing it before the Euro 2004 football championships and received many negative and pious reviews about working-class violence and hooliganism tarnishing the image of the country abroad. Its budget precludes spectacular special effects, but it achieves excitement and charge from its fast editing, loud house music soundtrack, the purposeful and aggressive parades to and from football stadiums calling attention to their identity, and the frenetic violence of the fights. Eimer praises its 'documentary-style realism' and authenticity (2004: 14), but the film is more hyperreal than realist. *Football Factory* demonstrates an aesthetic of seriality. Groups of young men rushing through council estates, South London backstreets and the no-man's lands of industrial decay, drinking sessions, conversations peppered with four-letter obscenities, the snorting of heroic quantities of cocaine and the close-in filming of the blood and gore of fights, are repetitive fragments which can be enjoyed as parts of the whole. Angela Ndalianis argues that neo-baroque repetition is not incoherent, but 'concerned with the reconstruction of order, an order that emerges from complex and expanding spaces' (2004: 69). The bigger picture constructed by the fragments is that of a working-class identity which rejects the polite acceptance of class inferiority and reclaims its territory.

The kinetic violence of the male protagonists materializes the constitution of the football hooligan heterotopia, allowing access to a closed society and understanding of why it differentiates itself and how it maintains its power. The fragmentation, violence and stressed visuals also suggest that there are problems in the attempt to fix a new sense of community because this rejection of middle-class culture operates at the margins of behaviour which will support a true community, in which young women have an equal part and are not consigned to sex objects to be 'consumed' on Saturday night after the pub.

Broadening the borders

Rebellion against 1980s' and 1990s' materialism is reflected in British films exploring other types of community. Britain's only surfer film, *Blue Juice* (Carl Prechezer, UK, 1995), set in Cornwall, explores the conflict for thirty-somethings between settling down and pursuing individual pleasures through the relationship of JC (Sean Pertwee), whose life is structured around finding the perfect wave, and his girlfriend Chloe (Catherine Zeta-Jones), who runs the beach café and wants to settle down. The spaces occupied by Chloe are womblike and enclosed, clearly signalling the containment which the feminine represents, and contrast to the green cliffs and wide seascape environments of JC and his friends, Dean (Ewan McGregor) and Josh (Steven Mackintosh). In the end JC achieves both aims by successfully surfing the ultimate wave over Cornish rocks and accepting the inevitability of domesticity.

What do these films suggest about contemporary British society? Firstly that the borders of narrative are being pushed and that behaviours regarded as aberrant 30 years ago are moving to centre stage. The big picture is not yet visible and so the homosocial worlds of British popular genre films incorporate both uncontested elements of the global capitalist culture of consumption (in the clothing uniforms of these sub-cultures) and the refusal to accept that the economic positioning that is the logical consequence of unthinking consumption is all there is to personal identity.

The famed liberalism of Scandinavian society creates different sorts of difficulties for films aiming to engage the young male audience in narratives of youthful revolt. Not all Scandinavian film-makers see opportunities in the Dogme95 manifesto; for Swedish director Josef Fares it makes 'the fun stuff with film disappear' (Lundberg 2003a: 22). The son of Lebanese immigrants, Fares shares Michael Winterbottom's creed of making the films you want to make. In his prolific teenage video shorts, Fares generally acted as director, producer, photographer, editor, stuntman on his no-budget car chases and with friends in front of the camera. He was accepted at Sweden's leading film school, the Dramatic Institute University College of Film, where Lukas Moodysson spotted his talent and went on to act as executive producer on Fares' first feature, *Jalla! Jalla!* (Sweden, 2000). One in ten Swedes is estimated to have seen this rites-of-passage film whose comedy resides in the culture clash between traditional immigrant values and liberal Scandinavian society, as experienced by the young and hormonal second generation. *Jalla! Jalla!* went on to achieve 1.3 million admissions in Europe and export to 30 countries worldwide (Lundberg 2003b: 22). Fares' second film, *Kops* (Sweden/Denmark, 2003), was also a successful action comedy featuring Fares' trademark explosions and frenetic action as an ensemble group of Swedish police fight to keep their station open in a crime-free community. Fares' film was again produced by Memfis Films, which put together a two-country co-production which qualified for Eurimages funding and support from institutions and television in Scandinavia. *Kops* was aimed beyond the youth market of *Jalla! Jalla!* and sales agents had to market it as an art-house film internationally, although Fares was regarded as a commercial director in Sweden.

The violence of popular films aimed at young males articulates a protest at the continuing disempowerment of working- and underclass youths in mainstream society which privileges conspicuous consumption as identifier of status. These films implicitly interrogate the values of globalized, multicultural society, by substituting other pleasures for the socially sanctioned ones of employment and stable relationships from which they are often excluded.

Middle-class tastes

Scandinavian cinema also provides examples of popular films with the potential to cross borders and appeal to middle-class audiences in other countries. All of the Nordic countries have small populations and therefore low numbers of cinemas and little possibility of amortizing production costs purely on their national market without state support and television distribution deals. Ib Bondebjerg suggests that the flourishing and well-supported Danish cinema has recognized its position as a small producer and developed particular globalization strategies (2005: 128–33). These aim firstly at a pan-Nordic, pan-European and global audience, using co-productions to access higher-than-average budgets and having a Hollywood style with Nordic elements. The second is the European co-production in the 'quality cinema' category explored earlier, and the third is the Nordic national heritage film. The effect of these strategies is that the Danish exhibition sector is shared mainly between national (25–30%) and US (56–64%), with very little interest in non-Nordic European films. To these should be added the localizing tendency, the low-budget national production which will cover its costs through generous state subventions, local and Nordic television deals. Sweden, Norway, Iceland and Finland conform to these models, although their share of their national markets is much lower than Denmark's. The transnationalism of Nordic production and distribution arrangements is not entirely synonymous with globalization, more a pooling of economic resources in the region (Hjort 2005: 193). The Nordic countries are united by a sense of common history, geographic proximity and marginality both inside and outside national borders, but they are not homogenous. Some of them achieved the status of nation-states only in the last century and all have had to grapple with the effects of globalization on traditional industries and ways of life. The desire for stasis and order can be seen in films drawing on Norse sagas, reworkings of older popular films, or the conventions of bourgeois heritage, but these too (such as the *Raven* cycle of films in the early 1990s) are conflict narratives, featuring disruptive characters representing modernity. Tom Hedergaard's addition to a popular cycle of filmed adventures of a criminal gang, *The Olsen Gang – Final Mission* (*Olsen Bandens sidste stik*, Denmark, 1998), reveals its nostalgia for belonging in its depiction of the alternative family of the gang.

The increase in state funds and institutions to support the film and media industries in the 1990s resulted in an increasingly wide variety of film genres produced. Lukas Moodysson's films have become darker in recent years but his first two, internationally popular films, *Show Me Love* (*Fucking Åmål*, Sweden, 1999) and *Together* (*Tilsammans*, Sweden, 2000), are lighter dramas in which ensemble actors represent different facets of social change. *Show Me Love* centres on a teenage girl's growing realization of her lesbian attraction for her best friend, allowing her personal drama to be contextualized against reactions in a variety of social spheres, school, community, home, peer group and relationship. It is a very gentle film, its young actors (one shy, dark-haired and reserved and the other bouncy, confident and blonde) playing against sexual stereotypes. *Together* also features a multi-generational ensemble cast representing a group of aging members of a commune coming to terms with partnerships, break-ups and teenage children. Much of the comedy resides in the ironic distance between the liberal, hippy precepts of the adults and their actions, amplified by the cringe factor experienced by the teenagers at the behaviour of their elders.

Funding also trained film-makers. Dogme95 revitalized Scandinavian film production to the extent of giving the area a higher international profile, but it is still hit and miss which films succeed in non-national markets. *Italian for Beginners* (*Dogme 12: Italiensk for Begyndere*, Lone Scherfig, Denmark, 2000), produced by Zentropa, Danmarks Radio and the Danish Film Institute, is a romantic comedy in which the Dogme precepts of rejection of intrusive special effects focuses attention on the psychology, desires and emotions of the group of adult Danes learning Italian, but beginners in forming relationships. The Dogme rules to avoid genres and extra-diegetic music were ignored. Scherfig's gentle humour earned her nearly 1.8 million admissions in 29 European countries and a Miramax distribution opened up the lucrative American market. Similarly, Susanne Bier's Dogme film *The One and Only* (*De eneste ene*, Denmark, 1999) was a huge national and international success.

Generous state funding in the Nordic countries has resulted in increased production and a greater share of national markets, but this does not infer a stable situation. State funds derive from taxation and are subject to the democratic authority granted to different ideological positions of right- and left-wing governments. As has been observed previously, box-office success leads to bigger budgets and a less Nordic profile, but transnational co-productions also mitigate the effects of political change. Lone Scherfig's English-language film, *Wilbur Wants to Kill Himself* (Denmark/UK/Sweden/France, 2002) is a black comedy, set in an eccentric bookshop in Glasgow. Its owner, Harbour (Adrian Rawlins), falls in love with regular customer Alice (Shirley Henderson), a single mother who augments her income by selling the books left behind by deceased patients in the hospital where she works. Alice and Harbour marry but she falls in love with his suicidal brother, Wilbur (Jamie Sives). The film features the interestingly dark and claustrophobic interiors, quirky humour and 'ordinary' physical appearance of the characters also visible in *Italian for Beginners*. Made with a complex production package including Zentropa, two Scottish regional funds and Nordic television companies, *Wilbur* is global in a Northern European rather than Hollywood sense, representing the positive side of pan-European production. Scandinavian cinema demonstrates that a combination of national and pan-Nordic financial support can result in local films demonstrating an engagement with change and disorder, resulting in popular films of the clash of city and countryside, the threat of transnationalism on local culture and the effects of modernity on traditional gender relations. These concerns resonate with other countries and ensure regular success for Nordic films outside Scandinavia.

Since the 1980s tastes of the British middle-class audience have been associated with the historical or heritage films which will be explored in Chapter Eight. Andrew Higson identifies a gradual 'embourgeoisement' of the cinema audience from the 1980s onwards as older, middle-class audiences were drawn back into cinemas (2003: 103). By 2001 the ABC1 audience was larger than the C2DE and although the former category does not visit cinemas as frequently as the 15–24 age group (Dyja 2004: 42), they are an important demographic category at whom the middle-class dramas and gentle comedies of other European nations are aimed.

France, with its highly regulated film industry and high output, is able to produce a wider range of film genres than any other country in Europe. It supports the careers of popular and prolific film-makers such as Patrice Leconte and François Ozon, the former having been critically ignored for years by virtue of his successful bourgeois comedies and the latter taken up by critics interested in his ability to attract iconic French actresses to his productions, his youth, and the gay subtexts which abound in his films. *Time to Leave* (*Le temps qui reste*, François Ozon, France, 2005) follows the last days of a young photographer, Romain (Melvil Poupaud), whose relief at being told that he has not got AIDS is undermined by the news that he has untreatable cancer. For the European audience part of the pleasure is watching decisions being made which are not part of the template of Hollywood 'dying young' narratives. Romain refuses to tell his family or partner, is rude and cruel to them and confides only in his grandmother, Laura (Jeanne Moreau). Laura provides a key to his behaviour, bringing all our intertextual knowledge of her cinematic and personal past to our reading of a worldliness which is largely unsaid but hinted at by her warning that she always sleeps naked when Romain has to stay the night and share her bed. Romain is brought to a realization of the contrast between her sensual engagement with living and his pursuit of recognition in the shallow world of the media. Ozon gives depth to Romain's predictable melancholy at his situation by briefly exploring his work milieu as a photographer, his relationship with the beautiful Sasha (Christian Sengewald) and the repeated inner flashbacks to himself as a young child, whose inquisitive face seems to interrogate the direction of his life. Romain comes into contact with a woman who asks him to impregnate her as her husband is infertile and in this difficult but selfless act, he discovers some meaning and closure to his life before he dies, peacefully, on the beach which was the scene of so much childish hope and happiness. This film was Ozon's 25th since 1991, a prolific career indicating a sure engagement with public taste. His recent films usually take a popular genre and give it a new twist. *5 x 2* (*Cinque fois deux*, France, 2004) tells the story of a marriage in reverse order, *8 Women* (*8 femmes*, France/Italy, 2002) is a whodunnit in which the characters frequently break into song and are all played by iconic French stars (explaining its €14.5 million French box office on a budget of €8 million).

These films for the educated middle classes reach smaller audiences, but as the earlier study of Eric Rohmer's career shows, the aggregate of audiences across many countries justifies their generally low- to mid-budget costs.

Local tastes: comedies which make it within national borders

Ozon's films, although popular and exportable, are not the most successful French productions. That honour goes to the *Taxi* series of films which has achieved enormous domestic box-office returns and has latterly been released internationally in dubbed DVD versions. The films display the seriality which is the hallmark of postmodern business practices (Harvey 1990; Ndalianis 2004) and whose fragmentation into episodes and vignettes resists closure and involves the audience in a continuous engagement with contemporary French life, as refracted through stories of a working-class, immigrant taxi driver, Daniel Morales (Sami Naceri). At the beginning of *Taxi* (Gérard Pirès, France, 1998), Daniel has moved from pizza delivery man to taxi driver, where he is able to indulge his expertise in high-speed deliveries of passengers rather than pizzas. When he inadvertently takes a police officer, Émilien (Frédéric Diefenthal), on a high-speed ride, he has to accept a deal to act as Émilien's driver to keep his licence. There are several running gags which prolong from film to film, such as Émilien's total incompetence at (among other things) driving and his inability to seduce the Amazonian fellow police detective, Petra (Emma Sjöberg), and Daniel's constantly interrupted lovemaking with his girlfriend Lilly (Marion Cotillard). Moments of romance are always a problem within male genres like *Taxi* in that they arrest the narrative and threaten to divert their audience from their real interest – the car chases – but the *Taxi* films overcome this by structuring in repeated interruptions which reinforce Daniel's heterosexual credentials, while getting down to the real boys' stuff. *Taxi* is enormously appealing by virtue of its protagonist, whose amiable and attractive personality is enhanced by his wearing the distinctive blue, Number 10 football strip of Zinédine Zidane, the hero of Marseilles, and his readiness to launch into a car chase at the drop of a hat. And although Daniel has a thick southern accent and proletarian occupation, narrative twists and turns reveal his superior intelligence, resourcefulness and planning in capturing the gang of German bank robbers. When Émilien's plans fail, Daniel calls on his network of ace pizza delivery boys to change traffic lights and control each stage of the inevitable final car chase. Moreover, each pursuit is carefully situated in wide-angle long-shots which privilege the cityscape of Marseilles with its narrow streets and vistas to the cathedral on the hill or the port below, bathed in blazing sunlight.

Taxi 2 (Gérard Krawczyk, France, 2000), again produced by Luc Besson's company, increased the budget from FF53 million to FF70 million by virtue of the first film's success. Daniel becomes involved with Lilly's bourgeois family and the attempts by her father, General Bertineau, to thwart the kidnapping of a visiting Japanese Minister. Needless to say, the French army is depicted as incompetent and the despised southern French proletarian, Daniel, saves the day. Given the budget, this involves the taxi flying over the French capital, aerial shots being prolonged to invite admiration at the successful, spectacular stunts.

The Spanish film industry is polarized between art film productions which aim at the international market, including the big-budget, English-language film *The Others* (*Los otros*, Alejandro Amenábar, Spain/France/USA, 2001), and distinctively local films which rely on

Spanish production and distribution expertise and detailed knowledge of their audiences. Producers have learned that Spain's core audience consists of 15–34-year-olds, the most numerous being 15–24 years old, giving them the choice between budgets of $2–3 million for films aiming at domestic distribution or $6–12 million for those aiming internationally (Green 2001: 11). Targeting Spain's core audience resulted in three mega-hits whose success has primarily been generated on home ground. *Mortadelo and Filemon – The Big Adventure* (*La gran aventura de Mortadelo y Filemón*, Javier Fesser, Spain, 2003) was the third top-grossing Spanish film ever. The Sogecine and Pendelton Picture co-production earned almost €15 million in two weeks from 3.2 million admissions generated by its Warner Sogefilms distribution. Inspired by Francisco Ibañez's comic books, the film features two strange characters whose anarchic adventures have their own peculiar logic. The two friends are sent to retrieve Professor Bacterio's dangerous invention, which has been stolen by the dictator of Tirania, but the quest is an excuse to explore the mind-set of the two protagonists and to scan the cinematic frame admiringly to appreciate its zany visual details. *Torrente: The stupid arm of the law* (*Torrente: el brazo tonto de la ley*, Santiago Segura, Spain, 1998) and its sequel *Torrente: Mission to Marbella* (*Torrente: misión en Marbella*, Spain, 2001) feature a sexist, egotistical, politically incorrect slob of a policeman who frequently breaks the law and makes gross gags and football jokes about Atlético Madrid. The *Torrente* films clearly have their young, male audience in mind, in much the same way as their French counterparts. With slightly higher than average Spanish budgets of $2.6 million, these films have generated returns of around $20 million.

Comedies formed the mainstay of Italy's historically prolific film industry but have rarely been exported. Although Italian production has fallen and US companies and subsidiaries dominate distribution and exhibition, the industry still makes films starring local comics which make no claims to the status of high culture and which make a lot of money. Although certain directors, actors, screenwriters and producers are recurrent presences in Italian comedy, it is not a genre in the Hollywood sense as serious issues, historical settings, stars and the use of realist conventions have all built on the template (Aprà and Pistagnesi 1986: 17). Italian comedies are essentially franchises built around the figure of a comic who is a product carefully differentiated by class, and especially geographical region – Benigni's early comedies played on his Tuscan characteristics. Leonardo Pieraccioni and Carlo Verdone's films feature in European top 50 lists, but achieve enormous financial success in Italy alone and have legs in terms of subsidiary media markets (Wood 2005a). Verdone draws on earlier comic traditions creating characters who are less perceptive than his audience, but whose incompetence rarely results in female characters getting the better of them, and Pieraccioni's films pander to the sexual fantasies of young single males in complicated plots featuring many scantily clad female characters. Without doubt the most sustained franchise is the 'Christmas' films, which has lasted almost 20 years from *Christmas Holidays 1990* (*Vacanze di Natale '90*, Enrico Oldoini, Italy, 1990). Gathering momentum from the mid-1990s, the franchise now has an established profile and package, represented by titles which promise a variation on the formula each year, the same producer, Filmauro, director, Neri Parenti, and stars, Christian De Sica and Massimo Boldi.

The actors adopt different characters in each, to enable them to vary their attempts at holiday sexual adventures. Budgets have crept up to €7 million for *Christmas on the Nile* (*Natale sul Nilo*, Neri Parenti, Italy, 2002), which generated €28 million in Italy, and although *Natale in India*'s gross of €19 million was regarded as unsuccessful, it is many times more than that of films more familiar outside Italy and the franchise shows no sign of reaching its end.

Zdenek Troska is one of the older generation of Czech film-makers who has 'churned out fairy tales and country comedies at the rate of one per year since 1999' (Macmillan 2003: 21). Some of them have a contemporary relevance to the socio-political situation of Eastern Europe, such as *Kamenak* (Czech Republic, 2003), in which the motive for post-communist restitution of a palace by English aristocrats is revealed to be hidden treasure, a metaphor for the capitalist sacking of Eastern European assets. Czech and Slovak support for the film industry has also produced a young generation of film-makers, such as Alice Nellis, who manage to achieve critical success at film festivals, but foreign distribution deals are still difficult to obtain. Nonetheless, box-office success in popular genres can propel directors, producers and members of creative teams on to bigger and more complex projects until they can no longer find the level of work they want in Europe and are snapped up in Hollywood. A Dutch television adventure epic, *Floris*, started the collaboration of Paul Verhoeven and Rutger Hauer in 1969, both of whom worked together on locally popular productions which fuelled their move into international production.

German films have a large language area in Central Europe from which to cover their costs, and comedies and popular genre films appear in the European Audiovisual Observatory top 50 list. German film-makers have a complex reality to draw on, the common history being interpreted differently along opposing ideological lines in west and east prior to unification after the fall of the Berlin wall in November 1989. As Daniela Berghahn has claimed, the 'asymmetry' between the cinemas of West and East Germany derived from their different pasts and the fact that, in the wake of unification, West German business and media interests moved into the East to take over Eastern industries without integrating the demands of capitalism with the direction desired by the population of the East (2005: 213–225). Moreover, while the West's cinematic output encompassed social comedies of angst among urban yuppies trying to find a meaning to life, or dramas of multicultural Germany, post-1989 films made in the East included dark films interrogating the socialist past, and the unemployment and sense of inferiority of the present. It took a decade for comedies to appear about life in the former DDR and the biggest success, the prize-winning *Goodbye Lenin!* (Wolfgang Becker, Germany, 2003), built on the positive impact of *Run Lola Run* (*Lola rennt*, Tom Tykver, Germany, 1998). Stefan Arndt of the production company X-Filme Creative Pool claimed that they made *Run Lola Run* because it was ready to go and they were bankrupt (Blaney 2001: 9), but the company has capitalized on its success to make a regular stream of low- to medium-budget ($2–5 million) films, increasing its slate from 1 or 2 to 4–6 films a year. *Goodbye Lenin!* grossed $4 million in the USA and $55 million outside the USA, a factor in X-Filme's expansion to open an international subsidiary aiming to make co-productions. Based in the Wolfsburg Studios, the project clearly takes advantage of funds available to facilitate commercial development in the East. It is supported by the Lower Saxony *Land* and the Medien und Financial Engineering section of Commerzbank, Berlin.[1]

Germany's Neue Constantin Film, led by Bernd Eichinger, is the country's leading producer/distributor, its acumen in backing successful films and distributing films, videos and DVDs reflected in its winning €22.6 million in 'reference funding' for its success in backing *Nowhere in Africa* (*Nirgendwo in Afrika*, Germany, 2001) and *Naked* (*Nakt*, Doris Dörrie, Germany, 2003). Eichinger's aims do not appear to have changed since he set them out in 1987:

> '... if you really want to persuade someone to leave their house, get into a car, look for a parking space and then squeeze between other people in the cinema, you have to provide not just entertainment, but something that really moves them, that really lasts beyond the two-hour film
>
> (Fisher 1987: 12)

With the changes in the social use of film which have taken place since then, Eichinger's vision and his attention to scripts and planning have been vindicated. His aim of building stars and roles for them has been facilitated by the stream of German comedies and genre films coming out of Constantin Productions and the ability to access funds from the *Länder*. A sound grasp of popular taste resulted in Germany's most popular international hit, *Manitou's Shoe* (*Der Schuh des Manitu*, Michael (Bully) Herbig, Germany, 2001), a send-up of Karl May's Indian novels which are very popular in Germany. The comedy outperformed *Titanic* at the German box office and achieved over 12 million viewers when broadcast on the Pro7 channel. Until the 1990s the words 'German' and 'comedy' seemed a contradiction in terms, but the increased profile of German cinema has facilitated video and DVD distribution outside the German-language 'footprint'. German distributors have also moved into the former Eastern bloc countries to exploit the vacuum left by the collapse of state-funded cinema.

With rare exceptions, European popular comedies do not travel well, perhaps because they achieve their audience response by their narrow focus on national characteristics, tastes and concerns. Their pleasure lies in their addressing contemporary problems obliquely, using chaotic and disruptive situations, irony and varieties of comic excess to question social values and rehearse or reject change.

Horror audiences

I will conclude with a few remarks about two film industry sectors which are rarely considered in film industry yearbooks, but which provide huge profits and steady careers for specialist producers and creative teams: horror and pornography. Horror films in particular have the potential to achieve cult status as the most successful include plot twists, dialogue and repetitive visual motifs which allow their generally young, male audiences to use movie trivia moments to communicate with each other (Telotte 1991). With some notable exceptions (Dario Argento, Alejandro Amenábar, Michele Soavi), films by European horror specialists are usually low-budget (around $2 million), but do not depend on a good theatrical release to generate their profits. After their rental and sell-through outings on video and DVD they form the bedrock of enterprising internet sales opportunities, with many specialist interests catered for (Wood 2005a: 59–60). Dario Argento is an example of a cult director who has conquered the quality sector of the film industry, achieving international recognition on the basis of his creativity and visual flair and use of recurring motifs (black rubber gloves, saturated red colours in cloths used to wrap knives, ultra-violence and the use of baroque architectural motifs). His successes in the 1980s increased his budgets to $7–10 million in the 1990s, but *The Stendhal Syndrome* (*La sindrome di Stendhal*, Italy, 1996), *The Phantom of the Opera* (*Il fantasma dell'opera*, Italy/Hungary, 1998) and *Sleepless* (*Non ho sonno*, Italy, 2000) were less visually complex than his earlier films. *The Card Player* (*Il cartaio*, Italy, 2003) marked Argento's return to a $2 million budget and to shocks and greater visual complexity. The twist of the serial killer who engages the police in games of cards, the winner saving or murdering the screaming girls on his webcam increases the tension. The use of new technology is contrasted to the painstaking examination of evidence and clues by the detectives, Anna Mani (Stefania Rocca) and John Brennan (Liam Cunningham), and to the neo-baroque architecture of the killer's lair.

The Others (*Los otros*, Alejandro Amenábar, Spain/France/USA, 2001) built on Spain's local horror tradition so that the horror resides in suggestion and atmosphere rather than gore and shocks. Suggestion is made easier by the plot concerning a neurotic mother, Grace Stewart (Nicole Kidman), constantly seeking to shield her photosensitive children from the light, resulting in velvety-black darkness and high-contrast lighting and a jerky pace as Grace constantly strives to shut doors behind her before doors can be opened ahead. In scenes where Grace is alone, or interrogates the mysterious and slightly sinister new staff, cold tones dominate the *mise-en-scène*, and mist outside the house enhances the claustrophobia. Although conventional in its 'things are not what they seem' plot, Nicole Kidman's performance, the production values and baroque look of the film captured audience interest worldwide. With an estimated budget of $17 million, *The Others* grossed around $17 million in Spain and, with energetic Miramax publicity, $96 million in the USA.

Recent British horror films *Dog Soldiers* (Neill Marshall, UK/Luxemburg, 2002) and *The Descent* (Neill Marshall, UK, 2005) achieved critical and financial success by tapping into the contemporary taste for extreme violence. In the first, six soldiers on a military exercise in Scotland are hunted down by a band of werewolves, genre conventions being enhanced by throwaway humour, fast pace and brutal encounters. *The Descent* profited from the rave reviews of frightened newspaper critics and enthusiastic word of mouth to more than cover its costs in Europe alone. It is unusual in having a group of young women cavers being menaced by a subterranean race of monstrous mutant humanoids, although the Final Girl (Clover 1992) fits genre stereotypes in being more resourceful in adapting her survival behaviour to the monsters' weaknesses. *The Descent* plays on archetypal nightmares of helplessness in the face of invisible horrors, hinted at in the opening sequences after the accident when Sarah (Shauna Macdonald) races along a hospital corridor with the lights going out behind her. Having survived a car crash in which her husband and child were impaled by copper water pipes, attacks by hairless, pock-marked mutants can be overcome. Attacks underground are played out in the beams of light from the girls' safety helmets, emphasizing gaze direction, their desire to know and knowledge withheld. The cave system of *The Descent* is, in effect, a neo-baroque labyrinth which is understood by virtue of the conventions of story and representation, but whose multiple and contradictory paths ask its audience to discover order out of chaos (Ndalianis 2004: 90–3).

The difficulties of distribution were recently overcome by the micro-budget Italian horror film *Hate 2 O* (*H2odio*, Alex Infascelli, Italy, 2006), which was distributed straight to newsstands by the daily newspaper *La Repubblica* and the monthly news magazine *L'Espresso*, as an experiment and a protest against the difficulty in getting a theatrical release. Following a group of girls who sail out to an island in the middle of a lake in order to spend a few days purifying themselves by consuming only water, there are predictable results when a mysterious presence starts to observe them. *H2odio* illustrates an attempt to bypass traditional theatrical distribution channels which do not serve the horror film well.

Horror films have a long life and retain premium prices on video/DVD. Successful directors specializing in this area of popular cinema achieve lucrative careers, as the filmographies of Umberto Lenzi and Michele Soavi testify.

Soft porn: a parallel universe

Since the 1970s a vast porno film industry has grown up, now estimated to be worth $40 billion a year (Iosifidis et al 2005: 106). The gradual increase in media outlets from the beginning of the 1980s ensured that the market for soft and hard porn films grew exponentially, with video, cable, satellite, DVD and specialist outlets being energetically developed. As public tolerance increased, soft-porn films aimed at middle-class sensibilities started to feature in box-office listings (Minnella 1998: 162–7). The porno film industry is a mirror image of the officially sanctioned industry, with the difference that it is carefully excluded from all state subsidies. It has its own star system, production companies and differentiation into genres and, in Italy alone, is estimated to produce over 1,000 films a year (Ventavoli 2000: 151). The industry has its own film festivals, usually held back to back with more respectable festivals such as Cannes (the *Hot d'or* festival) and Venice. Its revenues are difficult to establish, but it has never been prey to changes in fashion of other European genres.

Conclusion

In this chapter I have shown that, although European art film-makers bemoan the lack of finance and career opportunities, there exist areas of popular cinema (in the widest sense) which have nurtured prolific careers, of both directors and creative personnel. Sometimes with the protection of national and transnational subsidies, and often without them, the most successful of European low-budget films achieve good box-office returns by targeting a precise constituency identified by studying industry demographic information. The most successful rework existing popular genres, tapping into the contemporary ability to read ironic and multigeneric texts and responding to a taste for an active reading of chaotic narratives and visuals, of puzzles and fragments which resist closure and suggest that, through film, new systems of stasis and order are being sought after and rehearsed. Another area where low-budget films designed for the mainstream audience are produced – the co-production with television – will be explored in the next chapter.

Notes

1. www.x-filme.de/htm/news/html (accessed 22.8.2006).

chapter six

Cultural identity and the importance of television and satellite co-productions

Medium- to low-budget European cinema may have limited distribution opportunities but television has provided the ability to communicate with the mass audience. The importance of interpreting national contemporary reality and giving a voice to domestic concerns and minority interests has interested the majority of European states and the European Union itself. Since the early 1990s, however, the European media map has changed markedly and, while state-funded terrestrial TV channels may have a public service remit to reflect the diversity of their populations, this does not apply to satellite channels which are the preferred viewing of sections of it. Moreover, although terrestrial TV came to be regarded as the saviour of European film industries in the 1980s, state funding from tax payers brings political considerations into the arena of this type of film production and a different set of financial arrangements between production partners. As Dennis McQuail has pointed out, there are sharp differences in the extent to which party politics in any one state has a grip on the media (2004: 2).

Chapters Two and Three plotted the restricted possibilities of the traditional authorial mode of film-making and the resulting growth of international auteurist cinema. Arguably, Jean-Luc Godard remains the sole *auteur* who can demand artistic freedom in his co-production arrangements today; other directors working with television encounter tight budget restrictions and an overarching channel identity which impinges on their creative choices. Chapter Five, however, suggested that the survival of some types of popular European film has been assisted by co-production with, or diffusion by, television. Distribution differs because, after the initial transmission, a film's further progress depends on questions of channel ownership and vertical integration. In this chapter I will consider the film genres favoured by European TV and satellite channels. I will use the example of France to examine some models of co-production and will consider the effects on form and subjects. I am also interested in how film-makers articulate concerns with the preservation of European cultural identities, and the focus of the latter part of the chapter will be on representations of children on film and the production sector making films for children.

A complex media map

The European Audiovisual Observatory gives a figure of 1,678 TV channels in Europe, excluding small local and regional channels, video on demand (VoD) services and channels aimed at mobile phone or digital video broadcasting-handheld (DVB-H) reception (EAO 2005/5: 12–3). Over 55.2 million households in the 35 countries of Europe have direct-to-home or collective satellite reception (EAO 2005/2: 34). Not only do individual countries predominantly have one or more state, publicly funded channels, but many also operate a dual economy between public and private channels. In addition these are complemented by participation in shared programming – Austria participates in the European German-language channel 3SAT, which is jointly managed by four public-service broadcasters in Germany, Switzerland and Austria. The satellite company Canal Plus operates in Spain, Belgium, Italy and Poland as well as France, while Luxembourg's liberal media legislation has led to the setting up of numerous satellite channels targeting countries with stricter legislation, especially regarding pornographic content (Hirsch 2004: 141).

Cable and satellite technologies were introduced in Western Europe in the 1980s, and the 1990s saw the acceleration of the postmodern business practices identified by Harvey as 'flexible accumulation' – new services and the commodification of information technologies (1990). The commercialization of television services took place in successive phases which, in the 1990s, 'suited the development of vertically integrated, transnational media conglomerates, such as Bertelsmann, News Corporation, Vivendi-Universal (reconfigured as NBC-Universal) and the now defunct KirchMedia' (Iosifidis et al 2005: 157). The 2000s, particularly after the attack on the Twin Towers in New York of 11 September 2001, have been marked by a recession and loss of advertising revenue which have affected television budgets. However, Figure 6.1, extrapolated from the European Audiovisual Observatory's analysis of genres–channels supplied by European TV/satellite companies, indicates some of the factors impinging on film producers.

Country	Adult	Pay-per-view Adult	children	cinema	culture	documentary
AT	6	1				
BE		1	1	1		
CY (North)				2		
CZ				11		
DE	2	3	7	12	3	8
DK				3		1
ES	2	4	7	16	1	4
FI					1	

Country	Adult	Pay-per-view Adult	children	cinema	culture	documentary
FR	2		13	18	2	7
GB	30		53	32	3	88
GR				7		
HU			3	14	1	
IT	6		8	8	1	10
LV				1		
MT				1		
NL	11		1			2
PL			2	5		3
PT			1	5	1	1
SE			2	49	1	14
SK						1
Total	59	9	98	188	14	139

Figure 6.1 Channel supply by genre in the European Union (January 2006)
Source: European Audiovisual Observatory Yearbook 2005, vol. 5: 12

These figures provide some understanding of the presence in contemporary European film production of feature-length documentaries, children's films and pornographic films. They also demonstrate the symbiotic relationship of film and television and the continued attraction of feature film production to fill the hungry maw of terrestrial and satellite schedules.

France: vertical integration and a differentiated slate

As the Introduction explored, the French have been the most active in maintaining that cinema is a 'cultural exception' and should not be regarded as a commodity, subject to quotas or included in the free trade of goods and services. France is still a strong film-making nation and this section will consider how this has been achieved and maintained in the face of media globalization and changes in how people access and use films.

In the 1970s relatively few films were shown on French TV stations so that films had event status. With the launching of new channels in the 1980s (Canal Plus in 1984, M6, La Cinq and ARTE from 1986), television's use of film accelerated, with films becoming used as tools to win subscribers or attract viewers in the 1990s (Creton 2002: 10–12). TV investment in production became a logical step in order to maintain some control over channel identity and continuation of products which would attract viewers. French TV commissioning editors have been unable to rest on their laurels in the 2000s as some of the sources of film finance have changed in importance and, as Laurent Creton defines it, French cinema is increasingly commodified and labelled according to its use in TV schedules, so that it exists in a state of tension between its commercial attraction, its symbolic importance, cultural influence and artistic ambitions (2002: 14). From a funding high point in 2000, the TV investment package has changed considerably. Investors are having to increase their stake in the financing of French films to cover the decrease in TV co-production and pre-sales investments, and distributors, DVD distributors and foreign investors have filled the gap (CNC dossier 298-06: 6). These statistics indicate extremely important developments for the film industry as a whole. It is now possible to access TV programming on home computers via the internet, obviating the need to subscribe to terrestrial channels. Since terrestrial and satellite television depends for its income on the purchasing power of the very demographic which now has the possibility of avoiding the licence fee or subscription fee, the future of the TV sector sets fair to be plunged into chaos and, even as this chapter is being written, many communications consultants must be drawing large fees to suggest ways around these developments. In the meantime, in France at least, it is clear that DVD financing is becoming increasingly important in the production package of French films. DVD finance is a form of the distributor's *avance sur recettes*, or minimum guarantees, whereby a distributor would calculate the amount of future revenue from a film's exploitation in cinemas in a particular geographic area and invest accordingly. Figure 6.2 shows the proportions of investment from different sources in 2005.

Claude Forest accuses producers of not caring about the future of their film after it has been delivered to the TV co-production partner and therefore covered its costs (2002: 186), but channels themselves are clearly interested in audience response in order to make judgements about which time slots to use to attract maximum audiences and advertisers. Forest suggests that box-office success is a crucial factor in successful TV scheduling, which is borne out by CNC statistics for best audiences for French films in 2005. *Chouchou* (Merzak Allouache, France, 2003) came 50th in the European Audiovisual Observatory's top 50 European films, with almost 4 million admissions, predominantly in France. *Chouchou* is a frenetic comedy which plays with stereotypes of homosexuality, with transsexuality and immigration through its protagonist, Choukri/Chouchou (Gad Elmaleh), a Moroccan immigrant who finds it easier to get work when dressed as a woman. France 2 and Canal Plus were part of its production package, the rights involving first programming on Canal Plus and subsequent exploitation on the terrestrial channel. France 2's investment paid off when *Chouchou* attracted 15.3% of its audience when shown in primetime in April 2005 (CNC 298/02: 7). There is a direct correlation between a successful cinema release and a good TV audience. Moreover, these can generate good prices when a film is subsequently bought by other satellite or specialist channels.

French terrestrial, cable and satellite channels have invested so constantly in French cinema through co-production or participation agreements that their centralized purchasing and distribution systems give them effective mastery over a commercial system in which they control access to the end user (Creton 2002: 17). A particularly powerful position is held by Canal Plus, which invested €126.04 million in 120 films in 2005, 13.7% of all

	1996	1997	1998	1999	2000	2001	2002	2003	2004	2005
Producers' finance	21.9	33.1	27.7	28.0	31.2	36.7	28.9	24.8	27.4	28.4
SOFICA	4.8	4.5	4.3	4.4	5.7	3.3	4.6	4.5	3.1	3.1
Automatic finance	11.5	7.2	8.1	6.7	7.4	7.0	7.6	6.6	6.0	6.3
Selective finance	5.2	5.2	4.4	4.4	3.6	3.2	3.4	3.5	3.5	2.9
Regional finance	—	—	—	—	—	—	1.0	1.1	1.2	1.3
TV coproductions	8.9	7.2	7.0	6.0	9.0	3.7	4.6	3.8	4.3	3.8
TV pre-sales	34.3	29.4	31.5	34.2	31.2	32.0	29.8	26.3	28.3	25.7
Distributors' advance France	5.5	3.5	6.8	8.8	5.5	6.0	7.5	6.8	6.0	9.8
French video distributors' advance	—	—	—	—	—	—	1.5	2.0	2.0	3.1
Foreign funding	7.8	9.8	1.3	7.5	6.5	8.2	11.0	14.9	11.6	10.3
Foreign sales outside co-production area	—	—	—	—	—	—	—	5.6	6.5	5.3
Total	100%									

Figure 6.2 Sources of finance for French films in 2005 (%)
Source: CNC dossier 298–Bilan 2005/06. La production cinématographique

French investments and 56.7% of all French films (CNC 298/06: 5). In 2005 Canal Plus also purchased presales rights to 81.2% of French films with budgets of €2–15 million, 21.6% of films with a budget of less than €2 million and 66.7% of those with budgets over €15 million. Recognizing that this level of vacuuming up films for exploitation in various video and satellite windows would distort the exhibition of films in cinemas, Canal Plus has been obliged to contribute 1% of its profits to the French exhibition sector. Canal Plus was bought out by Vivendi (formerly Compagnie Général des Eaux, a water utility company) in 2000 for $12.5 billion as part of a strategy to create a global media business. Jean-Marie Messier, Chief Executive of Vivendi, successfully created a merger with the Bronfman family's American media holdings (Seagram which included PolyGram's film and music interests; Universal's film and media interests bought from Matsushita) to create Vivendi-Universal, a logical development in global corporate business terms, given the increasing size and closeness of the American and European media markets. However, by 2002 it had become clear that Vivendi-Universal had an enormous debt burden of €17 billion, due to Messier's passion for the acquisition of a wide range of companies (Iosifidis et al 2005: 52–3). Messier resigned in 2002 and the new management sought to reduce the debt by selling off companies, including a number of Canal Plus interests in Europe. In 2003 Vivendi-Universal's entertainment arm in the USA merged with General Electric to form NBC-Universal. GE owned 80% and Vivendi 20% of NBC-Universal, and NBC-Universal owned a share of Vivendi.

The recent history of Canal Plus reflects the increasingly global and transnational nature of the media industries and local concerns that aggressive commercial practices could and would destabilize domestic film and media interests. This was particularly worrying in Canal Plus's case because of the company's central role in propping up the French film industry which appeared to be alone in Europe in its ability to face up to American competition. Following Messier's bringing of Vivendi to the brink of bankruptcy in 2002, French legislation was amended to consolidate the company's obligations to contribute to the French media economy. Canal Plus was obliged to prioritize investment in films with budgets below €5.34 million; a clause now requires it to reflect cultural diversity and the priority budget ceiling has been lowered to €4 million. The immediate impact in 2005 included the doubling (to 41) of the number of micro-budget films costing below €1 million, half of them documentaries.

The influence of Canal Plus is not only financial. Whereas audience figures for terrestrial channels show the continual popularity of comedies, thereby influencing and perpetuating TV investment in that genre (Forest 2002: 195), Canal Plus has invested in a wide variety of genres and types of film, reflecting the composition of the different channels it has to schedule. Dominik Moll's career has been nurtured by Canal Plus's policy of supporting young directors, the success of *Harry, He's Here to Help* (*Harry, un ami qui vous veut du bien*, France, 2000) leading to *Lemming* (France, 2005). *Harry* was a co-production between Diaphana Films and the M6 commercial TV channel, with funding from the Soficas and participation of Canal Plus, and therefore destined to travel from cinema release to video, to Canal Plus's movie channel, to terrestrial screening and beyond. Miramax distribution generated an unusual $3.8 million in the USA and it was also released in Spain where Sergí López (Harry) has a career. *Harry* is a multi-generic crossover film from art to middle-class comedy thriller. The tension between these genres and audiences is exploited to the full in the story of Michel (Laurent Lucas) who, pausing in his journey with his wife and fractious children en route to their holiday home, meets Harry, who declares himself to be an old school friend. The subtle concatenation of small events whereby Harry, offering his help, takes over Michel's life gradually displaces the comedy elements. The sense emerges that Michel is somehow complicit in events when his latent selfishness and long-buried ambitions to be a writer are encouraged into the open. Michel's potential for instability is expressed in his holiday home, which remains in a state of DIY chaos, apart from the bathroom, resplendent in its kitsch pink perfection. Harry kills Michel's parents but it is only when Michel realizes Harry's helpful ploy of eliminating human distractions from his writing that he reacts to save his family. *Lemming* is also ambiguous about the middle classes. Alain Getty (Laurent Lucas) works for a high-tech company specializing in surveillance equipment and lives in an anonymous modernist house with his wife, Bénédicte (Charlotte Gainsbourg). There are elements of neo-*noir* visuals in long-shots of the house and the lakeside second home of Alain's boss, Richard Pollock (André Dusollier), and in the surreal and disruptive events which move the narrative forward. In the dinner-party-from-hell, Alice Pollock (Charlotte Rampling) accuses her husband of using whores, throws her wine in his face and scornfully describes the Gettys' house as *merdique*; she later commits suicide in her hosts' spare room, splattering the white walls with her blood. At the same time, the Gettys' kitchen sink blocks up and Alain's investigation discovers a small rodent stuck in the pipe. The presence of a Scandinavian rodent famed for its propensity to rush in crowds over cliffs towards its doom provides a correlative to the unravelling of the young couple's lifestyle. Bénédicte opts for a transfer of her erotic focus to elderly Richard, for which the audience has to make its own interpretations about her motivation. Alain is reduced to turning his flying surveillance camera onto his wife's lovemaking in the lakeside house and, at the end of the film, the only resolution concerns the admission by the neighbour's young son that he smuggled the lemming into the country. Both Moll's films are aimed at the educated middle classes who are one of Canal Plus's audiences, providing plenty of clues for them about conventionality and conspicuous consumption, the selling of ideas for corporate security, discarding of ethics and the commodification of sex.

Sergí López specializes in characters whose bluff façade gradually slips to reveal a slightly manic edge of incompetence or amorality. In *Byways* (*Chemins de traverse*, Manuel Poirier, France/Italy/Spain, 2004) – also supported by Canal Plus, the Brittany region and Eurimages – he plays Victor, a father dragging his adolescent son along and constantly moving from rented lodgings as he seeks investors for his commercial schemes. In *Dirty Pretty Things*, a BBC co-production (Stephen Frears, UK, 2002), he plays Juan/Sneaky, the evil hotel manager who runs a trade in the body organs of illegal immigrants. And in *A Pornographic Affair* (*Une liaison pornographique*, France/Switzerland/Belgium/Luxembourg, 1999) he plays an anonymous man who answers a woman's (Nathalie Baye) advertisement for adventurous sex. Sex is, however, never fully displayed on the screen; their initial encounters take place behind the red door which resolutely closes on them as they enter their hotel room, and the film is more interested to reveal, through voice-over confessions to their psychiatrists, the extent of their self-delusion and growing involvement with each other. The film can be described as soft-porn art cinema for the middle classes (a genre which the Italians have also perfected since the 1970s) and its complex funding from state and TV sources reflects its 'end user' destination in Canal Plus's adult channels in the countries of its French-language 'footprint'.

Besides the films of Ozon, von Trier and Varda, Canal Plus has supported small comedies such as *The Heat's On* (*Travail d'arabe*, Christian Philibert, France, 2003). This turns racist French stereotypes about Arab workmanship on its head when Momo (Mohamed Metina) is assigned to help a French plumber install central heating in an old lady's home, discovers the full horrors of her defective pipe work and attempts to put it right. Momo is a rather reticent, highly competent tradesperson who has to bite his knuckle in dealing with his white French boss's desire for maximum profit for minimum effort. *Red Satin* (*Satin rouge*, Raja Amari, France/Tunisia, 2002) is an example of one of Canal Plus's many international co-productions, this time concentrating on a middle-aged Tunisian woman's journey of self-discovery in the world of belly-dancing clubs. Lilia (Hiam Abbas) is a lonely widow with a daughter, Salma (Hend El Fahem), who discovers a belly-dancing club on an evening walk. Lilia is gradually drawn into the dancers' world, helping them with their dress and then learning to dance. In doing so she discovers her own suppressed sensuality and changes from a timid woman in a grey cardigan to the dancer resplendent in bright colours and red satin. Conflicts with the club's owner and romance with the musician whom she discovers is also seeing her daughter develop her self-reliance, and the film conveys the pleasure, professional satisfaction and excitement of women's dancing for their clients and themselves. *Red Satin* was also a complex co-production with support from CNC, Canal Plus and the Franco–German arts channel, ARTE.

ARTE has a small but considerable role in international film production through its funding (an average of €300,000 per film in 2005) of films of cultural importance. Its cultural remit acknowledges that cinema, far from being a mass medium, is mainly seen by people with a high level of education and disposable income. ARTE has no limit (except financial) to how many films it can show, but organizes its film screenings on three nights a week. Pierre Chevalier, a former head of subsidies for shorts and features at CNC, is credited with developing the idea of grouping ARTE's films in thematic 'collections' and for creating a space for directors to stop and think creatively by commissioning films which would occupy a boundary zone between film and TV. ARTE's view of film is closely aligned to high-cultural validation of the artist as exceptional individual, creating works of art in liminal spaces from which she or he gains a critical distance from the vulgar herd. This view belongs to the early nineteenth century when artists were marginalized from political endeavour but given cultural power and status which masked the commercial channels by which they earned their living. ARTE's schedules constitute it as deliverer of quality television, defined by the cultural capital of the audience rather than the professional culture of the 'well-made' programme of its producers (Cook and Elsaesser 1994: 68–9). Claire Denis's film *Beau travail* (France, 1999) is a typical 'quality' television product in its lack of cause-and-effect narrative, its structured ambiguities, its visual beauty and formal use of language. It is set in a French Foreign Legion camp in Djibouti, recalled through the memories of a former soldier, Galoup (Denis Lavant). The minutiae of everyday life, his strong feelings for Commandant Forestier (Michel Subor) and the enigmatic soldier, Sentain (Grégoire Colin), structure the narrative. Denis delights in filling her film with references to other texts, multiple interpretations of *Billy Budd* by Melville, Britten and Ustinov, Genet and Fassbinder's *Querelle*, Godard's *Le petit soldat* (France, 1963), all outsider figures who disturb unproblematic notions of masculinity. The notion of gender as performance underpins Denis's tableaux of soldiers exercising in static poses in the stark desert light, ironing their uniforms with neat, measured gestures and bonding with each other in visits to the brothel, in which the African women's words are not translated and they remain voiceless and exotic. The beauty of the framings and compositions and of the soldiers' bodies prevents recourse to any templates of soldier narratives. There are no roles to play or battles to be won. *Beau travail*'s beauty and ambiguities have earned it a cult following, particularly among academics who find it a fruitful subject for interpretation. It has acquired art film credentials and had successful cinema, video and DVD releases. *Beau travail* was part of ARTE's 'terres étrangères' (foreign lands) collection. It is an example of a cross-border film, defined by Mike Wayne as films which 'inscribe travel and a certain porosity of national identities within their narratives as a precondition of the co-productions which funded them' (2002: 45), and the crossing of borders is inscribed at every level within it.

Relationships between cinema and television in France have favoured the continuing image of French cinema as flourishing and successful, while concealing the commercial imperatives underpinning decisions on which type of films get made and which do not. The symbiotic economic relationship between French cinema and TV has favoured the convergence of the two systems, to the mutual advantage of both.

Who will be part of the family?

Outside France, and particularly in the UK, there has been no pretence that TV has not been the saviour of cinema. Film-makers and commissioning editors have recognized that 'the social experience of the audio-visual is now overwhelmingly in the home' (Stoneman 1998: 119). Faced with the dominance of American films on European cinema circuits and in satellite TV schedules, European countries have put in place a variety of measures to protect their film industries, often attempting to impose quotas for the number of domestic films to be transmitted on TV. The proliferation of public, commercial, cable and satellite TV channels has given impetus to European film production, but also to measures to ensure that programming reflecting domestic culture and history finds its way onto the small screen and that new talent is nurtured. While the last aim seems uncontroversial, critics, academics and programme-makers are divided on the efficacy of legislation to ensure that Europeans see themselves on the screen. Much academic writing, for example, is obsessed by the question of national identity and the cultural spaces available to explore and define it when films are increasingly transnational. Hoskins et al have attempted to navigate contemporary government intervention in TV and film production using the term 'external benefit' (1997: 81–2). External costs are well understood and include pollution or environmental problems not taken into account in an economic transaction. Education is an example of an external benefit but, for this to take place, a film must be watched by an identifiable number of people. TV and film industries' collection and display of audience figures have both a commercial purpose as explored above and external benefits in generating a sense of belonging to a different world from that depicted in mainstream American films. The popular *Taxi* films described in Chapter Five are made as mainstream comedy entertainment, but may also dispel stereotypes of French southerners, men of Arab origin, pizza delivery boys and the police as lazy, stupid and incompetent when the characters of Daniel and friends clearly are not. Rather than concentrate on narrow questions of national identity, I find the German film-maker Sandra Nettlebeck's favourite question – 'Who is going to be part of the family? – more productive. The rest of this chapter will therefore consider recent films with child or adolescent protagonists and films made for children.

Both Pavel Pawlikowski's co-productions with the BBC address this question. In *Last Resort* (UK, 2000), a young Russian mother, Tanya (Dina Korzun), and her son Artyom (Artyom Strelnikov) arrive in Britain to join her fiancé, but are sent to a 'designated holding area' in a run-down seaside resort where she is given a flat, food and shopping vouchers and told she must stay there until her case for political asylum can be considered. Tanya's status represents a clear attempt by officialdom to mark off outsiders and contain them. Tanya's flat is bare and uncomfortable, the lurid orange palm trees on the wall an insistent metaphor for her exotic 'otherness'. She has nothing in common with the Kosovan and Albanian men who also queue for the public telephone and finds herself the prey of the local provider of internet porn, who offers her cash to strip in front of his webcam. Artyom meanwhile has made friends with local British children who steal things to sell to the asylum seekers, but is taken in hand by Alfie (Paddy Considine), the only positive British character in the film. Alfie helps Tanya to furnish her flat and create a home and, when she decides to return to Russia, he helps her to elude the CCTV surveillance cameras. Like many of the films discussed in the next chapter, the presence of children indicates what is at stake in creating a national family, but full integration of Eastern Europeans in the formation of the couple cannot be achieved. The town is bleak, but the cinematography finds a beauty and hyperreality in empty, rain-washed streets, street lamps marching up hills and the graphic patterns of concrete housing blocks. *My Summer of Love* (UK, 2004) is the story of two adolescent girls from different backgrounds who meet one summer, become friends and fall in love. The *mise-en-scène* of place emphasizes the beauty of the Yorkshire countryside, epitomized by repeated long shots from the heather-clad hill over the neat rows of houses in the town below. Like Higson's 'long-shot of our town from that hill', the golden beauty of Pawlikowski's shot is not mere spectacle but has a narrative function. It expresses both the spatial freedom to explore their own personalities and the emotions of Mona (Natalie Press) and Tamsin (Emily Blunt), and the class differences which divide them. Working-class Mona's home is the pub in the town below, but her life is in a state of flux as her reformed criminal brother Phil (Paddy Considine) has discovered religion and emptied the alcohol down the sink. Tamsin is a spoiled, upper-class girl from a house on the hill, neglected by her parents and ready for rebellious experience – for a short time. Tamsin never quite tells the truth and uses Mona for her holiday adventure and, when it's time to go back to school, Mona is dumped and the clothes she has been lent are demanded back. Subtle upper-class exploitation is revenged when Mona nearly drowns Tamsin in the local river.

Belonging and not belonging are addressed in two films which foreground race: *Bullet Boy* (Saul Dibb, UK, 2004), produced by BBC Films, and *A Way of Life* (Amma Asante, UK, 2004), produced with funding from ITV Wales, the UK Film Council and the Arts Council of Wales. Both include younger figures observing older adolescents making huge mistakes which will affect their lives. These are not representations of a panoptic social control, but a hopeful insertion into the narrative of figures who might be persuaded to avoid similar mistakes. In effect, the characters of both films have eluded social control, but whereas in *A Way of Life* Leigh-Anne's (Stephanie James) only allegiance and anchor is to her baby, conventional ethical and moral frameworks being foreign to her, Ricky's (Ashley Walters) spell in prison in *Bullet Boy* has given him a determination not to become involved in gangs and gun culture again and a moral obligation to prevent his young brother from emulating him. Leigh-Anne can make sense of her life only by immediate personal reactions to conversations and encounters, her own powerlessness provoking violence without thought of the consequences. Ricky becomes a victim of other people's perceptions of him and of the masculinist gun culture of London's Hackney, where reactions to accidental slights (such as breaking a car's wing mirror) lead to disproportionate violent retaliation. In both films, spectacular long-shots of urban London or the Welsh port are excess to narrative requirements and, together with the violence, signal these as dysfunctional worlds not to be emulated, but about which something has to be done.

Disability and bullying also raise issues of tolerance, inclusion and exclusion. In *Bluebird* (Meijke de Jong, Netherlands, 2004), Merel (Elske Rotteveel) suddenly encounters bullying at school, which affects her relationship with her disabled brother Kasper (Kees Scholten). Merel's gradual acquisition of distance from her pain and hurt lead to understanding of social power and disempowerment. Following football-mad teenager Remco's (Yannick van de Velde) ambitions to play for the Dutch under-14 team after the sudden death of his father allows *In Orange* (*In Oranje*, Yoram Lürsen, Netherlands, 2004) the narrative construction of an alternative family which will support national ambitions. Both films were co-produced by Dutch television companies.

Children are constant figures in Italian cinema, representing positive elements of Italian society. *Domenica* (Wilma Labate, Italy, 2001) is a young girl (Domenica Giuliano) from an orphanage who must accompany police inspector Sciarra (Claudio Amendola) to the local Naples mortuary to identify the body of the man who may have raped her. In their journey across Naples, Sciarra witnesses Domenica's novel and unconventional ways of making people's lives better, which is contrasted to the official neglect which has made him cynical. Through the exploration of the space of Naples, Domenica's fresh and caring interactions with sections of the southern population generally ignored in cultural texts make a connection between the child and the city, and the necessity of giving both a future. *Domenica* is a small film, produced by Italian state TV, RAI, which had some success on the festival circuits. Co-production finance from Medusa, the distribution arm of Berlusconi's Mediaset, enabled Gabriele Salvatores' *I'm Not Afraid* (*Io non ho paura*, Italy/Spain/UK, 2003) to have a US distribution and an eventual passage through Mediaset's terrestrial, pay-TV and satellite channels. Opening shots of the black crow poised over a dark hole in the sunlit cornfield presage Michele's (Giuseppe Cristiano) discovery of the kidnapped boy hidden in a dark pit outside a ruined farmhouse and the dark side of the adults in his life. Michele sees the vanity of his father, who is tempted by the financial rewards of kidnapping, and the powerlessness of his mother, who will not intervene. In the material deprivation of his home (repeated in other village homes), and the comparison with the comfort of the prisoner's northern family, there is a suggestion that the unequal relationship of the couple is mirrored by that of the south and north of Italy. Salvatores' film offers layers of moral dilemmas for his audience to consider, but it is the child – the hope of the future – who rights the wrong and brings his father to realization of the ethical solution.

Children's films

The context of the production of children's films since 1991 is especially interesting as the sector exists as a microcosm of developments in mainstream cinema. A sector of the film industry rather than a genre in itself, the children's film reflects the globalization of the market and the entry of non-traditional investment sources lured by the potentially huge revenues from licensing and merchandising. Producers specializing in this sector can attract commercial investors and a glance at the shelves of any local video/DVD retail outlet provides an indication of the long-term rewards for investors if a programme or film gets it right. Arguably the film itself merely serves as a loss-leader to the much more profitable exploitation of the film-as-game, although there are signs that teenagers in particular are turning away from computer games (Mitchell 2006b: 35). While the ideal production is a series, which allows the build-up of familiarity and a long window for the exploitation of characters in toys, books, videos and DVDs, children's TV and dedicated satellite channels are also big consumers of film. Publicly funded terrestrial/satellite channels' regulations usually include the obligation to provide children's programmes. There is no equivalent requirement for satellite, but the provision of dedicated children's channels is an attractive part of the various packages available to subscribers. The European Audiovisual Observatory's analysis of the genre spread of the TV offering in Europe points to a stark difference between publicly funded and commercial TV. Where the obligation exists to carry children's programming, it exists as a small but significant element in a varied spread of genres. If private channels are not required to invest in children's programmes, a very much less varied offering results – usually based on sport and feature films. Children's programmes are absent and hived off to the niches of dedicated channels.

Children's films are a critically neglected but substantial area of European popular cinema, drawing on classic children's literature and more recently television programmes. The main actors, being children, are not expensive, nor are the adult actors as they generally come from television (like Rowan Atkinson) or the local theatrical tradition. In the case of the former communist countries of Eastern Central Europe, a flourishing industry of children's films answered both the objectives of the state to inculcate correct socialist values and ideals in the younger generation and a space for film-makers to explore social issues through fantasy (Hake 2002: 104; Berghahn 2005: 43–5). Children's films easily find television co-production partners and, having no controversial sex or violence, they find international distribution in a variety of forms. Germany, Scandinavia and Britain are the most successful producing countries and it is worth considering the dynamics of this invisible industry.

The majority of films which European children will be taken to see in the cinema, or will see on television, are US productions with huge publicity budgets and a plethora of tie-ins in the form of games and give-aways in fast-food outlets. Against the high profile of American films, European production is disadvantaged not only by the low numbers of children's films produced but also by the fact that future audiences for European films will not have become used to seeing films depicting cultures near to their own on the screen. Children's films have institutional support through the MEDIA programme's Kidflix events, which support exhibitors committed to programming films for children and schools by offering annual prizes of €500–1,000 to cinemas offering events and programmes to appeal to young audiences. Coming under the Media Salles umbrella, Kidflix draws on films which have been recommended by a number of film festivals with an international reputation, such as the Giffoni Film Festival (Salerno, Italy), BUFF in Sweden (Mallmö International Children and Young People's Film Festival), Zlin in the Czech Republic and Castellinaria in Switzerland.

State funds also support initiatives to introduce European films in schools, such as Skolbio through the Swedish Film Institute, and the Italian film industry initiative, Agiscuola.

Like other niche markets, festivals, prizes and subsidies are crucial for publicity, but this sector of the film industry also parallels European mainstream production in its range of budgets and financial success. *Bibi Blocksberg and the Secret of the Blue Owl* (*Bibi Blocksberg und das Geheimnis der blauen Eulen*, Franziska Buch, Germany, 2004) came 47th in the 2004 top 50 European film admissions with almost all of its 1.2 million admissions in Germany alone. Co-produced by Bavaria Filmproductions, like *The Flying Classroom* (*Das fliegende Klassenzimmer*, Tomy Wigand, Germany 2004), both films were nominated for Germany's Oscars, the Lolas, and therefore qualified for the nomination premiums paid out by the State Minister of Culture in the Best Feature Film, Best Film for Children and Young People, and Best Documentary categories. Aiming at the less populated children's film category makes considerable sense. Bibi (Sidonie von Krosigk) is a witch and her previous outing, *Bibi Blocksberg* (Hermine Huntgeburth, Germany, 2002), was set in Altenburg Castle boarding school and also featured magic animals, laying it open to claims of imitation of *Harry Potter*. The films were based on a successful TV series from 1999 to 2003, which was itself the product of the writer Elfie Donnelly's 1970s' books, which had later featured in comics, cartoons and cassettes. Bibi's parents were played by well known German actors, Katja Riemann and Ulrich Noethen. *The Flying Classroom* was also adapted from a famous book by Erich Kästner, which had already been filmed twice before, in 1973 and 1945. The film updated the book, post unification, by including two characters from the former German Democratic Republic (DDR) and rap music and, although hardly any boarding schools exist in contemporary Germany, Kästner's book remains part of each generation of adults' cultural memories. Both films were sold for airline in-flight entertainment which, as we have seen, provides an additional source of distribution revenue.

Children's films are also a popular category in Scandinavia, helped by the fact that, although budgets are low, Nordic films do well in their home markets. The *Pippi Longstocking* films have also been remade several times, most recently in animated versions (Michael Schaack, Sweden/Germany/Canada, 1997; Paul Riley, Canada/Germany/Sweden, 1998) based on Astrid Lindgren's stories of the destructive, naughty girl who also featured in TV series. Perhaps inevitably, nostalgia gave way to pastiche in *Kaka Ferskur (Fresh Rolls) or The Nude Adventures of Pippi Longstocking* (Todd Hughes, USA, 1988). Although the Danish Film Institute assists distributors by matching their investment in a film's minimum guarantees finance, only family films justify one-company production and distribution arrangements. Neiiendam suggests that the 'prolific' producer/distributor, Regner Grasten, has transformed the market by collaborating with Buena Vista on blockbuster releases of family films such as the *Anja and Viktor* series with as many prints as *Harry Potter* (2003: 20). Nordic children's films are often criticized for depicting a 'squeaky-clean, often complacent world', but Peter Cowie identifies small signs of change in *Schpaaa* (Erik Poppe, Norway, 1998), which represents Oslo as a concrete jungle along the lines of Matthieu Kassowitz's *La haine* (France, 1995) in its depiction of adolescent friends of different ethnicities coping with drugs, police and school homework (1999: 30).

Children attempting to come to terms with their world are one of the standard templates of this genre. In *Polleke* (Ineke Houtman, Netherlands, 2003), the 11-year-old eponymous heroine (Liv Stig) lives in a single-parent family as her mother has left her drug-addicted father. She falls in love with Mimoun, a Moroccan boy in her class. *Wondrous Oblivion* (Paul Morrison, UK/Germany, 2003) also explores issues of race through the story of an 11-year-old cricket-mad Jewish schoolboy, David (Sam Smith). When a Jamaican family move next door, David is overjoyed to be coached by Mr Samuels (Delroy Lindo). Set in 1950s' England, *Wondrous Oblivion* shows the development of racist attitudes to immigrants, the Jewish family being tolerated because they are white but the Jamaicans standing out by their darker skin. Recourse to an earlier time allows issues of gender stereotypes to be explored in *Billy Elliot* (Stephen Daldry, UK/France, 2000), set in Northern England in the 1980s at the time of the miners' strike. Depicting Billy's father (Gary Lewis) as a widower avoids too much stereotyping as Mr Elliot has to fulfil both the male and female family roles, motivating his eventual openness to Billy's future career as a dancer. In frustration at his brother's and father's reaction to learning that he is taking ballet lessons instead of boxing, Billy takes off, roughly dancing and kicking against walls along the terraced streets. Movement encapsulates the prejudices which he is literally fighting against and, in the image of the sailing ship in the blue waters in a vista from the hills of 'our town' (Higson 1996: 138), the possibilities of new worlds. Billy fetches up against the dead end of a street, providing a metaphor for the lack of opportunities for a boy of his talents. *Billy Elliot* clearly touched a nerve in British culture and has been made into a long-running London theatre production.

School stories provide another template for children's films, delineating closed worlds in which heroism can be rehearsed. *Les choristes* (Christophe Barratier, France/Switzerland/Germany, 2004) was typical in being set in a postwar school for disadvantaged children from broken homes, orphans and delinquents who are all given a fresh purpose by a new teacher (Clément Matthieu) who enthuses them into singing in his choir and performing his compositions. The film's framing narrative indicates from the beginning that the boy with the wonderful voice, Pierre Morhange (Jean-Baptiste Meunier), has become a world-famous conductor (Jacques Perrin), predisposing the audience to acceptance of the trajectory of discipline and artistic endeavour while avoiding the narrative complications of the ethnic diversity of contemporary French schools. *Les choristes* was produced by Perrin's production company, Galatée, which his nephew, Barratier, had joined in 1991. It was enormously popular in France, recouped its modest €5 million budget many times over and gave rise to a surge in applications to join choirs.

Films about animals also constitute a cross-over to the mainstream market, cashing in on the increased concern about the environment and the popularity of documentaries. Such films have legs, but can be expensive to produce. A film about two tiger cubs, *Two Brothers* (*Deux frères*, Jean-Jacques Annaud, France, 2002), worked hard to cover its £59 million on theatrical release, whereas *March of the Penguins* (*La marche de l'empereur*, Luc Jacquet, France, 2005) achieved the producer's dream of small budget ($8 million), large return ($77 million in the USA, €8 million in France), riding on its 2006 Oscar for best documentary, its César and other awards and nominations for its story, sound and stunning cinematography.

Old American cartoons and children's programmes are cheap and dominate terrestrial and satellite television schedules and channels, putting European production in this sphere into perspective. Yet the European children's film sector has a long history of providing an antidote to the violence and often unwelcome ideological underpinning of American output. For those who find this market niche congenial, children's films provide an opportunity to develop a taste for the quirky and fantastical, and support for a solid career. Chapter Four identified the strategy of American finance behind productions which looked European but were conceived with global reach in mind. The annexation of European expertise by American companies is amply demonstrated by the success of Britain's Aardman Animation company. Aardman's reputation was built on its award-winning stop-motion animation using the quirky plasticine animals it had created for gas central heating adverts on British television and for many short films – early appeal to the cross-over audience. Stop-motion animation is a slow process which suits independent individualists prepared to devote the considerable time it takes to set up the models. Aardman's adverts and short films were voiced by vox-pop interviews and British actors in a variety of class and regional accents, which provided a pleasurable ironic space for the British audience to appreciate the often inspired match between the voices and the plasticine animals. The move into feature films clearly required more investment than could be provided by the UK and an understanding investor who would appreciate the time-investment necessary for this type of animation. Dreamworks, which was independent and had already produced children's animation, had the potential to be a good partnership. *Chicken Run* (Peter Lord/Nick Park, UK, 2000) was an escape narrative set in a 1950s' battery chicken farm, using all the conventions of the Second World War prison camp genre, which grossed $106 million worldwide. Its successor, *Wallace and Gromit: The Curse of the Were Rabbit* (Steve Box/Nick Park, UK, 2005), was based on previous successful short *Wallace and Gromit* films and took five years to make. Here Wallace the inventor and his dog, Gromit, investigate the disappearance of vegetables destined for the village show and discover the existence of a monster rabbit. The directors won an Oscar for Best Animated Feature. *Were Rabbit* conforms to the pattern of European blockbuster success in earning less in the USA than on its worldwide run, and in its wide appeal in key Asian territories (Mitchell 2006a: 34). It was also exploited on airlines at the end of 2005.

The children's film seems set for a boost to mainstream cross-over with the release of *Stormbreaker* (Geoffrey Sax, Germany/USA/UK, 2006), the adaptation of one of a series of eight books hugely popular with boys and their fathers. When American action-adventure blockbusters have reached the preposterous stage, and hopes to revive the tired James Bond franchise have been pinned on the inclusion of Daniel Craig, the spy adventures of 14-year-old protagonist Alex Ryder (Alex Pettyfer), set in a recognizable London, are designed to satisfy desires to break out of an increasingly regulated social world. Those desires will, of course, be channelled towards satisfaction via a plethora of purchases. The merchandising deals for the $40 million-budget film include two video games with USA- and UK-based THQ, a global (excluding UK) agreement with Disney Wireless for ringtones, texting, screen savers and a downloadable video game, product placement of a Nintendo handheld device in the film, many toys, and book reissues (Goodridge 2006: 10). *Stormbreaker* is conceived as a franchise and (as Goodridge notes) the author of the book franchise selected UK producers Marc and Peter Samuelson to handle the sort of complex merchandising and promotions usually associated with *The Lord of the Rings* trilogy. Macnab cites the *Cody Banks* ($59 million worldwide) and *Spykids* films (which grossed $117 million internationally) among the benchmarks for this ripping yarn, which is significant in view of The Weinstein Company's purchase of US rights. *Stormbreaker* is clearly regarded as the next lucrative franchise film series (2006: 23).

Conclusion

The parallel universe of the children's film sector demonstrates both the continued importance of the feature film format and established distribution patterns and its dependence on the small screen for its lucrative merchandising possibilities. It also shows the tension between local desires to educate and inform European children about the realities of their world, usually with guidance on preferred behaviours, and global media companies' strategies to maximize profits in as many ways and for as long as possible. This chapter has considered whether European film form has been affected by the dominance of television in production partnerships and has concluded that it has. Film-makers have, however, been entrepreneurial in adapting the comedy format to encompass a range of more taxing ideas. On the positive side, concern that European children should be exposed to values reflecting generally accepted ideas of family, community and ethical action has led to the institution of cultural spaces for the production of films for children, and to mainstream films which utilize child characters to express those qualities regarded as essential for future health and happiness. If European films are marginalized in their national markets, then television co-production partnerships of all sorts provide a mass audience, but it remains difficult to express national particularities in channels dominated by multinational media interests. As I have demonstrated in this chapter, TV co-productions are predominantly small affairs compared with Hollywood blockbusters but nonetheless have the power to reach large audiences. The next chapter will continue the discussion of the spaces available to Europeans to see themselves on screen and to voice their concerns about cultural pluralism.

chapter seven

The irrelevance of borders?

Before the death of Tito, the break-up of the former Yugoslavia and the subsequent ethnic conflicts in the Balkans of the early 1990s, Europe considered itself to have been at peace for almost 50 years. The Balkans were considered to be a peripheral area on the borders of Europe, barely featuring in the news or in the holiday brochures. Since the start of the Cold War, Western European audiences had been able to see films from the Eastern bloc which had been successful on the art film festival circuit, or which reflected communist cultural ideals, but very little else. The disturbance to rigid categories of West and East brought about by the fall of the Berlin Wall in 1989 has been followed by the gradual breakdown of the cultural wall. The dire financial situation in Eastern bloc countries and the removal of shelter from market forces have made the position of studios, production companies and creative personnel very difficult. Yet those very market forces have also enabled video and DVD copies of films to circulate in Europe, even if to very restricted diaspora and academic audiences.

In the case of the former Yugoslavia, a Europe which regarded itself as civilized and modern had to take account of ethnic civil war and decide whether to become involved or not. But the Balkan conflict reverberated in many directions. It was suggested at the time that the development of satellite television was a considerable factor in informing the populations of Eastern Europe about the consumer delights which they were missing and the rejection of Marxist governments occurring in other parts of the Eastern bloc (Rantanen 2002: 107–10). Similarly, Western populations could not ignore the Balkan conflict because it intruded daily into their living rooms, provoking involvement by its very brutality. This chapter will discuss some contemporary representations of the Balkan conflict and how those images evolved at the turn of the century, faced with the influx of migrants from the Eastern Mediterranean, Russia, Poland, Hungary, the former Yugoslavia and Albania. My concern is not with how film-makers from the former Yugoslavia have engaged with the political reality and day-to-day experience of civil war, which has been explored by Dina Iordanova (2001, 2003), but how an area traditionally regarded as on the margins of Europe has intruded into the mainstream cinematic discourse of European countries. This chapter will discuss how the 1990s' conflicts have been represented and will comment on the sorts of stories, the types of narrative events, that the Balkan conflict enabled. The types of narratives are important in teasing out how countries outside the Balkans made sense of their social world and particularly how Balkan stories were used in the construction of images of national identity. In attempting to make sense of events and peoples, film-makers have drawn on pre-existing images of otherness, simultaneously modifying them and challenging accepted notions of national culture and identity (Naficy 2001: 8). How these representations have evolved and been incorporated into the concerns of the 2000s, that is with fears associated with what is perceived as mass immigration from the Eastern Central Europe, will also be addressed.

Global and local

The Berlin Wall fell in 1989 amidst great optimism on both sides of it that subsequent developments would confirm democracy and Western capitalism as desirable, hegemonic models for a modern society and that greater prosperity and freedom of expression for all would result. In fact, the subsequent economic and social difficulties in the East highlighted the less appealing side of advanced capitalism, large-scale poverty, civic violence, social alienation and ecological problems among others. As already discussed, these negative phenomena are features of globalization, the new metanarrative which seeks to explain why the same media products and clothing styles are available from Cardiff to Karachi. However, whereas communism, the grand metanarrative of equality and the suppression of individual desires for the greater good of the collectivity, has been discredited by its failure to deliver prosperity, the grand metanarrative of capitalism is for the most part unchallenged. Ulrich Beck has suggested that 'globalization shakes to its foundations the self-image of a homogeneous, self-contained national space …' and that borders are 'markedly less relevant to everyday behaviour' (2000: 14). The increasing importance and presence of the local is visible within the globalizing tendency. Robertson explains this as two sides of the same process. 'Cultural globalization thwarts the equation of national state with national society by generating cross-cultural and conflicting modes of life and communication' (quoted in Beck 2000: 47). The intrusion of the Balkan conflict was part of this process of globalization, so that both the Balkans and our own national space have been experienced simultaneously, rather than either/or. The conflict was experienced via the presence of that marginal world on mainstream, national television news and through the physical presence of refugees and immigrants in European national territory. It would, therefore, not be surprising if events on the borders of Western and Eastern Central Europe were interpreted differently in different cultural contexts. The *European Journal of Communication* devoted its entire September 2000 issue to 'The Media and the Kosovo Conflict', and Italian state television, RAI, published a thick volume on TV reporting of 'the war for Kosovo' (Pozzato 2000). The articles tested globalization theory, which argued that 'the transnational flow of media products is associated with the local appropriation of meaning' (Nohrstedt et al 2000: 400). The general conclusions were that the globalizing effect of media ownership, the use of news agency footage, had a synchronizing effect in the homogenization of public discourse. That is that, generally, the NATO propaganda view predominated. NATO propaganda personalized the conflict, demonising Slobodan Milošević as evil, irrational, vicious, acting as a metonym for the Serbian people as a whole. *Le Monde* and the French quality press attempted balance in reporting the Serb point of view. The German press had recourse to analogies with Nazism, and the idea of the *Voelkermord*, in order to engage the sympathies of a profoundly pacifist younger generation. The unwelcome spectre of the holocaust precipitated a transfer of guilt to Belgrade (Savarese 2000: 373–9). The British press marketed diplomatic initiatives as 'humanitarianism' in a Third World situation. Italians were the most virulent in their name-calling of the Serbs, while the mainstream Greek press rejected NATO's justification of bombing attacks on Serbia and was against any Greek intervention in the area.

These pieces of research are mentioned at some length because it would be expected that some of these ideas would be reflected in fictional works which, consciously or unconsciously, engaged with the presence of an ethnic war on the margins of Europe since the media, television and the press in particular actively shape our perception of the world in which we live. At the end of the 1990s and in the 2000s an evolution in representation can be observed. The lowering of borders between the former communist bloc and the Eastern Mediterranean resulted in cultural struggles between two conflicting economic and political systems, and the consequences of these struggles are laid bare in the *mise-en-scène* and narratives of films depicting the negative aspects of globalization.

British multiculturalism interrogated

The Balkans are present in a variety of British film genres. Contemporary cinema includes films made by British film-makers using the Balkans to rehearse drama and conflict, as well as people from Eastern Europe who have come to live in Britain. The films of the latter show the double perspective which Naficy suggests typifies the 'accented' style (2001: 22). The media themselves are embedded self-reflexively in film texts, in the form of films within films, TV footage and journalists, emphasizing the process of forming a point of view on events. The main protagonist, Alex Kirkov (Rade Šerbedžija), of *Before the Rain* (*Pred dozhdot*, Milcho Manchevski, UK/France/Macedonia, 1994. Golden Lion, 1994 Venice Film Festival),[1] is a photo-journalist and his lover, Anne (Katrin Cartlidge), is a picture editor. Both live in London, but Alex decides to return to his home in Macedonia. Visual motifs and the repetition of names link three stories; there is a suggestion that, by photographing someone, Alex contributed to their death and he is himself shot by his cousin at the end of the film for attempting to save the daughter of his childhood sweetheart, Hana. The nationality (Macedonian), religion (Christian) and ethnicity (Slav) of the main character are used to motivate the narrative oscillation between urban London and an unspecific, mountainous Macedonia. This is not free of exilic nostalgia, expressed in the heightened beauty of the blue colours and poetic use of space in the Macedonian sequences. The primitive interiors of the Orthodox monastery and the strongly Slavic features of the monks, the representation of the villages as underdeveloped (stone buildings, ruins, unmetalled roads) connote a 'Third World' reality. This finds echoes elsewhere in the film in the representations of Balkan women, who are accused in some nebulous way of being responsible for the conflicts – the first and second Zamira are both accused of murder; Hana is blamed for giving hospitality to Alex. All the women are powerless faced with the unpredictable and irrational brutality of the men. Abandoned cats roam the ruins or are shot by an armed man – a symbol of the destruction of the domestic sphere of normal relationships.

This brutal violence literally erupts into the diegetic space of London in the sequence where Anne asks her estranged husband for a divorce. The quarrel at the back of the restaurant is not translated, the two men being objectified as nameless, violent 'others'. The increasingly noisy quarrel imposes itself on the attention of those in the restaurant as muted conversations are disrupted. One of the men is ejected, but in the temporary calm which follows, the superiority of the English diners is punctured by the waiter's remarks making a link to Ulster. In *Before the Rain* a Balkan conflict moves from background to foreground when one of the men returns to spray the restaurant indiscriminately with gunfire, in the aftermath of which Anne discovers the bloodstained body of her husband. Goran Paskaljević was to make the link between religious conflict in Ulster and ethnic conflict more overt in *How Harry Became a Tree* (Italy/France/UK/Ireland, 2001).

Before the Rain is a complex film which, like many European films of the period after the Second World War, addresses social and political issues in a symbolic way. The depiction of women is particularly interesting. The passivity of the Macedonian women allows the slippage of guilt to be transferred to them for not contesting the brutality of the conflict. The bleakness of the position of women at the time of the Balkan conflict is foregrounded by the heightened realism of Manchevski's *mise-en-scène* and the ultra violence of the Macedonian men connotes the brutally patriarchal social system of the Balkans and anxieties about national identity. The film is also ambivalent about the figure of Anne, who is an emancipated, working woman in a sexual relationship outside marriage. Anne's actions lead to the death of her worthy but dull English husband, and her lover. In his masculine occupation as a photo-journalist and his relationship with Anne, Alex is portrayed as a modern man, exciting and compassionate, but his problematic backstory and nostalgia for his pre-modern country results in his occupying a liminal position in both London and Macedonia. His otherness cannot be assimilated.

In a similar way the Balkan conflict erupts into various narrative strands of Jasmin Dizdar's *Beautiful People* (UK, 1999). From the opening credits a running gag starts as a Croatian and a Serb slug it out on the streets of London. One is knocked over by a car; both end up in hospital and still attempt to kill each other. The hospital venue introduces the trainee doctor, Portia (Charlotte Coleman), who falls in love with the Serb, whose later admission of involvement in ethnic cleansing shocks her MP father. In another narrative strand, Dr Mouldy (Nicholas Farrell) is coping with marriage breakdown, his children and a pregnant Muslim woman patient urging him to abort her baby, the result of rape. Working-class Griffin lives on a council estate with his parents, spends most of his day in bed, emerging to roam aimlessly with his feral friends, indulging in casual criminality and drugs. Stoned out of his mind after a trip to watch an away game and indulge in some football hooliganism, Griffin falls into an airport baggage truck and is transported to Bosnia. Here he experiences at first hand the British United Nations force and becomes a hero in a field hospital in Srebrenice. By the splatter approach, Dizdar manages to hit a lot of targets, including ethnic differences between the English and the Welsh, the rape of Muslim women by Serbs, the difficulty of taking a moral stance (a pianist admits to having killed people in his homeland), issues of class and the persecution of refugees from other cultures. The film is ambiguous in its attitude both in respect of characters representing British class positions and of the representatives of the different ethnicities of the former Yugoslavia who are now living in London. The film shows the marginalisation of many groups in Britain – the elderly, young working-class males, health service workers, divorced fathers and so on. The very physical presence of Balkan refugees enables a multitude of stories to be told and comparisons to be made with divisions in British society, disintegration in one country rhyming with social disintegration in another. However, by its choice of characters, shots and framings, the film is generally positive about the pluralism of British society. This is represented symbolically in the second half of the film by the series of marriages or reconciliations. Portia and her pianist marry; the Muslim couple accept the baby; the film closing with images of the mother as an innocent bride dancing amid the flowers of her homeland. Both films conform to Naficy's definition of accented style, being fragmented, multilingual, the juxtaposition of liminal spaces inviting reflection on both national arenas.

Although films by British directors lack the double perspective of accented cinema, they still exhibit the oscillation between there and here, provoking the interrogation of values associated with British identity and providing an arena for the symbolic reworking of masculinity. Michael Winterbottom's *Welcome to Sarajevo* (UK, 1994: Channel Four/Miramax) foregrounds the mediation of events in Yugoslavia through following a group of journalists reporting the conflict in and around Sarajevo. On the one hand, the journalist figure is a common trope allowing a narrative to investigate a situation and explain it. On the other, it allows the film-maker to show the process of mediation through exposition of journalistic imperatives of the good story, the dramatic photograph, and meeting broadcast and copy deadlines. Typically, it is the central journalist figure, Michael Henderson (Stephen Dillane), who is the guide to Sarajevo and whose pursuit of stories allows a whole situation to be fleshed out. His recruitment of a local interpreter, Risto, then permits access to the lives of ordinary people, to the reality of hunger, lack of water and camping out in the ruins of houses, corroborated by reports from Henderson's press corp colleagues. The use of actuality footage adds an impression of overwhelming authenticity. Films about war reporting typically raise issues of good and evil, and this film is no exception. However, while the ordinary citizens Henderson meets are briefly fleshed out and their lives explored to the limits required by generic necessity, those shelling the city from outside and the snipers within are generally presented as casually brutal, shadowy figures. Henderson becomes emotionally involved in a story about an orphanage on the frontline and establishes a relationship with the little girl, Emira, and the baby she looks after, who is known only as 'Roadrunner'. Only when the film moves to an emotional climax as Henderson succeeds in getting permission to bus the children out does the enemy acquire a face. Henderson saves Emira, but at the expense of Roadrunner. The villains are represented as stereotypically macho, large, active men with guns, acting irrationally. Their motivation is not explored and the chaos of Sarajevo is not explained. Moreover, the Henderson/Emira story echoes many sentimental reports in the tabloid press of orphans or sick children being 'saved' by noble intervention on the part of kind Britons. The conflict is delineated in emotional terms. Figures of children in danger allow a narrative to express societal ideals so that Henderson's feelings of helplessness express anxieties about personal and national power in a globalized world. As Henderson becomes more involved with the orphanage, so his

Sarajevo experiences seep into his London, family world, through phone calls and then through Emira's adoption. The presence of ethnic conflict in the Balkans raises questions of effective power and moral force in Britain which, with the loss of Roadrunner and the saving of Emira, are only partially resolved.

The BBC film *Warriors* (Peter Kosminsky, UK, 2000) was especially commissioned by the BBC as part of its millennium programming. The documentary style again lends an enormous sense of authenticity to a story of British soldiers sent to the former Yugoslavia as part of the UN Peacekeeping force in 1992–93. The film concentrates on the characters of the soldiers and how they cope with a difficult situation. In the 1980s this film might have been set in Ulster, but wars move on. Ireland is quieter now and has moved towards a political settlement so that tales of heroism in the Irish war zone would be unpopular and inappropriate, and ambiguous in moral force. Not so with the Bosnian conflict. The almost daily presence of the war on television screens in the early 1990s resulted in familiarity with the main players and NATO propaganda provided a framework. Such a complex and constant war also enabled certain types of war stories to be rehearsed – dramas of self-knowledge and the rehearsal of masculinity, dramas of self-sacrifice and self-discovery, where male characters test themselves against the margins of acceptable behaviour.

The powerlessness of characters in these dramas express many anxieties, not least that of being unable to mark out and contain the Eastern European 'others'. Fear of the ultimate level of social disintegration into anarchy, brutality and civil war is compounded by the similarity of skin tone between 'us' and 'them'. These films are not quite brave enough, or certain enough, to suggest a moralising framework to the narratives, and the doubts and uncertainties which characterize them are reworked in the late 1990s when the influx of populations from Eastern Central Europe made itself felt. Altogether different are those films made by incomers to the UK. As I have mentioned, the characters of *Last Resort* (Pawel Pawlikowsky, UK, 2000), Alfie (Paddy Considine) and Tanya (Dina Korzun), are emblematic of the meeting of East and West. Through its delineation of the many bureaucratic agencies with which the Russian, Tanya, has to deal in order to gain food and shelter, and the reactions of British people to her situation, the film is able to show a complex moment of the assimilation of the outsider. Whereas Tanya encounters a few hostile reactions to her presence, the overwhelming reaction is of overworked indifference, or of fleeting sympathy while conforming to legislation. The practice of confining illegal immigrants to run-down seaside towns allows the attempt to contain outsiders to be compared with the neglect of peripheral populations who traditionally made most of their income during the summer months until the increase in foreign package holidays made their existence even more marginal.

Stephen Frears' *Dirty Pretty Things* (UK, 2002), set among illegal immigrants working in a London hotel, is the ultimate metaphor for shifting populations and meetings across cultures typical of postmodernity. The hotel, significantly named the Hotel Baltic and filmed in jarring shades of yellow and red, is ruled by the ultimate representation of the gross and mendacious capitalist, the manager Mr Juan (aka Sneaky) (Sergi López). López's persona is ideally suited to this figure, combining seductive friendliness, energy and intelligence with the suggestion of complete amorality and a manic pursuit of money.

Convinced of his own superiority, and that of Western medical technology, Sneaky uses hotel rooms as occasional operating theatres where nameless illegal immigrants are relieved of body organs in exchange for visas or passports, another metaphor for capitalist commodification and colonial exploitation. He despises his victims for their difference, while profiting from sale of their organs, arrogantly convinced of his business acumen. Okwe (Chiwetel Ejiofor), whom he co-opts as surgeon, and Şenay (Audrey Tautou) are easily marked as 'different' from this capitalist entrepreneur by virtue of what Baudrillard identifies as 'signs of folklore', his colour, her Turkishness (her religion, dignity and virginity) (1993: 132). At the end, after Sneaky has raped Şenay, the tables are turned and those he has exploited display their ingenuity in constructing a makeshift operating theatre to relieve him of his body parts. By refusing to become assimilated, and by exacting revenge, the characters raise awareness of the disarray of Western culture, both literally and symbolically (Baudrillard 1993: 138). There is a suggestion that the world of illegal immigrants is invisible to London's regular inhabitants in Okwe's cynical claim that he and his kind carry out the functions that Britons will not do. The containment of Okwe, Şenay, Ivan (Zlatco Burić), Guo Li (Benedict Wong) and their friends in the hellish, anonymous netherworld is, however, a narrative device to bring them from the background to the foreground, to identify and examine them in relation to the values of contemporary Britain. In reality, the multiculturalism of Britain's larger cities is everywhere apparent and anxieties about assimilation or rejection of British society were regularly rehearsed in the media before 7 July 2005, when the London underground was bombed by young men expressing their ultimate alienation from the British culture they had grown up in.

The difficulties of marking difference: Italy

Whereas the eruption of the Balkans into the diegetic spaces of British films is used to explore complex social and political situations in both countries, Italian films tend to demonize the outsiders. Since 1990 Italian cinema has grappled with questions of immigration in interesting ways, suggesting difficulties in Italian culture, as refracted through cinema, of conceptualizing borders and of imposing a view of what (or who) belongs within and what belongs outside the national space. Italy has always had a porous border with the Balkans; borders have become largely ineffective and irrelevant, but the desire to establish boundaries has become correspondingly important. Given the current difficulty that Italian cinema has in getting small-scale, social films into mainstream cinemas, the fact that television, the mass medium, considers Balkan subjects to be important is rather significant. If globalization is the direct result of the European colonial experience, then the Italian response to it is an expression of huge historical complexity. Italians are daily reminded of the conquests of the Roman Empire, but are less likely to remember Mussolini's colonial excursions in Africa and Albania. Italy was also colonized by France and Spain, among others, over many centuries, and more recent memories include their experience of being diasporic populations in North and South America and Australia, and the butt of racist and pejorative stereotypes.

When Italian film-makers have sought to engage with events at the end of the millennium they have been able to draw on existing stereotypes and narratives of social tensions. Italian films from the 1940s to the 1980s tended to displace anxieties about social change (class mobility, sexual freedom, etc.) onto narratives with Southern themes and to demonize Southern Italians as outsiders, unrepresentative of an imagined, Italian modernity. In the 1950s and 1960s, therefore, the South signified a disruption to the myth of prosperity and postwar boom and provided a rich repertoire of tropes of backwardness in social organization and relationships. The florid colouring, dark eyes and abundant hair of Southern actors were used to suggest a hypersexuality, an excess of passion and violence in opposition to Northern modernity and restraint. As part of the same process, the exploration of reasons for social problems have frequently been displaced onto other countries, so that Spain and the Balkans have been used to locate social critique in a narrative space resembling that of the national 'problem'. Žižek defines as 'reflexive racism' the construction of images of the multicultural Balkans as a theatre of ethnic horrors, and this displacement indicates the presence of a racist ideology of the 'other' (2000: 29–30). Analysis of how Italian cultural texts indicate how social tensions and non-Italians are to be understood is a fruitful area in which to study Italian national identity (Allen 1999: 29–30). One strategy is represented by recourse to Southern mafia stereotypes in the marginal presence on screen in *Bread and Tulips* (*Pane e tulipani*), Silvio Soldini, Italy/Switzerland, 2000) of Balkan conmen who rent the bumbling detective a houseboat when he is unable to find a hotel room in Venice. The feelings of inadequacy and menace in unfamiliar surroundings experienced by the protagonist are externalized onto stereotypical, swarthy foreigners, operating on the margins of society.

Similarly, the typical landscapes of the South are used to suggest the danger to the Italian body politic of backward social relationships in *David's Summer* (*L'estate di Davide*, Carlo Mazzacurati, Italy, 1998), made for RAI television, which rehearses the Italy/Balkans culture clash through the summer adventures of 19-year-old Davide. Contact with a young Bosnian, Alem, allows the story to become very dramatic and for sex and drugs and petty criminality to intrude into the rural space. Stealing heroin at the end of the film from the criminal boyfriend of Davide's lover, the boys go south to find Alem's contact (a man who smuggles Albanians into Italy) in order to make a big drug deal. The quarrel over payment in which Alem is knifed takes place on the dockside. The city and the port are framed to foreground the bright light and pictorial aspects of the Southern city. This heightened reality allows access to Barthes's *troisième sens*, the third sense which links the South, the Balkans and criminality (1970: 15). Although Alem is represented as a sympathetic character, blonde and energetic, the *mise-en-scène* attempts to contain him in visually as well as narratively closed spaces. He works in a bar, a narrative site which enables the protagonist to meet a variety of marginal characters. Interestingly, Alem lives in a church hostel with other *extracomunitari* (people from outside the European Union, the Italian euphemism for foreigners, blacks and Asians). Non-Italians are therefore marked out and contained within the rural space, but clearly cannot be controlled altogether. The margins insistently move into public space.

In the dramas of borders of the 1990s and 2000s, what is being made visual is the tension around national identity, between 'us' and 'not us'. Fluidity, ambiguity, doubts, excess expressed visually or in monstrous characters or in the performance of violence are all elements of the template of *film noir* and can also be used by film-makers as techniques to visualize the tension between one system which aims to present itself as simple, natural and incontrovertible, and another which threatens its stability. Italian films engaging with the Balkans draw attention to narrative space and foreground referentiality in order to establish links between the story world and the reality of contemporary Italy. The particular characteristics of Italian *film noir*, disturbing asymmetry, *chiaroscuro* lighting, showy visuals, narrative, kinetic, performative and visual excess, therefore function to draw attention to the presence of trauma, events which offend the democratic sensibilities, or which threaten traditional political and gender power relationships.

Whatever the target of their narratives, contemporary filmic *noirs* are ultimately about power. How power is exercised and how social stability and traditional gender relationships are destabilized by the demands of globalized capitalism. An interesting inflection of containment and recourse to images of Southern Italy occurs in Carla Apuzzo's *Roses and Guns* (*Rose e pistole*, Italy, 1998), featuring two characters called Rosa. The action is set on the edge of Naples, between the run-down, working-class, industrial Bagnoli area and the Phlegrean Fields (themselves an unstable part of the earth's crust). The low-life, marginalized characters therefore inhabit a border zone on the outskirts of Naples and 'work' in the telephone sex industry or armed robbery. Through the character of the Serbian hitman who pursues the younger Rosa, a link is made between social breakdown in Italy and the extreme violence of the Balkans, connoting fears present in Italian middle-class society at the Balkanization[2] of the Italian body politic.

Although his film *Lamerica* (Italy/France, 1994) follows two Italian conmen in their attempts to set up a lucrative scam in Albania, Gianni Amelio's purpose was to make a film about Italy and its past (Amelio 1994: 4–7). *Lamerica* is unusual not only in making connections between Italy's colonialist adventures of the fascist period and the current exodus from Albania but also in emphasizing the physical resemblances between Italians and Albanians. When its Italian protagonist, Gino (Enrico lo Verso), loses his passport and belongings, he is framed in the midst of crowds, rather than surveying them from the comfort of his 4 by 4. Placing Gino among a 'sea' of faces and part of a crowded 'flow' of Albanians evokes the 'flood' metaphor which is a standard media trope to construct immigration as a threat (Horsti 2003: 47). By putting the camera in his subjective viewpoint as he becomes one of the hopeful *clandestini* (illegal immigrants) trying to get to Italy, the film forces an identification with the position of the Albanian 'other', reminding Italians of their own past as economic migrants and despised immigrants in Argentina, Australia and Northern Europe.

More recent films of immigration, such as *Across the Border* (*Oltre il confine*, Rolando Colla, Switzerland, 2002), *Burning in the Wind* (*Brucio nel vento*, Silvio Soldini, Italy/Switzerland/Jamaica, 2002) and *Letters on the Wind* (*Lettere al vento*), Edmond Budina, Italy, 2002), give more narrative space to the development of character and motivation of Eastern Europeans, Bosnians and Albanians. These recent films continue to have recourse to the visual containment of the 'other' in restricted spaces and to the depiction of foreign outsiders as brutal criminals or victims, but their narratives are interesting for their portrayals of families and the difficulties these stories have in achieving convincing resolution. They reflect Italian middle-class concerns that they have lost control of political power and that the national family is under threat from immigration (Wood 2005a).

Set in 1991, at the height of violent conflict in the Balkans, Colla's *Oltre il confine* has two attractive protagonists but they are unable to form a couple because of the trauma the male protagonist, Reuf, has experienced in losing his wife. Todorov suggests that massacre, the extermination of victims without remorse, reveals the weakness of the social fabric whereas sacrifice testifies to the power of the social fabric (1984: 143–5). Like *Before the Rain*, Colla's film oscillates between these two poles and uses visual excess to indicate the difficult and unfriendly nature of the Balkan terrain and the difficulties of crossing borders. The Italian heroine, Agnese (Anna Galiena), does, however, undertake a transformative journey from a hard, selfish career woman, reluctant to care or connect emotionally with her father, to a woman prepared to suffer personal danger to rescue an immigrant's daughter. While fitting Iordanova's template of the Westerner through whose actions a Balkan situation is delineated and mediated (2001: 56–64), Agnese's heroic and humanitarian rescue successfully reconstitutes Reuf's (Senad Basic) family and rehabilitates Italy itself. The foreign family is integrated into Italian national space. Total integration as represented by the formation of a couple is, however, too much for the narrative to handle (Wood 2005a: 152).

Children in Italian cinema always have the significant function of representing what is at stake for Italian society. Marco Tullio Giordana's *Once You're Born* (*Quando sei nato non puoi piú nasconderti*, Italy/UK/France, 2004) uses the character of the rich Italian child, Sandro (Matteo Gadola), to confront the ethical issues of relationships between the citizen and the 'other'. While sailing with his father and friend, Sandro falls off their yacht, unremarked, in the middle of the night. Just as he is about to drown after hours in the water, Sandro is saved by Radu (Vlad Alexandru Toma) and hauled aboard a boatful of *clandestini*. Radu introduces him to his sister, Alina (Ester Hazan), and the boy shares their meagre resources until the boat is intercepted and captured by the Italian coastguards. As Áine O'Healy has remarked, the film contains one of the most pejorative representations of Southern Italians in the persons of the two boatmen (2006), whose performances stress their unpleasant appearance and amorality. Giordana emphasizes their exploitative greed, thereby implicating Italy in the transnational people trafficking which is a negative consequence of globalization.

Once Sandro reveals his nationality, he is returned to his distraught parents, but finds it difficult to reintegrate. His desire to thank his rescuers sets in train a quest narrative which, in common with other films of this genre, introduces disorder. Chaos and disorder in this case are generated both by the *clandestini* and by Italian bureaucratic measures to contain them. In the course of his quest, Sandro peels away the tissue of lies Radu told him, discovering that Radu was trafficking the teenage Alina into prostitution, and he also achieves a sense of the consequences of untrammelled capitalist exploitation, of which his father's business represents a more benign part. Sandro's crossing the border has been transformative in raising moral questions and starting his search for answers with profound implications for Italian society and a new, pluralistic national identity. Sandro's desire to understand is epitomized by his committing to memory the phrase spoken by the disturbed immigrant near his school, whose meaning (and the title of the film) is revealed at the conclusion. During his quest Sandro discovers Alina in the imaginatively named *Centri di Permanenza Temporanea* (Temporary Stay Centres), located in a huge abandoned factory where she alone has a well-furnished room where she sells sex. The factory is full of the dark enclosed spaces typical of this genre and is difficult for Sandro to break into. The Italian state has made this liminal space a border zone within national space, thereby seeking to contain and control non-nationals. All borders are 'meaning-carrying entities', sites of cultural heterogeneity and battles over cultural and racial difference (Donnan and Wilson 1999: 4–5). The importance of Sandro's personal engagement with the non-Italian 'other' is its expression of what anthropologist Eric Wolf calls 'personal power' and 'structural power' which 'shapes the social field of action so as to render some kinds of behaviour possible, while making others less possible or impossible' (Wolf 1990: 587, quoted in Donnan and Wilson 1999: 155). In a situation of transnational movements of peoples, political power as exercised by the state is not the arena in which a new national hegemony evolves at the beginning of the twenty-first century.

The irrelevance of borders

Like English actors in Hollywood, Balkan characters in the 1990s and 2000s are permitted the dubious honour of portraying villains and monsters whom the texts license us to loathe, thereby deflecting attention from the fact that the richer EU countries are implicated in the drugs trade and the brutal sexual traffic from the Balkans to the West, and particularly in the abuse of young women. Chaos and barbarism are not confined to the non-national and the ultra-violence of Nicholas Winding Refn's films constitute the overcoming of limits, breaking 'the borders of a system of social or cultural norms' (Calabrese 1992: 49). Gangster and thriller film conventions in *Pusher* (Denmark, 1996) centre the narrative on Frank (Kim Bodnia), desperately seeking to repay a drug debt to representatives of the Eastern European drug mafia in a violent and unglamorous Copenhagen. The tension from knowing no more than Frank does about events focuses attention on the everyday reality of illegal economic enterprises, prompting comparison with the operations of global capitalist corporations. Refn claims (like Rohmer, Belvaux and others before him) to have devised the 'trilogy thing' to force investors to give him money (Charity 2000: 78). In the event, *Pusher* and its sequel, *Bleeder* (Denmark, 1999), were so successful that they spawned *With Blood on My Hands: Pusher II* (Denmark/UK, 2004), focusing on Frank's sidekick, Tonny (Mads Mikkelson), and *I'm the Angel of Death: Pusher III* (Denmark, 2005), in which the drug boss, Milo (Zlatco Burić), reappears and his deterioration involves psychopathic violence and the destruction of his family.

Lukas Moodysson's *Lilya 4-ever* (*Lilja 4ever*, Denmark/Sweden, 2002) also deals with family breakdown resulting from the collapse of the Soviet Union through the story of Russian teenager Lilya (Oksana Akinshina), who is abandoned by her mother, falls victim to a young man's promises of a better life in Sweden, is given a fake passport and is trafficked into prostitution. The horrors of Lilya's new life are graphically and remorselessly shown by concentrating on her-point-of-view shots of grotesque male faces as she is repeatedly raped.

Films about immigrants and asylum seekers, and particularly about the traumas of sex slavery, are regularly released or feature as television co-productions. The obsessive return to these narratives of social and sexual violence and exploitation, to the lack of comforting narrative closures, to the inability to impose an overarching meaning on the political void in East Central Europe and to control mass population movements, all are ways of figuring trauma and, as E. Ann Kaplan suggests, to performing it (2001: 205).

Repetition, obsessiveness and fragmentation are also visible in *Distant Lights* (*Lichter*, Hans-Christian Schmid, Germany, 2003), an ensemble film set along the river at Slubice, the border between Germany and Poland. The lights of the title represent the dreams of the characters and five struggles to realize their dreams structure the narrative. There are no happy endings, not for the man who has fallen for the seduction of capitalism and opened a shop selling mattresses no one wants to buy, or for the Polish girl whose linguistic qualifications and ambition to work in public relations have not protected her from her predatory boss and the realization that what she is doing is upmarket prostitution, or for the Ukrainian couple and their baby who mistake the lights of Slubice for Berlin. The film's tagline, *Willkommen in der Wirklichkeit* – welcome to reality – exposes the disjunctures between the myth of Western prosperity and reality, and leads to a radical understanding and critique of globalization.

Turkey: meeting of East and West

I mention Turkey for two reasons. Firstly, there are European narratives which find it necessary to go to the edge of Europe in order to raise positive images of otherness. Secondly, there is a considerable Turkish diasporic population within Western Europe, mostly but not exclusively in Germany. The position of cinematic representations of Turkey raises fundamental questions for critics wishing to consign Turkish/German films to a convenient category. If they are made in Germany by a film-maker of Turkish origin, with German finance, are they to be categorized as 'world cinema', 'transnational cinema', 'postcolonial hybrid cinema' or even 'Turkish/German cinema', even if the film-makers have lived their entire lives in Germany and such films have cross-over appeal to the mainstream (Göktürk 2002: 248–9). Turkish immigration dates from the 1960s when 'guest workers' were lured to West Germany to do the jobs Germans rejected. Early Turkish/German films posited the Turkish immigrant as a problem and/or indulged in miserabilist dramas which reproduced clichés about immigrant culture. We are in effect occupying a transitional moment in Western cinema history, in the same way that films of the early 1950s depicted working-class boys and girls as a problem, whereas by the late 1950s, girls with jobs and boys moving up a class were 'just there' and not signalled as narratively significant. While in British cinema the populations of the old Commonwealth share certain experiences of the exercise of the law, education and the colonial experience and, even when feeling the tug of tensions between British culture and the patriarchal culture of origin they form the unremarked characters of everyday British life, in German cinema the patriarchal nature of immigrant culture still intrudes, generating interesting conflict narratives. There is not enough space here to address the complexity of films by Turkish/German film-makers about their world which is a rich source of research for the cultural critic. However, to choose a few examples, writer/director Fatih Akin's *Short Sharp Shock* (*Kurz und schmerzlos*, Germany, 1998) recalls Matthieu Kassovitz's *Hate* (*La haine*, France, 1995) in its choice of three representative young characters to explore the dead-end options open to ethnic minority Germans. Exploring the origins of Gabriel (Mehmet Kurtulus), Serbian Bobby (Aleksandar Jovanovic) and Greek Costa (Adam Bousdoukos) show the limited opportunities open to minority populations in Hamburg and the temptations represented by local gangsterism. Produced by German television station ZDF (Zweites Deutsches Fernsehen), it shows the inexorability of the incorporation of the three youths into a criminal subculture.

Head-On (*Gegen die Wand*, Fatih Akin, Germany/Turkey, 2004) is less usual in focusing on the difficulties experienced by a young woman of Turkish descent in carving out a life for herself in Germany. Sibel (Sibel Kekilli) meets Cahit (Birol Ünel) in hospital in the aftermath of their failed suicide attempts. She wants to escape the strict rules of her conservative family and he his pointless existence collecting glasses in a bar. Sibel dragoons Cahit into marrying her, going through a traditional wedding ceremony, furnishing Cahit's seedy home and launching out into the sexual adventures proscribed by Turkish patriarchal culture. Inevitably they develop feelings for each other; sexual jealousy provokes Cahit to fight and kill one of Sibel's lovers. His prison sentence and her ostracism by her traditional family after the trial leave Sibel adrift between two cultures and she escapes to Istanbul to try to make a new life. There her angry alternative existence leaves her open to violent abuse and beatings for which she is hospitalized. When Cahit is released from prison and goes in search of Sibel, he finds her calmly accepting her female fate, married to the taxi driver who saved her from beating and the mother of a young child. *Head-On* is ambivalent about Turkey. It is punctuated by a carefully staged folkloric band performing in front of the mosque of Aghia Sofia. The German sequences show Sibel in enclosed, garishly coloured spaces, and the fast editing ratchets up the tension as Sibel tries to combine sexual freedom and personal expression. The Turkish sequences are characterized by cool, predominantly blue tones and by performative restraint in the final sequences. As in the films discussed earlier, different visual paradigms signal the tension between different explanations of social positioning. The lack of narrative resolution in *Lola and Billy The Kid* (*Lola und Bilidikid*, Kutluğ Ataman, Germany, 1999) reflects the fact that, although the mother and brother of the murdered belly dancer, Lola, reject the hypocrisy of the patriarchal murderer, Osman, they end up in the no-man's-land of the street. The film also uses visual excess and *noir* visuals in its melodramatic story set in the Berlin transvestite community, enabling a sense of the fluidity of gender and ethnic identities to be experienced.

By contrast, Ferzan Ozpetek has the protagonist of *The Turkish Bath: Hamam* (*Il bagno turco, hamam*, Italy/Turkey/Spain, 1997) leave Rome to take possession of and sell the property (a Turkish bath) his aunt has left him in Istanbul. He delays his return as he experiences the warmth of his aunt's friends and becomes fascinated both by Turkish culture as represented by the baths and by the son of his hosts. Ozpetek does not entirely escape the orientalist tendency in Western culture, which uses spaces outside Western Europe as arenas where sexual and other fantasies can be enacted. Moreover, the tension between Italy and the 'other' is expressed visually through the choice of architectural paradigms and the *mise-en-scène* of place. The protagonist's home in Rome is a high-level, modernist apartment contrasting with the house and bath he inherits in the old quarters of Istanbul, characterized by dark, closed, mysterious spaces, jumbled streets, labyrinthine passages, spyholes and sexual ambivalence. Movement within these spaces reinforces the contrast. The relationship of the architect and his wife is shown as strained and non-communicative, whereas the closed spaces of Istanbul provoke a change in him, from reserved, time-conscious business man to a defender of Istanbul's architectural heritage. This oscillation between order and disorder structures the narrative visually and narratively. Both architectural paradigms coexist as signifying systems, inviting the conclusion that personal truth and authenticity do not necessarily reside in what seems regular, functional and ordered. Modernism's claim to honesty and rationality is represented, at a metaphorical level, both as insufficient to explain the complexity of contemporary life and unattractive in its cutting off of the possibilities of other ways of being.

Balkan directors

With the exception of a few directors who have achieved international, *auteur* status, such as Emir Kusturica, the films emanating from the Balkans themselves have been small films, put together with packages of finance from many sources and often visible only on festival circuits outside their countries of origin. This is 'poor cinema', but producers have often taken advantage of the lean state of Balkan economies 'as actors and crew are willing to work for very low fees rather than not work at all' (Petkovic 2000: 23). Critics have remarked on the verve and visual flamboyance of these films and especially their grotesque and frequently black humour. Iordanova attributes these expressions of suffering and excitement to attempts by film-makers to grasp the contemporary world of crumbling borders, migration, dispersal, exile and profound change which has replaced a socially and geographically static society and is linked to 'diasporas in the making' (2000a: 68). To the traditionally negative view of migration are added feelings of lack of personal and collective control over one's destiny in a time of conflict, fear and anxiety at the surrounding violence, and of inferiority in the face of NATO and United Nations involvement. Inhabitants of the region are aware of their representation in the West as primitive, irrational and stupid, as can be seen from the ranting of the master of ceremonies in the Belgrade nightclub, Cabaret Balkan, in Goran Paskaljevic's *The Powder Keg*, aka *Cabaret Balkan* (*Bure Baruta*, Yugoslavia/Republic of Macedonia/France/Greece/Turkey, 1998). In fact, the sense of excitement at the possibilities unleashed by social breakdown – opportunities for personal expression unfettered from very rigid, hierarchical and patriarchal social organization and the old national identity – is compounded by the traumas of war. Visual and narrative instability are expressed in the often frenetic pace, strident colour tones and the grotesque in setting, colour, character and performance.

Conclusion

How the Balkan conflict has been incorporated into European cinematic discourse, and how incomers to European countries have been represented and constructed as 'others', are crucial issues for understanding our world at the beginning of the twenty-first century. The bombardment of images from outside national spaces of the destruction, violence and brutality and the total breakdown of civic life in disorder, displacement and death entered Western European public consciousness and formed a repertoire of 'media templates', helping to shape narratives about the past and present (Kitzinger 2000: 61). The suggestion that borders are irrelevant in the contemporary world has some validity, since it is possible to simultaneously sit in one's living room, safe in national domestic space, and watch and grasp some of the experience of the complete collapse of what Europeans have regarded as civilized society. Films treating Balkan events provide evidence of the anxiety and fear which they occasioned, and demonstrate the mechanisms through which experience can be ordered to be assimilated, understood, accepted or rejected. The templates then provide a repertoire for public understanding of subsequent disturbing events, such as the mass immigration of peoples arriving in Western Europe via the Balkans, or other media 'issues' about social breakdown. The construction of images of lawless, inner-city underclasses, criminality, drug culture are such events which, like the Balkan conflict and its aftermath, run through 'every level of the circuit of communication, including journalists' thinking, the media content and people's conversations' (Kitzinger 2000: 75).

As we have seen, the different inflections of the templates discussed in this chapter disprove the idea that the borders are totally irrelevant and that globalization of the media leads to homogenization. The mobility of information which modern communications technologies deliver does not transcend common-sense experience of time and space. Rather, as Ferguson suggests, our experience of time and space is rendered more complex, other realities presented via the media acting as layers among other layers in our experience of our world (1992: 79). The richness and complexity of cinematic attempts to come to terms with ethnic conflict, social breakdown and mass immigration are not only indications of how threatening these events are perceived to be to notions of personal and national identity; they also provide ample evidence that mainstream, commercial cinema on the American model is totally inadequate to explore and express these perceptions in any meaningful way. Where they have tried, as in *Behind Enemy Lines* (Mark Griffiths, USA/Philippines, 1998), the results have been simplistic tales suggesting the supremacy of the American ideology of individualism.

The templates which have evolved to explain these particular events appear closed. The Italian incorporation of previous negative templates of southern underdevelopment and lawlessness into representations of characters associated with the former Yugoslavia is an example of how meanings, once established, tend not to be questioned. The Italian example indicates the presence of coded racial attitudes towards darker-skinned Europeans, often standing metonymically for Arab or African populations. The demonization of the Serbs as backward, violent and tribal in their centuries-long harbouring of grudges skates over the inconvenient evidence that they are members of a modern society; the power vacuum in Albania justifies commercial intervention, while Turkey's violent oppression of its own Kurdish population is ignored by the media. In examining the nature of these particular templates and how they are constructed it is possible to question them and to perceive in whose interests they remain unchallenged.

Notes

1. *Before the Rain*'s funding package included finance from small production companies, British Screen, the European Co-Production Fund, PolyGram and the Ministry of Culture of the Republic of Macedonia.
2. The spectre of Balkanization, or the breakdown of society into 'tribal' factions, the suspension of accepted morality, chaos and violence, is regularly evoked in Italian political and social discourse. The Northern League political party advocated drawing a line just below Rome and letting the southern part of the peninsular and Sicily go to the dogs.

Top-earning European history films/costume dramas

Notes

(a) All data are taken from European Audiovisual Observatory Yearbooks, 1998–2005; (b) EU7 relates to information on the major cinema markets; (c) EU15 relates to members of the EU prior to 1 May 2004; (d) EU25 relates to expanded membership including Eastern European states post 1 May 2004; (e) EU29+ relates to the 25 states of the EU, plus Switzerland, Iceland, Norway, Romania and Turkey.
The European Audiovisual Observatory has changed its methodology slightly from year to year, for example initially giving dollar earnings of European films in the US market, then reverting to figures for cinema admissions. Although a few successful films appear to have had no release in the EU, the global, EU29 figures indicate that these gained their success in Eastern European accession states.

The ranking is based on figures for the top 50 films of any nationality by admissions in Europe. Where the letters 'EU' follow the ranking, this denotes the film's placing in the top 50 European films by admissions in Europe.

Film	Date	Country of prod	US earn $/ admissions	Ranking/year	Released in no of EU countries	Total admissions (millions) EU7	EU15	EU25	EU29+
Shakespeare in Love	1998	UK/US	6.2m/1998	8 1999	14		17.3		
The English Patient	1996	US/UK	55m/1997	7 1997	12		14.7		
La vita è bella	1997	IT		17 1997 EU	1		2.1		
			10.3m/1998	26 1998	7		6.7		
			45.4m/1999				13.1		
Van Helsing	2004	US/CZ		14 2004	14			12.9	
The Others	2001	ES	17.9m adm/01	4 2001	6		11.2		
				12 2002 EU	11				3.5
King Arthur	2004	US/UK/IE		18 2004	14				10.9
Sense and Sensibility	1995	US/UK	39m/1996	10 1996	13		9.4		
Chocolat	2000	UK/US	12.5m adm	4 2001	11			8.9	
Gosford Park	2001	UK/US/DE/IT	7m adm/02	29 2002	13			6.7	
The Hours	2002	US/UK		30 2003	14				6.7
Cold Mountain	2003	UK/US/RO/IT	8.4m adm/04	38 2004	14				6.7
Der Untergang	2004	DE/IT		43 2004	3				5.5

Film	Date	Country of prod	US earn $/ admissions	Ranking/year	Released in no of EU countries	Total admissions (millions) EU7	EU15	EU25	EU29+
Billy Elliot	2000	UK		38 2000	7		5.0		
Un long dimanche de fiançailles	2004	F/US	0.4m adm/04	49 2004	2				4.6
The Talented Mr Ripley	2000	UK/US		40 2000	12		4.3		
Quo vadis	2001	PL		47 2001	1		4.3		
Enemy at the Gates	2001	DE/US/UK/IE	9.5m adm/01	48 2001	11			4.3	
The Pianist	2002	F/UK/DE/PL		45 2002	9				4.9
			5.2m adm/03	9 2003 EU	14				3.6
Captain Corelli's Mandolin	2001	UK/F/US	4.7m adm/01	13 2001 EU	9			3.9	
Girl with a Pearl Earring	2003	US/LU	1.7m adm/04	15 2004 EU	14				3.7
Jeanne d'Arc	1998	F	14.1m/1999	7 1999 EU	3		3.1		
				27 2000	9		1.3		
Angela's Ashes	1999	IE/US	2.3m adm/00	9 2000 EU	9			3.1	
Il postino	1994	IT/F	12.7m	47 1996	10			3.0	
Belphégor – Le fantôme du Louvre	2000	F		16 2001	4			3.1	
East is East	1998	UK	0.7m adm	10 1999 EU	5		2.77		
Elizabeth	1997	UK	15.5m/1998	11 1998	5		2.3		2.1
Alexander	2004	UK/F/NL	5.5m adm/04	23 2004 EU	8				2.2
Vidocq	2001	F		27 2001	3			2.1	
				43 2002 EU	3				1.0
Ridicule	1996	F	1.2m/1996	17 1996	5		1.7		
			1.3m/1997	20 1997 EU	13		1.9		
Lucie Aubrac	1997	F		23 1997 EU	3		1.74		
Le bossu	1997	F/IT/DE		24 1997 EU	3		1.72		
Kolya	1996	CZ/F/UK/US	5.8m/1997	30 1997 EU	14		1.4		
East is East	2000	UK	0.7adm/1999	24 2000 EU	13		1.4		
The Wings of the Dove	1998	UK	5.5m/1998	17 1998 EU	11		1.3		
Aimée und Jaguar	1998	DE	0.1m adm/00	26 1999	3	1.2			

Film	Date	Country of prod	US earn $/ admissions	Ranking/year	Released in no of EU countries	Total admissions (millions) EU7	EU15	EU25	EU29+
Le barbier de Sibérie	1998	RU/F/IT/CZ		28 1999	4		1.2		
A Midsummer Night's Dream	1999	UK/IT/US		17 1999 EU	10		1.7		
The End of the Affair	2000	UK/US	1.6m adm/00	20 2000	9		1.5		
Iris	2002	UK/US	0.9m adm/02	33 2002 EU	10				1.3
La veuve de Saint-Pierre	2000	F/CA	0.6m adm/01	33 2000 EU	8			1.1	
Jane Eyre	1995	UK/IT/F	5.2m/1996	30 1996	6			1.0	
An Ideal Husband	1999	UK	18.5m/1999	40 1999	9		0.98		
				32 2000 EU	10		1.1		
The Magdalene Sisters	2002	UK/IE	0.8m adm/03	47 2002 EU	2				0.94
				28 2003 EU	11				1.7
Brassed Off	1996	UK	2.9m/1997	43 1997	11		0.93		
				37 1996	1		0.78		
Plunket and Macleane	1998	UK		37 1999	8		0.93		
Her Majesty Mrs Brown	1997	UK	8.5m/1997	46 1997 EU	4		0.89		
Le libertin	2000	F		50 2000	5		0.7		
Malèna	2000	IT/US	0.5m adm/01	49 2000	2		0.69		
The Legend of 1900	1997	IT		32 1998	1		0.69		
I cento passi	2000	IT		50 2000	1		5.7		

chapter eight

Theme park Europe?

Costume drama and the historical film are *genres* which Europe is considered to do really well. Historical films, whether adaptations of famous classics of European literature, period romances, epics, costume dramas set in the recent or remote past, horror films or other genres, all have made regular appearances in charts of box-office popularity. The form which they take, and the historical periods that come and go in fashion, are indicative of the complexities of notions of nation and identity. As Pam Cook suggests, 'The historical film re-presents the past for the purposes of the present and the future' (1996: 67). Study of historical re-presentation allows a more nuanced analysis than many discussions focusing on the faithfulness of transposition of a literary work, or the authenticity of historical re-creation. Following Gramsci's notion of folklore 'as a particular form of popular oral representation', historical films bear the mark of 'reigning social discourses' (Landy 1996: 86). As this chapter will explore, the popularity of historical fiction films is an indication of the nearness of the match between 'common-sense' (in Gramscian terms) beliefs about the past and present and their representation on screen. These representations often illustrate the conflict between the desire for stasis, or what Landy calls a 'relatively rigidified phase of popular culture' (1996: 86), and the warring presence of complexity, which threatens the neat closure of incorporation into a hegemonic view of history.

Chaos and complexity tend to complicate the discourse of historical films, making them an interesting and important area of study. In this chapter I want to focus on films considered to present a static view of the historical past – the historical costume dramas – and the war films which have become a noticeable sub-genre since the mid-1990s, which by their very nature materialize opposing discourses. I will question whether their seductive visuals incorporate them into the 'theme park' notion of being formed for pleasurable, uncritical consumption. I will also attempt to bring together commercial concerns (budget, audience, distribution) and the 'collage of beliefs' and attitudes in the world presented to the spectator by the films (Landy 1991: 484). Given the prolific nature of these genres, my choice of films will be eclectic, but my main interest will be the extent to which spectacle, chaos or complexity are able to problematize beliefs about the past and suggest (however elliptically) ways of understanding the new European present.

The heritage film and the British costume drama

Heritage cinema was the term applied to a significant group of 1980s' British films by critics attempting to understand their use of history, their nostalgic yet aggressive mood, their spectacular visuals and their enormous financial success. It is a complex field, which, as Andrew Higson has mapped out, now contains hybrid categories, sub-genres and films which overlap the categories of heritage film, costume dramas and period films (2003: 9–13). Heritage films of the 1980s were cheap by Hollywood standards, but were very successful in the USA; *A Room With a View* (James Ivory, UK, 1985) cost around $3 million but grossed $30 million. Higson crystallized discussions about the heritage cycle of British films of the 1980s, attempting to place them in the complex context of Britain's decline as a major international political power and manufacturing nation (1993: 110–15). Heritage cinema was placed within the context of legislation to preserve old buildings and landscapes, and an enterprise culture which validated the 'selling' of the experience of history (Corner and Harvey 1991: 46). Both represented right-wing Prime Minister Margaret Thatcher's attempts to manage the conflicts between old and new, and what particularly interested those studying heritage films was their iconography and the extent to which they were able to offer a critique of the values of the political conservatism, while offering a seductive spectacle of environments and landscapes. The genre was often disparagingly referred to as the 'National Trust School of film-making' or 'white flannel films' due to their use of National Trust properties as sets and locations, and the propensity for the male protagonists to take part in that arcane ritual conflict known as the English cricket match. Higson argued that the evocation of a historical past was created by illusionistic detail in the 'fetishization of period details', creating an imaginary past 'invented from the point of view of a present that is too distasteful to be confronted head-on' (1993: 113). He identified the camera style as 'pictorialist' in that views of landscapes or covetable objects are unmotivated by the gaze of characters, their excessiveness to narrative requirements transforming them into something to be used and admired (1993: 117).

If the James Bond films can be called 'consumerism dressed up as jetset sophistication' (McKay 2006: 26), then heritage cinema can be categorized as consumerism in the service of cultural competence (Bourdieu 1993). The repeated adaptations of E. M. Forster's and Jane Austen's novels on film and television have provoked many articles on product placement and lifestyle; where the Merchant Ivory team got the wallpapers (Swengley 1992: 6), how to get the romantic Austen look in your home furnishings (Parkin 1996: 7) and garden (Anderton 1996: 5). Not surprisingly, the National Trust and other historic properties started to use heritage film images in their marketing, 1995 being a bumper year for visitors (Kennedy 1996: 8). British heritage cinema also spawned British Tourist Authority maps of film locations, exhibitions of authentic costumes and a coffee table book (Pym 1995). One of the Conservative government's last Heritage Secretaries, Virginia Bottomley, provoked angry reactions among British film-makers by calling for more heritage films 'to encourage tourism and our great traditions' (Brooks 1996: 12). The social changes identified in previous chapters which resulted in economic circumstances no longer being the prime indicator of social difference have led to a situation in which 'questions of culture and cultural difference become paramount to our understanding of the manner in which hegemony and social order are both maintained and reproduced' (Lee, quoted in Rice and Saunders 1996: 93). We become what we consume.

Purchasing the desired objects reveals the aspirational objectives of classes whose historical representations are almost always excluded from the heritage genre, or whose present circumstances bear little relation to images of servants, clerks or aristocrats who might have been their forebears. Class movement, education and social change create an ironic distance for the viewer of the heritage film. Julianne Pidduck suggests that if the films are pleasurable because of their 'offer of a retrospective belonging to conservative myths of privileged Englishness that glosses over the class struggle', they rarely identify totally with class hierarchies and usually include a character whose class marginality licenses them to comment critically (2004: 123–4). What Jameson identifies as a postmodern characteristic, that is 'the idea of the simultaneity of the nonsimultaneous, of the coexistence of distinct moments of history' (1991: 307–8), is fundamental to the heritage and historical film. The genre invites the acquisition of cultural knowledge and skills of evaluating objects, architecture and interiors (without necessarily reading the book or seeing the painting), while marking oneself off as different from an aristocracy or upper class whose views are now construed as classist, racist and/or philistine. I will argue that difference, resulting from the inbuilt trope of ironic distance from the milieux described, is a key to understanding the function and importance of historical films.

Cultural capital aligns with a contemporary liberal view of society, thereby mapping onto the past a common-sense appreciation of the present. Thus, Helen Schlegel's (Helena Bonham-Carter) rebelliousness in *Howards End* (James Ivory, UK/Japan, 1992) and her love affair with the working-class Leonard Bast is revelatory about early twentieth-century patriarchy in which unmarried motherhood meant social exclusion and a contemporary rejection of ideas of upper-class superiority. Rosina's (Minnie Driver) concealment of her Jewish identity in *The Governess* (Sandra Goldbacher, UK, 1998) gives ironic distance to the depiction of the suppression of female autonomy and the delineation of upper-class life in a remote Scottish house, while her independence shows traces of contemporary feminism. Fanny's (Frances O'Connor) status as poor relation in the grand Bertram house in *Mansfield Park* (Patricia Rozema, USA/UK, 1999) motivates her point of view on their moral values and (unusually) the source of the money which underpins their lifestyle, slavery.

British heritage cinema evolved during the course of the 1990s as it changed from being a relatively low-budget form of British art cinema to a higher-budget mainstream genre. Its success attracted American and Japanese investment and the incorporation of non-British directors. As a result, by *Howards End* there were implied criticisms of the crass materialism of the 1980s through representations and dialogue of the Wilcox family, but they were outweighed by the flamboyance and pleasures of the spectacular construction of cinematic space. Architecture and space delineate differences in values and class interests for an international as well as a British audience. The artistic Schlegels are associated with the white Georgian/early Victorian town houses with their neat, black metal railings and cluttered arts-and-crafts interiors; the nouveau riche Wilcoxes live in a red-brick, nineteenth-century mansion block whose rooms' proportions, wood panelling and bought-in portraits are designed to impress. The working-class Basts live in dark and dingy rooms dominated by the sounds of steam trains. The struggle between stasis and historical change is also represented spatially. The Schlegels are being obliged to move home because their London house is required for development, the sequences in their Devon house and at Howards End representing the power shift that removal of their class from the centre of London symbolizes. Higson suggests that *Howards End* is an example of narratives of instability, in which the house materializes questions for the future – who is to inherit England – raising questions about the nature of Englishness and how that functions for social cohesion, while reaching a conclusion pleasing to its middle-class audience (1996: 238–9). The house, Howards End, itself seems to have captured the imagination of English audiences who wanted to see it (Pym 1995). From early sequences in which Mrs Wilcox (Vanessa Redgrave) walks along the front of the house in the early evening light, looking in at her family, to the Schlegels exploring the empty rooms prior to moving in, the house is depicted as a desirable commodity, reflecting the contemporary British obsession with property. Changes structure the narrative, from the initial meeting of Helena with middle-class aspirant Leonard (Samuel West), the death of Mrs Wilcox and her husband's (Anthony Hopkins) cheating Margaret Schlegel (Emma Thompson) out of her inheritance, Margaret's marriage to Mr Wilcox, Leonard Bast losing his job, his affair with Helena and subsequent murder by Charles Wilcox (James Wilby). However, questions of how to reconcile stereotypes of national identity with the pluralism of contemporary society resonate across European borders.

Sense and Sensibility (Ang Lee, USA/UK, 1995) also spatializes power relations. Inez Hedges suggests that women characters are 'conventionally positioned in the three-dimensional diegetic space in a manner that makes them seem more passive than the male characters' (1991: 88). In Lee's film, this convention is actively used to connote their possibilities of activity. Mrs Dashwood (Gemma Jones), Elinor (Emma Thompson), Marianne (Kate Winslet) and Margaret (Emilie François) are often framed by doorways, as in the sequence where the younger Mrs Dashwood's (Harriet Walter) brother, Edward Ferrars (Hugh Grant), arrives. Only he breaks the frame and it is in his company that Elinor is able to go riding and, freed from passivity, to comment that his sense of uselessness can be overcome when he inherits his fortune, while she cannot even earn hers. Moreover, the moral framework which informs the source texts means the absence of representations of sex and nudity which would limit distribution to the Far East. Although the trade paper, *Variety*, uses the term 'polite costumer' for these films, erotic content is still present. In fact, eroticism seethes beneath the surface of stilted dialogue and spectacular images, but represented in the coded forms considered appropriate for expressing British, or English, restraint and sexual repression. Costumes are part of the pleasure of filmed historical fiction, becoming, as Stella Bruzzi notes, 'significant components of a contrapuntal, sexualised discourse' (1997: 36). In *Sense and Sensibility*, the colours of the Dashwood women's day-to-day clothing are muted, the contrasting textures of muslins, linens and sacking aprons providing interest. Their formal evening clothes tell a different story in the drawing of attention to breasts and cleavage in an erotic display which signifies both a woman's fitness for motherhood and the economic necessity of trading sexual possession for financial security. The particular characteristics of the Regency empire-line frock to draw attention to the breasts was clearly a subject of fascination at the time of the BBC's *Pride and Prejudice* (Simon Langton, UK/USA, 1995) and conjecture about how to achieve the requisite level of uplift (Frean 1996: 8). The very rigidity of the male characters, and particularly the unmoving necks swathed in elaborate neckerchiefs, materialize female desire for the male as erotic object, costume in both cases indicating the importance of female desire rather than the fetishization of the woman as object of the look (Mulvey 1990).

Female desire is central to *The Governess*. The early scenes in Rosina da Silva's Jewish family and London community are marked by complete segregation from the world of upper-class Englishness described above. Rosina and her sister, Becca (Emma Bird), are at the same time sexually innocent and sexually frank, signalling their otherness in relation to the repression and silence of the upper-class English. Their conversations wonder about the nature of the male penis and whether sperm really resembles semolina pudding, and Rosina is hailed as 'Jewgirl' by prostitutes flaunting their breasts as she walks from the synagogue to home. The openness and curiosity about the world is signalled by the predominance of warm red tones in the *mise-en-scène* associated with her, contrasting to the cold, green-grey tones of the country home of the Cavendish family, with whom she takes a job as governess when her father is murdered. Rosina gives up her distinctive Jewish hat and hairstyle, dresses in monochrome and dons glasses and a new Christian name, Mary Blackchurch, but opening her trunk in the privacy of her room lets out the fiery reds of her shawls, the colour of appetite. Her first scientific discussion with her employer, Mr Cavendish (Tom Wilkinson), happens against the backdrop of the seashore lit by the orange rays of the setting sun. The vista is both spectacular and, in the asymmetry of its diagonal composition, disturbing. In a reversal of the static 'woman at the window' shots identified as typical of costume drama (Pidduck 2004: 25–7), Rosina observes her employer entering and leaving his workshop and races through the house and outside to gain entry to it. Immobility provides a metaphor for women's disempowerment under patriarchy, whereas Rosina embodies female aspirations for autonomy and self-assertion. As she takes on a more proactive role in assisting Mr Cavendish in his photographic experiments, warm colours move into his cold workshop realm. Rosina puts together a still life consisting of a Turkish rug, fruit and dark cherries, and she is an active partner in their love affair. Mrs Cavendish (Harriet Walter) is distinguished by her immobility within the house, by her soft, ringletted hairstyle and the display of her body in excessively low-cut dresses, the fetishization of her body signifying her acceptance of powerlessness in the patriarchal order. In the workshop Rosina, by contrast, is licensed to actively look at the world rather than to be looked at. There are many shots of her eyes gazing to camera and Cavendish's camera's lens, and point-of-view shots of her stroking Cavendish's soft, hairy chest foreground her desire. It is her photograph of his naked body resting after lovemaking which is her downfall. Rosina leaves the house when her lover cannot commit to her and her racial identity is revealed. Much later, back in London, Mr Cavendish visits Rosina's photographic studio, declares his submission to her will and is rejected. A medium shot of Rosina's emotional reaction behind the studio curtain indicates her pain, but it is momentary and followed by a voice-over announcing her recognition as a portraitist of her community. Described on the DVD box as a tale of 'a remarkable woman, ahead of her time', *The Governess* answers a question of importance to Western women at the cusp of the millennium. Can women have it all? Represented as able to sublimate her sensuality in her creative work and earn recognition and a living from it, Rosina has nonetheless to renounce the complications of a sexual partnership.

Although the contemporary world of multi-ethnic Britain and working women is absent from adaptations of seventeenth- and eighteenth-century fiction, allusions to it surface in country-house dramas set in the nineteenth century and in Patricia Rozema's Austen adaptation, *Mansfield Park*. The latter transforms Austen's colourless character, Fanny Price, into a feisty girl whose writing of stories while seated at her window aligns her with the author, Jane Austen, rather than the heroine constrained to domestic powerlessness. Fanny is shown actively rushing through the spaces of house and landscape, and it is she who reveals the basis of the family fortune in slavery and who excites the lesbian attentions of Mary Crawford (Embeth Davidtz).

The world below stairs and its class antagonisms are foregrounded in other films, either by making these the narrative focus, as in *The Remains of the Day* (James Ivory, UK/USA, 1993), or by casting famous British actors in lower-class roles, as in *Gosford Park* (Robert Altman, UK/USA, 2001). Like *The Governess, Mansfield Park* was produced by the BBC with contributions from the National Lottery via the Arts Council of England. The former was distributed by Sony Pictures Classics and the latter by Miramax. With a budget of £2.8 million, *The Governess* successfully grossed $3.9 million in the USA which, given its predominant use of interior and exterior location shooting and limited cast, must represent a good return, in contrast to *Mansfield Park*, whose Miramax distribution was unable to deliver American success. Claire Monk surmised in 1995 that, although the mid-1990s' heritage cycle of films was becoming more overtly concerned with sexuality and gender, particularly non-dominant and ambiguous sexual identities, the films were in fact less radical than some of the 1980s' cycle which contained enough sexual ambivalence to appeal to a variety of tastes (1995: 32). She defined films like *Carrington* (Christopher Hampton, UK/France, 1995) as post-heritage, so it has to be seen as significant that, since then, the heritage film has shed explorations of sexuality as it has acquired larger amounts of American co-production financing and distribution, reverting to more elliptical representations.

As Chapter Three has explored, there is a pattern for entry into the sphere of the international quality film, a commodity identified by global media companies as capable of achieving good returns on the investment in prints and other media forms. The reward of film festival prizes to actors, cinematographers, set and costume designers, sound engineers, special effects designers and CGI engineers enhances their career profile, making them attractive options in the 'package' of future films. A quality creative team is important for all types of period film, depending as they do on an impression of authenticity in the creation of 'pastness'. In the British case, historical drama is now produced in a range of budget categories, but with fewer low-budget costume dramas as their potential to cross over into mainstream, multiplex distribution has become apparent (Higson 2003). Their success has disturbed the traditional view that the mainstream worldwide audience requires action blockbusters. Claire Monk's analysis of British audience statistics challenged prevailing industry ideas that the mainstream UK cinema audience consisted solely of 18–34-year-old men and sought to interrogate the patronizing critical assumption that the heritage film audience consisted of women, 'conservative, bourgeois and short on cinematic taste' (1999b: 25). Her preliminary analyses concluded that heritage films had a less élite appeal than claimed and that, although they did appeal to an older audience, that group were also regular cinema-goers. Crossover films such as *Howards End* also drew in a male as well as a female audience. A particular insight was the revelation of a small but significant audience of older women which, because of demographic change, is increasing. In Britain, as elsewhere in Europe, the cinema audience is largely defined as middle-class, i.e. ABC1, and this audience also goes to see foreign, art-house films. As Britain, with France and Germany, is one of the three most important film markets in Europe, these figures suggest that global reach has been a factor in the historical film's success.

Given the technological developments of the last 11 years, these findings are interesting in suggesting explanations for the longevity of the exploitation of heritage films in various media and the diversification of this type of historical cinema fiction into various sub-genres. British studies wonder why Britain is so obsessed with class when it is not more unequal or less socially mobile than other countries, Cannadine in particular concluding that this is because, for historical reasons, Britain has a larger repertoire of vernacular models than most nations to describe and discuss them (1998). As I have suggested before, the division by advertising industry categories of class is a blunt instrument, taking no account of social change, taste or sexual orientation. Arthur Marwick's analysis posits the existence of 'not one middle class, but a range of middle classes, amazingly variegated in educational backgrounds, in burdens and privileges' (1998: 14). Those depicted as middle-class by heritage films are now firmly upper-class, joined by an assortment of city traders, currency millionaires, pop and media stars. The British working class has shrunk, supplanted by a proletariat whose tastes are answered by satellite television, or who are unemployed and marginalized and therefore of little interest to cinema exhibitors or advertisers. Moreover, the industry has itself woken up to the fact of the existence of the regular female audience, mainly through monitoring DVD retail sales. The heritage genre itself has become more hybrid, so that elements of it are discernible in the rom com, such as *Notting Hill*, in which the heritage film is specifically referenced in the sequence where Anna (Julia Roberts) appears in a location at Kenwood House in London.

The acknowledgement of a variety of class positions and tastes explains the presence of working-class costume dramas in British cinema whose heightened drama and affective elements provide a space in which personal issues are made to stand for social uncertainty and the incapacity to resolve some of the conflicts of the fraught modern world. Peter Brooks's (1976: 13–22) contention that melodrama comes into being 'in a world where the traditional imperatives of truth and ethics have been violently thrown into question, yet where the promulgation of truth and ethics, their instauration as a way of life, is of immediate, daily, political concern' offers an immediate insight into the appeal of historical fictions in which questions of right action can be rehearsed at a distance and modes of conduct explored. In this light, films like the enormously popular *Elizabeth* (Shekhar Kapoor, UK, 1998) and *Mrs Brown* (John Madden, UK/Ireland/USA, 1997), although both about famous female monarchs, embody questions about women wielding political power and what they have to give up to do so, cross-class romance, duty to family and nation. *Hideous Kinky* (Gillies MacKinnon, UK/France/Morocco, 1998), set in the 1960s, resonates both with the baby-boomer generation of women who tried voyages of self-discovery at that time and with their daughters who still have to juggle their desires and those of their children. *Vera Drake*'s (Mike Leigh, UK/France/New Zealand, 2004) tagline, 'wife, mother, criminal', situates the film at a time in the 1950s when abortion was illegal. Working-class Vera's aim is to 'help girls out' when their pregnancies would spell disaster, and the film contrasts her situation and that of the middle-class girl who is able to pay more and get a legal abortion. The uncommunicative dynamics of working-class family life at that time clearly struck a chord with an American IMDb user who grew up in Britain, also recalling the drabness of her home. The synchronicity of her recollection and the recreation of the past valorize the present by stabilizing the idea of a dystopic past. Returning to a time when families were together but at the price of enormous suppression of women's needs, *Vera Drake* is unusual in that the female protagonist is a mother, but she is seen acting autonomously, rather than through the eyes of children or husband. Mulvey suggests that melodrama provides a 'safety valve for ideological contradictions' under patriarchy, in which the moulding of the feminine unconscious 'leaves women largely without a voice, gagged and deprived of outlets' (1987: 75). For Marcia Landy, family melodrama 'offers a window on the world of female identity, desire, and sexuality' (1991: 191). For Vera's family, she is just 'mother', performing the tasks underpinning family life, but her occupation as abortionist introduces a thoroughly disruptive element to male control of female reproduction, which literally erupts into the public sphere when she is arrested and tried for her crimes by the legal establishment. Within this trajectory, the reality of young women's lives at the time is brought into the light, suggesting a space to make comparisons with the present.

The achievement of autonomy, a creative outlet and artistic recognition is represented as massively disruptive in *Hilary and Jackie* (Anand Tucker, UK, 1998), which interweaves the career of world-famous cellist Jacqueline du Pré (Emily Watson) with the personal relationship to her sister Hilary (Rachel Griffiths). The film is marked by postmodern excess at many levels. The violence and obsessive quality of Emily Watson's cello performances, the 'monstrous' nature of du Pré's self-absorption and selfishness in manipulating others and demanding sex with Hilary's husband, the display of emotion, and in the *mise-en-scène*. Costume (Sandy Powell has won two Oscars and many nominations for her designs) stresses Jackie's excessive personality through her performance dresses of red silk and her massively fur-trimmed coat. *Noir* lighting situates Jackie in cold blue, shadowed tones and she is often framed in low-angle shots, situated on stage with strong vertical graphic movements of décor and architecture reflecting both her artistic triumphs and the bursting out of limits that her talent required. The film's focus on her as exceptional individual reflects a contemporary obsession with celebrity, but also the stretching of limits which is a characteristic of postmodern culture (Calabrese 1992).

In the previous chapter I argued that representations of the Balkan conflicts provided a space in which contemporary multiculturalism, masculine identities and ethical dilemmas could be rehearsed at a distance. As I have demonstrated in the section above, historical costume dramas also offer a distant space, in which to reflect on class and social responsibility, female autonomy and desires, acceptable and unacceptable change. Visual spectacle functions not as 'theme park' consumption of beautiful images, artefacts and costumes but as a disruption inviting reflection beyond the nationally specific to appropriate behaviours in the contemporary world.

Sex and violence and the past

Engagement with the full range of French historical drama is beyond the scope of this chapter. It differs from the British generic trajectory in that historical films were from the start conceived as event films, designed to showcase the high cultural status of French literature, arts and fashion, and the spectacle and *mise-en-scène* of place is quite different. In *Artemisia* (Agnès Merlet, France/Germany/Italy, 1997), exteriors and interiors are subordinated to the story of the adolescent Artemisia's (Valentina Cervi) journey to become a painter but the saturated oranges and blue colour of costumes are a counterpoint to discovery of the sensual properties of paint and sex. The seashore is where she discovers perspective through the frame used by the painter Tassi (Miki Manojlovic); artists' *ateliers* are framed in long-shot for the eye to experience with Artemisia the technology of seventeenth-century artistic production. The historical controversy of her relationship with Tassi, who was tried for her rape, becomes reduced to the consequences of her adolescent curiosity about sexuality and fascination with his sexual freedom and licence. *Artemisia* was criticized on many sides; from feminists concerned at the reduction of a feminist icon's career to simplistic biopic (Pollock 1998: 26–8), or Lolita-drama whose protagonist 'gestures with the naturalness of a traffic policeman and whose voice resembles the emergency services' automated recording' (Lalli 1998: 42).

Artemisia was not criticized for its eroticism, a constant feature in French and Spanish historical films. In *A Horseman on the Roof* (*Le hussard sur le toit*, Jean-Paul Rappeneau, France, 1995), the erotic charge lies in the delay of sexual resolution between Angelo (Olivier Martinez), the Italian revolutionary fleeing through cholera-stricken Provence, and Pauline de Théus (Juliette Binoche), who helps him, especially in the scene where he reduces Pauline's fever by rubbing her naked body with hot cloths. Eroticism, and the foregrounding of Frenchness, marks them off from Hollywood films with which French historical films compete. *Horseman* draws on Provençal images familiar from earlier internationally popular films, *Jean de Florette* and *Manon des Sources* (both Claude Berri, France/Switzerland/Italy, 1986). Other costume dramas are adaptations of canonic French literary texts, foregrounding French expertise in theatre and costume design, acting skills and use of language, biopics of famous French men and women, or set in key moments of French history.

Eroticism is also a constant in Spanish cinema, which has plenty of history with which to come to terms and, in the 1990s, shifted rejection of fascism onto the sphere of sexuality where the erotic stood for repudiation of conservative patriarchy upheld by Franco and the Catholic church. *Lovers* (*Amantes*, Vicente Aranda, Spain, 1991) is set firmly in the 1950s, arguably a moment of consolidation of Francoist ideologies. That it was based on a real love triangle and murder indicates that there were already strains in aligning these ideologies with the reality of modern Europe, and Marsha Kinder sees the central figure of the former soldier, Paco (Jorge Sanz), as allegorizing the 1950s' generation caught between two Spains, the traditional one represented by his virginal fiancée, Trini (Maribel Verdú), and the emerging Spain of commerce and graft, represented by his older landlady, Luisa (Victoria Abril) (1993: 206–13). In Aranda's film, the autarchy and self-sufficiency typical of fascist politics are metaphorized in the claustrophobic *mise-en-scène* of Luisa's apartment and in the exploitative relationships between the characters. Luisa's manipulative and excessive desire, reflected in numerous shots of her exploring and arousing Paco's body, is problematic for Chris Perriam in perilously sliding close to soft-porn clichés (2003: 154), but her sexual control of the young man has to be regarded as subversive in its historical setting. The affair results in a plot to rob Trini of her savings, again materializing the woman's investment in the marriage bargain in return for the virginity insisted upon by the Church. As discussed above, Luisa's importance lies in the well-known exaggeration and disinhibition of Abril's performance (Stone 2004: 171), materializing the disruption caused by female autonomy, especially in the Spanish context of stereotypes of suffering Catholic womanhood.

Politics are firmly sidelined in *Belle Époque* (Fernando Trueba, Spain/Portugal/France, 1992), reaching the countryside only in brief snippets of news delivered by passing extras, or in the schoolteacher's (Gabino Diego) switching sides. *Belle Époque* won an Oscar for Best Foreign Film and was hugely popular in and outside Spain. In a review, Paul Julian Smith identifies it as a key text marking the entry of Spanish cinema into the international marketplace for historical drama by virtue of its polish and inoffensiveness (1994: 38). Young army deserter, Fernando (Jorge Sanz), on the run in rural Spain, is taken in by the artist father of four beautiful daughters. Sanz was a prolific popular star by this time, the type of actor described by Richard Dyer as condensing around his persona ideals of youthful masculinity and changes to ideas of masculinity at that time (1991: 57–9). The repetition of female sexual liberation and desire in the seductions of Fernando by all four sisters destabilizes gender values, further complicated by the range of sexual activity represented by the girls. The most interesting of these is that of Violeta, described by her family as 'a man', who seduces Fernando during a carnival evening when he is dressed as a maid and she is in his army uniform. The scene where her gaze is fixed on his red lips and she calls him a pretty girl is perversely and profoundly erotic, but deflated by comedy when she blows his bugle at the moment of orgasm.

In these two films, the period drama format cannot contain more than oblique mention of history, instead using violence and sexual excess to destabilize the gender ideology which was the mainstay of the Francoist regime. In the Spanish as in the French case, my analyses suggest that eroticism and excess contribute to unstable representations of history, which can be said to express anxieties about identity in a contemporary world dominated by the English language and Anglo-Saxon versions of global media and communications.

Constant engagement with history: Italy

An engagement with history has been a constant feature of Italian cinema from its inception and I have explored some of the favoured historical settings elsewhere, and particularly how certain directors associated with art cinema practice were able to move into the international quality sector (Wood 2005a: 63–81). Few contemporary directors have been able to cross over into this international market, but several set designers, cinematographers and costume designers have done so. Italy is renowned for its craft traditions so that Italian films often have a quality look way in excess of their budgets. Whereas lead actors in contemporary fiction generally get to keep their costumes, at the very top end of production reinterpretations of historical clothing is treated as museum quality. More generally, costumes are hired out to many films, or derive from recycled clothes bought in markets for minor characters. This gives Italian historical fiction an appearance of authenticity which is reflected in realist strategies to lend authenticity to the director's recreation of the past. At the same time, narrative, kinetic, performative and visual excess – *film noir* conventions, disturbing asymmetry, *chiaroscuro* lighting, showy visuals – function to draw attention to the view that simple explanations of historical events are inadequate. The history of Italy has been marked by massive social change and traumatic events – assassinations, murders, scandals – for which no explanations have been given and no one punished. Complexity and excess are therefore neo-baroque strategies to interrogate the past, which lies like an open wound in the present.

In the international, quality sector, Giuseppe Tornatore's films *Cinema Paradiso* (Italy/France, 1989) and *Malèna* (Italy/USA, 2000) are among the few which are internationally known. The earlier film was a co-production package with Italian and French television and the Cristaldi company (which produced an important range of art and popular cinema); the latter a fruitful alliance between Berlusconi's Medusa, and Miramax distribution which garnered many nominations and prizes for its music (Ennio Morricone) and cinematography (Lajos Koltai). Tornatore admits that his favoured style is to bring his characters' feelings to the fore, to use hyperbole to tell his stories (Toffetti 1995: 28). This is used to advantage in *Malèna* in which visually stunning use of the Sicilian landscape and a paucity of dialogue facilitates its international distribution. Set in the 1940s, the narrative viewpoint is that of a young adolescent who witnesses the young widow's (Monica Bellucci) 'horizontal collaboration' with the enemy in the 1940s after her husband has been killed. Compared with the films investigated above, Tornatore's film is interesting because of the anxieties it works to suppress. The adolescent viewpoint enables Tornatore to ignore feminist views and the wider political context (neither being known as the preoccupation of young boys) and to conquer a larger audience through the appeals of sex and Italian fashion.

Recent Italian cinema, however, returns obsessively to historical events, particularly those of the 1970s, such as mafia kidnappings and murders, terrorist atrocities of right and left, corruption, and the murder of Prime Minister Aldo Moro in 1978. Contemporary reworkings of these moments continue to display the conventions of Italian *film noir* described previously, in the oscillation of authenticity of place and visual excess and asymmetry (Wood 2006/7). They also differ from earlier *noirs* in including representations of domestic *milieux*, feminized spaces within which the protagonists move with confidence. The moral authority of the juridical investigators in films like *The Long Silence* (*Il lungo silenzio*, Margarethe von Trotta, Italy/Germany/France, 1993) and *Middle Class Hero* (*Un eroe borghese*, Michele Placido, Italy, 1994) derives from the fact that their competence in the spheres of both reason and emotion enables them to map an ethical position onto them as representatives of the national as well as local community.

The Eastern European epic

The collapse of institutions in postcommunist Eastern Central Europe had a deleterious effect on Eastern bloc industries, not least the film studios which had made films on the communist rather than the capitalist model. The more entrepreneurial establishments, such as the Czech Barrandov Studios, survived by courting foreign film and television productions with their low fees and high technical skills. It is not surprising that, threatened with loss of national prestige and the all-encompassing grand metanarrative of communism to explain and justify a way of life and ideals in opposition to the capitalist West, the former communist countries should have recourse to representations of the past to sugar the bitter pill of the present.

Poland experienced a brief blockbuster era, fuelled by the phenomenal success of the action-packed historical epic, *With Fire and Sword* (*Ogniem i mieczem*, Jerzy Hoffman, Poland, 1999). Dealing with a Cossack uprising in the Ukraine, under Polish rule at the time (Iordanova 2000b: 98), the film had a hitherto unprecedented budget of $8 million from the Polish government, TVP (Polish television) and private backing from Kredyt Bank, and went on to gross a record $25 million at the Polish box office (Franklin 2003). As Paul Coates has observed, in Polish culture 'both heroism and masculinity suffer the enormous shocks of recurrent military defeat and the encounter with modernity' (2005: 116–7). This is played out in numerous films from the 1950s, heroism usually being the purview of the workers' struggle. Proletarian heroism, associated with Soviet socialist realism, was always a problem in Polish culture. Situating an epic clash in a former republic of the USSR in the seventeenth century allowed the Soviet colonization of Poland to be the ghost at the feast of a conflict celebrating youthful Polish heroism. *With Fire and Sword* is based on Nobel prize-winner Henryk Sienkiewicz's book, read by every Polish schoolchild. The tragic love story of Helena (Izabella Scorupco – a former Bond girl) and the nobleman, Skrzetuski (Michal Zebrowski), parallels the military conflict. Although the director laid claim to dealing with eternal values and vices, Zebrowski likened his preparation for the film as becoming 'a sort of Polish cowboy', indicating the meld of genres which gave it contemporary appeal.[1]

But Poland succumbed to economic recession and government and television funding has dried up. The follow-up epic, *Quo vadis* (Jerzy Kawalerowicz, Poland, 2001), cost $10 million but was less successful and has not been followed, reflecting the difficulty of using the epic template in a political situation of mass emigration in search of work and encouragement of a more European identity.

War films and the attempt at closure

Contemporary European cinema includes a significant number of war films and their presence has to indicate an obvious conflict between cultural discourses. As the previous chapter has explored, the presence of ethnic conflicts, sieges, military campaigns and the consequences of war in depictions of refugees and the victims of torture and rape in the Balkans in the 1990s have disturbed widely held beliefs that modern society is inherently civilized, democratic, stable and just. The widespread European revulsion over the invasion of Iraq in the 2000s and the continued involvement of Western European countries in that conflict has also fuelled interest in representations of war, usually displaced to the more remote conflicts of the First and Second World Wars.

Dark Blue World (Jan Sverák, Czechoslovakia/UK 2001) uses flashbacks from a present in a postwar, communist labour camp to explore the lives of two young Czechs who flee the Nazi occupation of their country to volunteer for the Royal Air Force. Sverák's film, like his *Kolya* (1997) which won an Oscar for Best Foreign Language Film, represents an attempt to make a Czech film with international appeal and to move away from the communist cultural practices whereby productions had to conform to political orthodoxies rather than to capitalist laws of the marketplace. Sverák was able to make it because he had control over the project through his own production company and had put together a tri-partite co-production which was eligible for Eurimages financing and included distribution deals in Britain and Germany, and the support of the Czechoslovak government. These arrangements, and the appeal to British memories of East Central European assistance in the Second World War, justified his insistence on the use of the Czech language. Considering that war films are effectively costume dramas, in this case necessitating uniforms and aerial dog fights, the budget ($8 million/£6.3 million) was modest, but so too was the box office. The film appeared caught in the classic bind of expectations that an Eastern Central European film would be 'a small art-house film about some drama or psychology'.[2]

The film borrows story conventions from the war genre in the delaying of immersion in the fighting, in the structure of the aerial combat sequences and in the romantic sub-plot in which Franta Sláma (Ondrej Vetchy) and his young protégé Karel Vojtisek (Krystof Hádek) both fall in love with the same woman (Tara Fitzgerald). The film also betrays the presence of interesting discourses about Czech history, and the sheer emotionalism of its representations indicates the painful nature of coming to terms with facts of invasion and defeat which were suppressed and repressed during the period of Soviet domination. The framing narrative of Franta's suffering in the postwar prison hospital in Czechoslovakia returns at regular intervals in the film, providing a contrast both visually and in mood to the RAF sequences. The colour tones of verdant green and blue skies of wartime England also provide a metaphorical opposition to the darkness of the postwar scenes. Franta's prison doctor is German and from the dark spaces of the Nazi invasion, and the Soviet postwar oppression, come the repeated questions – 'Why did you Czechs capitulate to the Nazi demands to hand over your weapons and troops?'; 'Why didn't you shoot yourselves rather than capitulate?'; 'Why are you here [in the camp]?' This repetition indicates the presence of trauma and unfinished business in Czech history and establishes an atmosphere of tragedy from the beginning, generating an ironic perspective on the past.

The tragedy of Franta's later life, mistreated and imprisoned on his return to Czechoslovakia (as thousands were) because he was suspected of opposition to the communist regime, makes a connection between capitulation to the Nazis and capitulation to the Soviet annexation in the late 1940s. In a parallel elision, the light and airy atmospheres and green and blue colours enhance the sense of freedom in wartime England, jumping over the 40 Eastern bloc years to connect with contemporary freedoms. It also heightens the affective charge of what the DVD cover describes as a 'story about love, comradeship and sacrifice told with the nostalgic sentiment of classic Hollywood movies'. There are two, heavily affective moments at the beginning and end of the film, both set in Czechoslovakia. In the first, Franta's love for his dog, Borcha (a tawny spaniel), is established as he returns from a flight and calls her to him. When he decides to escape the Nazi occupation, there is a protracted emotive farewell scene between man and dog as he entrusts Borcha to his girlfriend and has to tell the dog to stop following him as he leaves. When he returns in his RAF uniform after the war, the girlfriend is married with a child. The dog recognises him, but the child won't hand her back. Love of country is displaced onto the feminine, one who has betrayed him and the other which is powerless. The film is therefore full of painful ambiguities about the legitimacy of actions in the past.

Complexity also surfaces in a simple tale of love in Jean-Pierre Jeunet's *A Very Long Engagement* (*Un long dimanche de fiançailles*, USA/France, 2003). One of the ways in which this occurs is in the oscillation between different visual regimes. Nineteen-year-old Mathilde's (Audrey Tautou) world is characterized by warm green and brown tones, whereas the First World War and its aftermath are depicted in *noir* elements of black and blue tones, darkness and obscured vision. When Mathilde's young fiancé, Manech (Gaspard Ulliel), goes missing in action, Mathilde refuses to believe that Manech has been killed in the battle of the Somme and her actions and voice-over detail the steps taken to discover what actually happened. Manech was left to die in no-man's-land, near a trench called Bingo Crépuscule, for the crime of self-inflicted wounding, in the company of four other men. Successive sequences construct the painstaking sifting out of evidence from Mathilde's meetings with the protagonists, accompanied by a voice-over which is scarcely more informed than she herself. She discovers the existence of a survivor and teases out the assumption of a false identity assumed in the front-line chaos. In doing so she meets and interviews the counterpart to herself, the performer, Tina Lombardi (Marion Cotillard), who is equally obsessed, but in establishing responsibility for her lover's death. Although Mathilde's story dominates the screen, Tina is her alter ego. Tina is represented as obsessive, a dancer/singer lover of the Corsican criminal, Ange Bassignano (Dominique Bettenfeld), single-mindedly pursuing the officers who concealed the fact that the men had been officially pardoned and murdering the man who shot her lover. In a sequence which uses all the conventions of contemporary *noir*, Tina lures one of her prey to a cavernous and deserted tunnel, killing him with a gun strapped to her body. An excessive *mise-en-scène* of place emphasizes the diagonal orthogonal lines and *chiaroscuro* visuals of the space, and the high-contrast lighting on Tina's body. She goes to the guillotine, her body being flopped brutally into the waiting coffin. For Sue Harris the film succeeds on both emotional and visual levels of painting a picture 'of a civilian population blighted by physical afflictions' (2005: 78). War is represented as impacting on the population at both psychic and physical levels.

Mathilde finds Manech, shell-shocked, in the final reel, but whereas the film concludes with the formation of the original couple, Mathilde's journey of competence in unravelling the truth, necessitating courage in travelling through France interrogating a diverse range of social types and engaging with military hierarchies, leaves the possibility of convincing narrative closure ambiguous. Although official histories have widened understanding of the role of women in times of conflict, Mathilde's journey in this film is privileged to such an extent that her intellectual growth indicates an unequal future relationship with Manech.

Films about the Second World War have also featured significantly in recent German cinema. Although the exploration of taboo areas of German history was a tenet of New German cinema of the 1970s, and television series such as Edgar Reitz's *Heimat* used the family saga to detail the complicity, implicit and explicit, of the German population in the rise of Nazi fascism, the recent spate of films reveals a new openness to examining national history and guilt in mainstream cinematic form. Whereas Rainer Werner Fassbinder used melodrama and excess to depict the camp aspects of Nazi culture, reaching its kitsch apotheosis in *Lili Marleen* (West Germany, 1981), contemporary films use illusionistic detail to carefully reconstruct historical moments. *Downfall* (*Der Untergang*, Olivier Hirschbiegel, Germany/Italy/Austria, 2004) is a big-budget production by Bernd Eichinger's Constantin film, German and Austrian television and the Bavarian Film Fund. It is based on recently published memoirs of Hitler's secretary, Traudl Junge, who was a witness to the German leader's final days in the secret bunker in Berlin, menaced by the Russian army's advance. *Downfall* engages its mass audience by attributing some psychological depth to the character of Hitler (Bruno Ganz) and by depicting Traudl (Alexandra Maria Lara) as pretty but ordinary in comparison with the stony-faced Magda Goebbels (Corinna Harfouch). By the end, the film becomes almost monochrome as it depicts the end of the Third Reich in scenes of the bloody and senseless self-sacrifice of Nazi and SS troops convinced of their continuing pact with the Führer, the obvious fear and confusion of Lara's performance generating empathy with Traudl's predicament. In a symbolic coupling, Traudl is offered the possibility of crossing safely through Russian lines by the young boy who has been a mute witness to the suicidal horrors of the Hitlerbunker. She is offered redemption by the younger generation. In a final coda, the elderly Traudl Junge herself affirms her ignorance of the Final Solution, but admits with emotion that on seeing a wall plaque commemorating the death of Sophie Scholl, she realized that she should have been more aware and active in finding out what was going on.

More recently, *Sophie Scholl* (*Sophie Scholl – die letzten Tage*, Marc Rothemund, France/Germany, 2005) brings to the screen a book studied in German schools from the 1960s onwards about a small group of very young students who formed the White Rose cell dedicated to resistance to the Nazi war machine during the Second World War. Sophie (Julia Jentsch) and her brother are caught leafleting their university, are arrested and interrogated. The long interrogation offers Sophie a way out, but at the price of identifying the other members of the White Rose organization. Sophie refuses and is executed. Again, the *mise-en-scène* is of a charcoal monochrome, lightened only by touches of rusty red in Sophie's jumper, lips and her interrogators' book of regulations. Attention therefore focuses insistently on her face, expression and words. It is interesting that the newly unified Germany needs this film, this reconstruction of evidence of opposition to the Nazi war machine, which was at its height in 1943. It has been rewarded with a Silver Bear at the 2005 Berlin film festival, three German film awards and three European film awards.

Recourse to considerably earlier conflicts features in *King Arthur* (Antoine Fuqua,

UK/Ireland/USA, 2004), in which Arthur (Clive Owen) is a Sarmatian general in the service of Rome, left behind with his knights by the retreating Roman military forces and having to accept the Roman terms of one last task on their behalf before they can return to their homeland. Nostalgic moments regularly freeze the narrative, repeating the information that this is an alien conflict. In the scene in the drinking den when Sir Bors's (Ray Winstone) woman sings longingly of the journey home, both song and Arthur's knights' noisy rejection of Roman objectives provide a homology, expressing in different forms an idea which is repeated throughout the text. It is hard not to interpret this insistent repetition in the light of Prime Minister Blair's defence of George W. Bush's war on terror and British army forces' presence in Afghanistan and Iraq. Arthur and his knights attempt to achieve their goal of rescuing the Pope's godson faced with pagan Celtic warriors, the duplicitous Bishop Germanus (Ivano Marescotti), whose agenda is the establishment of Christianity rather than the survival of Roman *polis*, and the barbarian Saxons, led by Cerdic (Stellan Skarsgård). Arthur's getting the Celts onside is assisted by his growing relationship with the young woman warrior Guenevere (Keira Knightly). This is a world in chaos in which one civilization is painfully acceding to another. Arthur's knights' activities take place on the chaotic cusp of change, as represented in their relationships. Sir Bors is a bluff proletarian soldier with families in both ends of the continent who eventually makes his commitment to Britain; Arthur sees himself as a Roman, but much is made of his being a Christian follower of Pelagius who preached equality and tolerance, rather than the hierarchical and absolute allegiance of Roman Catholicism. After Alecto (Lorenzo de Angelis) reveals that Pelagius has been assassinated, Arthur's seduction by Guenevere seals his commitment to the country in which he has fought his campaigns. As befits a depiction of the start of the Dark Ages, the film's tones are dark, with a predominance of grey and black, and smoke and mist veiling the green landscapes of Britain with its hills and characteristic oaks (filmed in Ireland). In one of the most spectacular set pieces, Arthur's small band of allies faces a Saxon army across an ice-bound lake. Through astute military tactics they force the Saxon army to clump together, provoking the cracking of the ice and the destruction of the Saxons in the icy depths. The sequence's icy tones enable the flights of arrows to be visible and the shots from beneath the ice generate considerable suspense.

It is tempting to make a connection between *King Arthur* and Britain's involvement with the war in Iraq and its consequences in the 7 July 2005 London tube bombings. Narrow attributions of good and evil to particular factions within and outside the film are difficult, and pointless. The film is far more interesting in indicating the presence of trauma in the face of chaos and uncertainty in British internal realities and foreign policy, faced with what is presented as an irrational and relentless Arab enemy. Arthur's world is one of spectacular excess in its violence and darkness. Only he and his band have positive attributes of fairness, intelligence, magnanimity attached to them, and the Saxon leader exists solely to maintain that, finally, he has found a worthy enemy.

These precepts underpin another, bigger-budget ($130 million) military epic, *Kingdom of Heaven* (Ridley Scott, UK/Spain/USA/Germany, 2005), set during the twelfth-century Crusades, in which the protagonist, Balian (Orlando Bloom), finds himself leading the defence of Jerusalem. The aristocratic Christian leaders are depicted as perfidious, evil and incompetent. Balian motivates the common troops by knighting them *en masse*, thereby increasing their commitment noticeably, and makes an impassioned speech for religious tolerance, attempting a redemption of violence which seems today as utopian as the idea that a blacksmith could command medieval Jerusalem. These are predominantly male melodramas, whose excessive elements are often expressed visually and performatively through spatial configurations. Conceived as multinational projects for global distribution, the conflicts central to films like the last two are curiously un-nationally specific, reflecting the fact that their ethical dilemmas resonate far outside their historical context. Where war dramas appear to respond to national concerns to come to terms with a problematic past, they still provide spaces to rehearse ethical questions current in the contemporary world.

Conclusion

Historical fiction is a staple of the film and television industries, with potential for exploitation in international niche markets in the future. Higson sees them as research and development opportunities for Hollywood, introducing an element of the local into globalized film culture (2003: 259–60). Paradoxically, these local expressions of history are, at the high-budget end, predominantly reliant on transnational funding. But the fact that institutional funding is also allocated to them reflects the fact not only that these genres have been identified as financially viable but also that they respond to both national and international needs to make sense of the present. The preoccupation with history results from the postmodern pull between uncertainty and the 'common-sense' stereotypes of nation which are unconsciously perceived as inadequate. The pull is towards simplicity, but complexity erupts. The spectacular elements of *mise-en-scène*, hyperreality in attention to objects and costumes, melodramatic plots and intense emotions, visual excess and violence are not, therefore, mere invitations to passive pleasure and consumption of a sanitized, theme-park view of history. The media provide contemporary European populations with the information by which they make sense of themselves and their circumstances. Filmed histories represent active engagements with that process via the interplay of co-existing moments, in which present circumstances are always structured within representations of the past. These films are thus far from simple and the range of interpretations different audiences take from them testifies to the importance of the local elements in this type of international cinema. The void of anxiety about identity and life's meaning has not been completely neutralized by what Jameson calls the 'visual culture of consumerism' (1998: 150), although that is there. Rather, the excessive elements attest to the fact that, for many audiences, pleasurable consumption is somehow not all there is to life. As I have demonstrated, ethical questions are not only rehearsed in the authorial cinema identified in Chapter Two, or the TV co-productions explored in Chapters Five, Six and Seven. Two recent films, *Black Book* (*Zwartboek*, Paul Verhoeven, Germany/Netherlands/Belgium/UK, 2006) and *The Life of Others* (*Das Leben der Anderen*, Florian Henckel von Donnersmarck, Germany, 2006) indicate the continued wide appeal of historical drama in working through questions of personal responsibility.

Notes

1. Advertisement feature, *Screen International*, 14 May 1999.
2. Jan Sverák quoted in Schwinke 2006: 16. The film was also released at the same time as *Pearl Harbor*. Since *Kolya* there has been a fruitful collaboration between British producer Eric Abraham and Sverák's company Biograf Jan Sverák, in which his father, Zdenek, takes part as writer and actor.

chapter nine

Case study: Ireland

Ireland has been chosen as an example of the complexity of the situation of cinema in the small countries of Europe, with the complication that the island is home to the Republic of Ireland and to Northern Ireland, which is part of the UK. 'Ireland' will be taken to refer to the whole island, otherwise I will distinguish between the two political entities. The Republic of Ireland has a population of just over 4 million, a little less than that of Croatia and Norway, and just more than that of Lithuania. At the time of writing the UK population has just reached 60 million, including the population of Northern Ireland (the six provinces of Ulster). Like the Benelux countries, Austria, Portugal and the countries of the Baltic, Central Europe and the former Yugoslavia, Ireland is usually ignored in statistical surveys, prompting the question raised in Chapter Two – in whose interests does this happen? *Screen International*'s Ireland correspondent, Ted Sheehy, concluded that the marginalization of Ireland happened because Hollywood was not interested enough in it (2002: 7). Just as American film industry statistics often subsume the picture of Canada, we have to assume that industry concentration on statistics of the main European markets, France, Germany and the UK, is a convenient smokescreen to conceal several US commercial strategies. Europe is lumped together for the purpose of obtaining maximum revenue from DVD sales by 'chipping' disks so that products marketed in one region will not play in another unless 'unchipped'. Yet Europe is currently a mere adjunct of North America where mainstream film release is concerned, as US films are now released contemporaneously in Europe as a strategy, among other things, of avoiding piracy. As Sheehy hints in the same short article, if Irish statistics were given separate exposure in the reports of multinational companies based in England (i.e. London), it might become clear that results were proportionately better in Ireland, although presumably not as a result of more effort! Ireland is coterminous with the UK as far as film distribution is concerned and is similarly dominated by American majors. Statistics show that in 2004, the Republic and the UK had very close rates of household television use (79% and 82% respectively) and close rates of VCR penetration (74% and 88%), but that Ireland has some catching up to do with DVD-player penetration (EAO 2005/2: 10–15).

Although there has been considerable multiplex development since the 1990s, the increase in cinemas from 172 in 1990 to 280 in 1999 and 335 in 2004 has been concentrated in the Republic's five main cities – Dublin, Cork, Galway, Limerick and Waterford (Forest 2001: 290–1) – and 36% of seats are in multiplexes (EAO 2005/3: 29). The Irish are second only to Iceland in having a high rate of annual visits to the cinema, an average of 4.29 (the UK average is 2.88). The Republic produces around ten feature films a year (with a low of two in 2002), but only four or five (nine in 2003) achieve a release elsewhere in Europe.

The advantage that the Irish film industry does have over Belgium, Croatia and the rest is the fact that it is English-speaking and the huge diaspora populations in the UK, as well as the USA, Canada, Australia and New Zealand, constitute a potential audience. Historically, though, Irish artists have always been conscious of their predicament in sharing a language with the coloniser and, within language, of being reduced to essentialist stereotypes of intellectual and physical inferiority (Said 1993: 269–85). The persistence of stereotypes of a predominantly rural, backward island on the margins of Europe is maintained in the service of powerful interests outside Ireland, and this chapter will aim to tease out both the singularity of Irish cinema and its context, and the shape of those interested in its occlusion.

Colonial and postcolonial

Part of the fascination of Irish cinema for those of us who write in the UK and who are not Irish is the 'like/not like' quality, which is also experienced when considering the cinema of Britain's former colonies, Australia, New Zealand, Canada, and how this sense of difference prompts a reconsideration of our own cinema and culture, and particularly the persistence of imperialist discourses within it. Britain and 'the English' are a constant presence as colonizing 'other' in Irish culture, giving rise to many mythic constructions of Irishness seeking to combat annexation by Anglo-Saxon discourses of identity. The contemporary triumphalism of celebrations of Irish culture often glosses over the financial colonization of Ireland by both the UK and the USA. Above all, Irish culture was concerned to distance itself from the suggestion that shared sets of practices and values existed between Ireland and the UK, but as Richard Kearney outlines, modern Ireland has to surmount several areas of difficulty in doing this (1997: 2–12). Conceptualizing the Republic of Ireland as state is difficult when a consensus of shared values between Ulster and the Republic fails; Ireland as territory raises the problem of both the UK and the Republic laying claim to Ulster; defining Ireland in terms of ethnicity is meaningless when not only does the Irish diaspora amount to some 70 million persons but the reality of a modern, multicultural reality is ignored; Ireland as Celtic culture ignores the fact that contemporary culture displays a greater diversity than the racial paradigm; and Ireland as the country of the Gaelic language is a problem when it is spoken by such a small minority. There is consequently a deep need to repossess a sense of identity in the imaginary, and cinema has been a key player in this task.

Irish culture has evolved several strategies in this regard and there exist interesting parallels between the overarching myths of Irish culture and those of the Basque country – another fiercely independent region obsessed with its own distinctiveness. The struggle to achieve separateness has predominantly taken two forms, that of sacrificial martyrdom and the myth of Mother Ireland – a myth which combines both nurturing and the fierce mother who incites her sons to sacrifice their blood in the fight for the nation (Kearney 1997:

116–19). The former is a very male struggle, the latter an idealized representation of the national, pre-existing the colonial rupture, and effectively limiting the possibility of contemporary Irish women's incorporation into active representation of the nation. There is a parallel between the Republic and the fragmented Basque identity described by Stone (2002: 133). *Euskal Herria, País Vasco* and the Basque country are three nations in one, like Ireland containing the construction of the nation as a mythic place of warriors 'hidden deep inside the impenetrable and ancient language'; the modern designation of the area which seems much smaller and limited; and the autonomous, industrialized nation as seen from abroad. The contemporary Republic is a place of potent myths, the name of a small country on the margins of Western Europe and an industrialized nation which has given rise to the nomenclature of 'Celtic tiger' in its aggressively capitalist success. In many respects it has been a richer, more successful economy than that of the UK until recently, and its population is widely perceived to be better educated and more entrepreneurial than its neighbours.

All these contradictions and emotional investments in these representations are structured into recent Irish cinema, especially in its use of stereotypes. As we have seen, the performance of peasant idiocy, of local yokelry has been a constant feature in cultures which, knowing themselves at a disadvantage, play to their stereotyping as a strategy to undermine their cultural enemies. The Irish have perfected this ploy and brought it to a fine art in playing with stereotypes of 'paddywackery'. *Hear My Song* (Peter Chelsom, UK/Ireland, 1991) displays many of these. Mickey O'Neill (Adrian Dunbar) is a small-time impresario who hears the rumours that the great, popular Irish tenor, Joseph Locke, has fled to Ireland to avoid the taxman and determines to find him in order to recoup his own fortunes. Hearing rumours of concerts by a singer bearing a remarkable resemblance to Locke, Mickey sets off with his friend, following the trail to the depths of the Irish countryside. The scene where the trail leads them to an archetypal Irish pub contains myriad character stereotypes. There are wide-angle long-shots of the greenness of the empty countryside, sparsely populated with low, white-painted houses, the drinking men playing their illegal poker games in the pub cellar including the rural idiot who goes to the pub to have his rotten tooth pulled, the beetle-browed vet who doubles as dentist, various local eccentrics, and the canny, reticent figure of the singer.

These stereotypes persist in recent films such as *Man About Dog* (Paddy Breathnach, UK/Ireland, 2004), which follows a group of three young men and their attempts to get rich with a 'winning' greyhound. Myths of Irish fecklessness, energy, violence and cunning combine in the antics of the three to reclaim the dog (which they have sold when it appears a loser) in the face of the interest of rural 'hard men'.

There are many ambiguities in the Irish use of stereotypical images of themselves. Helen Kelly-Holmes surmises that a change occurred when media and other texts originating outside the national or regional sphere started to become accessible, and the 'prescribed hierarchies' of representations preferred by Church and state, formed in the interests of national coherence, could no longer be controlled (2000: 20). The very knowingness and irony and frequent excess signal their disruptive nature, which Homi Bhabha recognizes as crucial disjunctive spaces and signs for the emergence of new historical subjects (1994:

216–19). That, in the Irish case, involves recognition of themselves as transnational subjects and part of cultural globality, and a population which is with difficulty evolving a new sense of nation which takes account of the presence of other migrants within it. The persistence of negative stereotypes of Irishness in British culture represents an attempt to normalize the colonial experience and the disruption which the conflict between Catholic and Protestant in Ulster creates in the picture of Britain as a modern, postcolonial state. The psychic struggle for a hegemonic view of territory results in the eruption of words, events and images which cannot be contained within dominant discourse in both the North and South of Ireland, and in Britain. The excessive cries of 'IRA propaganda' which greet any film or television programme in Britain seeking to explore historical moments such as the nineteenth-century potato famine, Easter Rising, the Irish Civil war or the Troubles in Northern Ireland are indications of unfinished business.

British representations of Irishness have tended to demonize the Irish. In *Odd Man Out* (Carol Reid, UK, 1947), the actions of the inept terrorist, Johnny (James Mason), are represented as irrational and beyond explanation and he is depicted as a victim, trapped by his environment of inward-looking community and hermetic politics. The *mise-en-scène* emphasizes the closed nature of his Ulster community through tight shots in enclosed spaces, *noir* lighting and low-angle shots which emphasize confinement and the lack of a wider view. The visual claustrophobia of the *mise-en-scène* is an objective correlative of ambiguous emotions around the limiting of opportunities represented by the weight of the historical past and the constant lure of escape which has resulted in the Irish diaspora.

An evolution in British versions of the stereotypes can be seen in *The Long Good Friday* (John Mackenzie, UK, 1980), in which London gangster Harold's (Bob Hoskins) acceptance of the stereotypes of the Irish as mad Micks prevents him from identifying his new enemies. Harold is on the verge of sealing a lucrative partnership in crime between his East End criminal empire and the American mafia for the exploitation of London's former docklands. His shadowy and violent enemy is revealed as the IRA, poised to establish themselves as sole operators in rake-offs from development contracts. The excessive violence of the bombings, knifings and abductions, and the metaphor of the abbatoir for both criminal activity and the turning upside down of received ideas, indicate problems with the administration of territory which can be read as an allegory of British difficulties with their colonial role in Ireland. However, cinematic and televisual constructions of Irishness in British productions have changed in the last 20 years, no doubt due to the rise of 'Celtic cool' displayed in beer advertisements, Irish-themed pubs and music.

Contemporary Irish cinema and its past

The history of film in the Republic is that of a poor cinema, intertwined with and less important than politics. After the Easter Rising of 1916 and the establishment by treaty of the Irish Free State in 1922, the main priority was to establish social and economic stability, and although a fledgling Irish cinema had existed from the late nineteenth century, political factionalism and the world economic recession made production problematic. Kevin

Rockett has charted the continual attempts to set up a modest infrastructure for the industry from the 1920s to the end of the 1980s, none of which was successful and most of which fell prey to the presence of Britain's more powerful economy and film industry (1988: 3–124). All of the measures tried, such as the establishment of Ardmore Studios, a trades union and the Irish Film Board, represented bids to take control of Irish culture. The Irish government established The Irish Film Board/Bord Scannán na hÉireann in 1981 and abandoned it in 1987. It was re-activated in 1993 as, by then, a slow groundswell of Irish productions had culminated in five Oscar nominations for *My Left Foot* (Jim Sheridan, Ireland/UK, 1989), Best Actor wins for Daniel Day-Lewis and Best Supporting Actress for Brenda Fricker, followed by the phenomenal critical and financial success of *The Crying Game* (Neil Jordan, UK/Japan, 1992) (Gibbons 2005: 215). As the next section will explore, Jordan is an Irish writer/director whose position on the national/diasporic cusp (Naficy 2001: 8) enables his work to challenge accepted notions of identity.

The event which brought the Irish film industry into the sphere of the postmodern, global economy was the appointment, in 1993, of Michael D. Higgins as Minister for Arts, Culture and the Gaeltacht (at a time when the UK had no equivalent, culture being a problematic term for the Thatcher government, depending as it does on a sense of community and a common memory of texts felt to be important). With his slogan of 'The last great colonisation is of the imagination', Higgins's overt agenda was to combat the Americanization of contemporary culture by putting in place the means by which the Irish could speak with their own voice, and he recognized the importance of postcolonial resistence by describing his country as a 'First World country with a Third World memory'.[1] The original Section 35 legislation put in place generous tax breaks in order to attract productions by offering individuals a tax-free deduction from total income and companies a deduction from eligible profits. Individual investors might claim up to I£25,000 ($38,000) annually; a company investing might claim up to I£350,000 ($530,000) per annum; corporate investors could choose to claim up to I£1.05 million ($1.6 million) in one single qualifying investment in one film in a three-year period (White and Sangey 1994: 17). Certification of projects using Section 35 finance was carried out by Higgins's Ministry, and conditions of tax reliefs and subventions were designed to ensure the commercial viability of the production, that 75% of the work (lower for co-productions) was carried out in the Republic and that the budget included provision for training. Productions supported had to make a significant contribution to the national economy and act as an effective stimulus to the creation of an indigenous film industry. The Irish Film Board was revived under the initial direction of Rod Stoneman (a former UK Channel 4 commissioning editor) and given a budget of I£15 million for production loans and script development. This legislation had an immediate effect in making Ireland a very attractive place in which to film, and the training requirement was influential in building up a creative industry infrastructure. Although the fund was criticized for supporting financially unsuccessful Irish films and foreign blockbusters, the initial legislation recognized that contemporary films were unlikely to amortize their costs in such a small cinema market and that partnerships with foreign companies would at least provide Irish men and women with the opportunity of acquiring key skills.

Section 35 was revised in 1997 with doubled funds, to attract big-budget international projects like *Saving Private Ryan* (Steven Spielberg, USA, 1998). Legislation has been renewed under successive Ministers (Sile De Valera and John O'Donoghue) and it is now known as Section 481 funding. The result has been big-budget international films using Irish locations and a small but significant number of local films which put Irish voices on the cinema screen and on television, and which are exported through globalized media systems to countries of the Irish diaspora. This solution has the virtue of overcoming one of the problems of small countries: it is difficult to maintain the level of your share of your own market if you have a small population. Ensuring that foreign film production takes place in the Republic keeps people employed and ideas in motion so that some continuity is generated. Since 1994 there have been interesting co-productions drawing on the Republic's tax break monies and on the relatively substantial budgets available to BBC Northern Ireland. In the Irish solution, financial success is not as important as cultural success in their version of the local solution. Minister of Arts, Sport and Tourism, John O'Donoghue, recognized the importance of culture as commodity by identifying it as 'perhaps the most resonant, identifiable and enduring aspects of our international identity'.[2]

This commodification of the local has to be seen in the context of the Republic's benefiting from the global largesse of the European Union in the form of the subventions available to small countries from the inception of the MEDIA programme in the early 1990s. Irish writers have benefited from SCRIPT, which has supported their pre-production work, and later training awards. Eurimages has also assisted co-productions.

Paul Greengrass's 2002 film *Bloody Sunday* (UK/Ireland) provides an example of the interesting work that producers and directors have to do to get their budget together. The subject – the dramatization of the Ulster civil rights protest march on 30 January 1972 in which 13 marchers were killed and four injured by British troops – was controversial. In the case of *Bloody Sunday*, this involved Granada TV arranging a co-production deal with Jim Sheridan's company, Hell's Kitchen, which meant that the project automatically accessed Section 481 money; and also setting up a company, January Films, in the Republic of Ireland, which allowed for 10% of the film's budget to be offset through tax. After this, a shortfall of £100,000 was met by the UK Film Council. *Bloody Sunday* was nominated for many film festival awards, the 2002 Berlin Golden Bear and prize of the Ecumenical Jury being awarded to Greengrass. The film's budget was $5 million and this was recouped by cinema release in the USA. *Bloody Sunday* had considerable appeal outside the UK and Ireland and its controversial subject has ensured its 'legs' in video and DVD issues and re-issues.

In the 2000s other regions and countries have got their act together to lure film production to their shores, the countries of Eastern Central Europe being particularly successful and cheaper than Ireland. New Zealand followed the Irish model in the interests of supporting its domestic film industry, playing on the variety of geographies and climates available. The Irish film industry has suffered from the competition, but plays the English-language card in attracting American productions.

Creativity and difference

Susan Hayward asserts the existence of seven discernible typologies which will assist the enunciation of the 'national' of a cinema – narratives, genres, codes and conventions, gesturality and morphology, the star as sign, cinema as mobiliser of the nation's myths and of the myth of the nation, and cinema of the centre and cinema of the periphery (1993: 8–9). Narratives draw on indigenous culture and provide a repertoire of forms by which a culture 'understands its own significance' (Turner 1986: 18). 'Gestures, words, intonations, attitudes' (Hayward 1993: 12) affirm a construction of nation, resolutely marking it off from the Englishness of Ireland's neighbour, but doubled as the speech patterns of Ulster and the Republic are quite different.

Ireland has a long theatrical history and the Republic's actors have a pre-eminent site of excellence in the Abbey Theatre in Dublin. As a result of the theatrical tradition and the possibilities offered by TV production, there exists a wide pool of Irish actors who can embody a range of cultural models. The speech patterns of Irish speakers of English differ greatly from English delivery, providing instant markers of difference. Those of the South are based on the sentence construction and expression of the Gaelic heritage. The expressiveness of gestures, based on an archaic slow delivery of meaning via speech and body movement indicating the psychic importance of the verbal message, derives from pre-modern cultural modes. In the twentieth century, the Irish reputation for wit and sarcasm, explosions of meaning in witty aphorisms, facilitated the quick-fire repartee characteristic of Irishness, in direct contrast to the pregnant pauses of rural dramas. Both modes are sides of the same cultural coin. In *The Field* (Jim Sheridan, Ireland/UK, 1990), the silence of Maggie McCabe (Brenda Fricker) is able to evoke female resistance to the patriarchal obsession with land and control of all aspects of family life which resulted in the suicide of her eldest son. The power of this control is visualized in the opening sequences in which Bull McCabe (Richard Harris) and his son, Tadgh (Sean Bean), undertake the painful journey from the seashore where they have gathered heavy burdens of seaweed, over dunes and hillsides to the verdant green of the field McCabe rents and whose fertility is the direct result of their labours. When an incoming American buys the field and has other plans for it, Bull kills him, setting in motion Tadgh's flight and death and the dissolution of the family. Richard Harris was nominated for an Oscar and Golden Globe for his performance, and *The Field* materializes Irish society's dependence on the family as a bulwark against outside exploitation, while also showing the psychic damage which it causes.

With the theatrical traditions and years of television drama providing training grounds for actors on both sides of the border and in Britain, there are now hundreds of actors who can people a range of genres from the classics to serious drama, soap opera, comedy, crime drama and science fiction. Many of those who have achieved international recognition – Stephen Rea, Gabriel Byrne, Liam Neeson, Colm Meaney, Ray McAnally, Ciarán Hinds, Brenda Fricker, Colin Farrell – also work regularly between Britain and Ireland in film and television. Others are familiar to Irish or art-house audiences, or – like David Kelly and Ruth McCabe – provide the 'typical' faces and voices which lend authenticity to Irish stories. The sheer range of talent enables a variety of cultural types to be portrayed, from traditional stereotypes of rural Ireland and the Church, tales of political conflict needing representations of leaders and factions, to comedy drama requiring actors of different generations to represent contemporary reality. Brendan Gleeson, for example, is able to play an inept minor Dublin criminal, Bunny Kelly, in *I Went Down* (Paddy Breathnach, Ireland/UK, 1997), whose expressions of puzzlement and non-comprehension do not prevent him from outwitting the Cork gangsters at the end; IRA leader, Thomas Macken, in *Love Lies Bleeding* (Michael Winterbottom, UK, 1993), whose charisma carries his foot soldiers along with him, while concealing layers of disinformation and manipulation; and the blunt and uncomplicated Father Bubbles in *The Butcher Boy* (Neil Jordan, Ireland/USA, 1997).

The increase in Irish film production from the 1970s had enabled some film-makers to get a start in the industry so that a small number of directors were already identified as being of international class. Many had moved from Ireland to Britain for several years and relished the idea of pursuing a career in the domestic arena. Neil Jordan, Jim Sheridan, Pat O'Connor and Joe Comerford achieved recognition in the 1980s, but only the first two have achieved authorial status and movement into the quality zone explored in Chapter Three. Jim Sheridan has to some extent been able to buffer his career from the economic ups and downs of the film industry by forming a production company, Hell's Kitchen. Neil Jordan is a writer as well as a director and producer. He has been recognized as one of the most interesting Irish film-makers but, like Michael Winterbottom, the range of genres which he has used and his regular forays into international productions make him difficult to categorize. The phenomenally successful *Interview with the Vampire: The Vampire Chronicles* (USA, 1994) was a spectacular, gothic adaptation of Anne Rice's cult horror books with American stars; *In Dreams* (USA, 1999) was a big-budget ($30 million) supernatural horror film; *The End of the Affair* (UK/USA, 1999) was another big-budget ($23 million) adaptation, this time of Graham Greene; and *The Good Thief* (France/UK/Ireland/Canada, 2001–2) was an international co-production set in the South of France about an aging gambler's (Nick Nolte) last heist. Jordan's career conforms to the patterns observed earlier in that his career was established in interesting, critically regarded films for Britain's Channel 4's Film Four production arm, but received a boost from the success of *The Crying Game* (UK/Japan, 1992) and the offer of increasingly large budgets. In effect, Jordan's filmography is revealing of the circumstances of Irish film-making. He achieved success before Section 35 funding was set up in 1993. His productions have never been wholly Irish and in fact reflect the reality of the transnational movements of peoples and finance. *Angel* (Ireland/UK, 1981–82) creates a heightened reality through the insistent colour tones of purple and gold and its use of saxophone music to emphasize the schizophrenic nature of modern Irish society through the young musician Danny's (Stephen Rea) journey to revenge the killing of a mute girl. His quest takes him through the muddy farmyard of Mary (Sorcha Cusack), whose desperation at the murder of her husband is one of the recurring (but subordinate) themes of the effect on women of political and sectarian violence. Besides the constant presence of American culture, the extreme violence of Jordan's films is another indicator of the difficulty of establishing a modern Irish identity which can incorporate the everyday elements of contemporary life.

History or heritage?

Chapter Eight has explored the nature of the historical fiction film which has been such a staple of cinematic production from the 1980s onwards and has suggested that the genre's interest for those who study film lies in the tensions between the desire for stasis and fixed 'common-sense' interpretations of the past and recognition that the imagined world requires less fixed notions of community, history, gender, sexuality and society. Lance Pettitt's analyses of certain 'key' Irish films started with the premise that they were 'largely uncontroversial and designed to be safe', but identified oblique explorations of 'institutional and collective silences about sexuality and racism in the public domain, repressed in almost a decade of social conservatism preceding this period [1988–92]' (2000: 115–16). In the period after 1990 which interests us here, 'structured absences' of attention to social change are not the norm. Difficulties and disruptions are therefore firmly structured into Irish cinematic reworkings of the past, even when they are set in the 1950s and 1960s, decades which often allow (usually male) film-makers to ignore feminism and women's demands for equality. Full consideration of the Irish cinema's engagement with its often emotionally contested past is lacking in published work, which usually focuses on films such as *The Butcher Boy* (Neil Jordan, Ireland/USA, 1997) or films about 'the Troubles' in Northern Ireland. In a land where versions of historical truth are hotly contested, such as the events surrounding the death of Michael Collins or the attribution of blame in sectarian murders, recourse to the past inevitably sets in motion conflicting discourses which often occlude realities of class and disempowerment. David Brett regards Ireland as an important area for study because there is no agreed 'national' narrative, 'nor a set of representative strategies around which an unproblematic "heritage" could be constructed' (1996: 8). Brett considers that 'heritage' is a product of the process of modernization, 'which, by eroding customs and expectations, forces us to re-articulate our sense of the past' and which is heavily concerned with legitimating the present. As this book has observed, a parallel process is taking place in German cinema to review national history from the perspective of unification rather than the ideologically different interpretations of the DDR and BRD.

In the hands of Neil Jordan, the complexity of the work of combining conflicting discourses finds expression in his adaptation of Patrick McCabe's well-known book. *The Butcher Boy* is set in a small Ulster town on the borders with the Republic, whose visualization casts it as a prison. At the centre of the town is a wide square with a fountain to which the young protagonist, Francie Brady (Eamonn Owens), obsessively returns. The film's plot charts his entrapment and escapes from his cramped and poverty-stricken home in an alley off the square, from the reform school, to the seashore of 'beautiful Bundoran' and to Dublin. The square is effectively a panopticon, furnishing a means of social control whereby the inhabitants are able to monitor each other's behaviour and to control it through the power of gossip which matches every action against preordained and sanctioned modes of behaviour. However, traditional social hierarchies and interaction have already been de-stabilized by the accelerating effects of colonization in the 1950s, embodied in the insertion into the community of the Nugent family who have returned from England and whose modern fitted kitchen symbolizes the buying into identical images of modernity required by contemporary capitalism. Here the panopticon is an ambivalent space. The image of the prison has been seen as both place of martyrdom and symbol of entrapment and desperation (Zucker and Moen 2000: 49). In Jordan's film it is both. *Mise-en-scène* accentuates the confined nature of the Bradys' cramped house; the parents' reaction to entrapment is alcohol and jazz for Da (Stephen Rea), frenetic cake-making and suicide for Ma (Aisling O'Sullivan). Francie's inadequate parenting has freed his imagination so that his experiencing of American culture through stories of cowboys and Indians has more reality than his indigenous culture. The exciting and longed-for visits of his uncle Alo (Ian Hart) from England are a narrative correlative of the tales of colonial conquest, which Francie enjoys in his comics and play. The child makes interpretations of his own condition and his relationships with others on the basis of the simple schemas of comic books and family and religious myths. Behaviour, knowledge or reactions which do not fit the stable world view which he has constructed are met with verbal or physical violence. Francie's response to losing his friend Joe to boarding school is excessive, but based on comic-book logic – if the hero wants something, he goes out and gets it. The imagination is the realm in which Francie seeks explanations for his condition and, since his version of the imaginary has to draw on the limited cultural tropes available to his marginalized existence, it is unable to sustain him. He is trapped as much by the formation of his imagination as he is by narrow and classist social conventions. The character of Francie constitutes a huge disruption to the process of historical closure and the progress of his increasingly inappropriate behaviour leads inexorably to Mrs Nugent's (Fiona Shaw) murder, allowing the sacred institutions of church and rural community to be examined, and found to be as mad as Francie, along the way. Jordan's use of the singer Sinéad O'Connor to represent the Virgin Mary in Francie's visions is at once the throwing down of the gauntlet to conservative elements in Irish society for whom O'Connor represents a transgressive model of Irish womanhood and, in its very excess of colour and representation, a signalling of the redundancy of the traditional use of the figure as solace for social disempowerment.

Helped by his voice-over, it remains ambiguous whether Francie (young or old) believes in his vision, but the juxtaposition of the visions to sequences in the reform school introduce another problematic element into this representation of Irish history. Francie's companions in the school are firmly designated as bogmen, the 'colchies' disparaged by contemporary Dubliners, who represent the rural backwardness which is perceived to hamper the Irish road to full modernity, while still being able to reap the rewards of government and EU subsidies intent on preserving a mythical ideal of nationhood rooted in the soil. As in many European cultures, the rural arena is fraught with contradictions and conflicting identities, from the incomplete incorporation of Sicily into Italian notions of nation, to the attractions of the Welsh and Scottish borderlands for British culture, the difficulties of incorporating the Basque homeland into images of Spanish modernity, and the construction of 'otherness' of the various 'nations' or tribes of the former Yugoslavia. The hyperreality of Jordan's representation of Francie's world, the casual violence of institutions towards him (the reform school and the paedophile priest), the panopticon and the *mise-en-scène* of excess and containment all indicate a problematic conception of the conservative past and the postcolonial present.

Michael Collins (UK/Ireland/USA, 1996) was a big-budget production which won Jordan the Golden Lion at the 1996 Venice film festival. Centred around an iconic figure in the struggle for national independence, the film raises many of the mysteries and ambiguities of historical representation, but is unable to escape the weight of representation of historic moments of nationhood. Jordan does achieve some complexity in his recreation of the storming of the Dublin central post office in 1916 and the struggle for nationhood by emphasizing the difference between Collins (Liam Neeson) and De Valera (Alan Rickman), but whereas De Valera's political career provides a succession of images of his place in Irish history from this iconic moment, the figure of Collins was a void into which many meanings could be poured. Jordan makes De Valera an ascetic, controlled and slightly Machiavellian figure, and his single-mindedness is stressed to the detriment of a more complex delineation of the conservative social legislation with which he was associated. In this he is helped by Alan Rickman's previous roles as softly spoken villains in Hollywood films. The strategy of the real Collins of avoiding historical fixity by immortalizing himself in photographs allows Jordan to depict him in Liam Neeson as a towering presence, a man of soldierly action and intellectual acuity. This means that the film can be read and appreciated on several levels and explains how it might be enjoyed in Britain, where the Irish war of independence was a symptom of imperial decline. Whereas in Ireland, Collins as hero is kept alive by the public narratives associated with the founding of the Republic, for such a story to reach a global audience it must detach itself from a narrow context and draw on widely accessible repertoires of cultural representations of masculinity. These include Hollywood genres such as the western and gangster film, the tragedy and historical epic with their roots in Greek drama, Western and Eastern myths of heroic male quests. In contemporary cinematic fiction these are joined by the counter-cultural stories of anti-heroes, of anti-imperialist struggles and exciting clashes with authority in ecological movements. When contemporary news programmes deliver images of modern warfare at the same time as reports of increasing state legislation to regulate behaviour regarded as anti-social, soldier narratives provide rich and complex forms of investment in the social world. As Graham Dawson explores, the 'narrative imagining of lived masculinities' in soldier narratives 'organizes the available possibilities for a masculine self in terms of the physical appearance and conduct, the values and aspirations and the tastes and desires that will be recognized as "masculine" in contemporary social life' (1994: 23). In the case of Neeson's performance of Collins, these include adherence to high ideals, selflessness in the service of the community, decisiveness, the ability to identify goals and plan to achieve them, ruthlessly if necessary, a sense of ease in the homosocial world of male endeavour, intelligence and humour – all qualities of use to men climbing the managerial ladder. The ability to command and lead is connoted by Neeson's physical size – his commanding presence – even if his ability to fully represent the nation is less well realized in the narrative space given over to his relationship with Kitty (Julia Roberts). *Michael Collins* made slightly more worldwide than it did in the USA, reflecting the appeal of this historical account.

Breakfast on Pluto (Neil Jordan, Ireland/UK, 2005) is another McCabe adaptation with a central character who constitutes the disruption which provokes a different assessment of both Ireland and England. The central character of Patrick 'Pussy' Braden ('Kitten' in the film) is a glamrock fan and transvestite who leaves County Monaghan to experience London in the 1960s and 1970s. McCabe saw this character as epitomizing 'a culture which isn't entirely First World yet' and who lacks the generations of urban knowledge to take part in global culture and survive (Case 1998: 22–3). In the film, Kitten (Cillian Murphy) brings his rural Irish mentality into the First World of London at a historical moment in which stable ideas of politics and sexuality are breaking down. S/he occupies plural liminal spaces as a transgressive presence from a political border and a liminal presence in a chaotic historical moment. Kitten's moulding of his body in simulacra of femininity in make-up and perfectly co-ordinated suits, dresses, shoes, gloves and hats is an attempt to negate difference, while the excessiveness of transvestite recreations of femininity is a visual marker of it (Naficy 2001: 24). *Breakfast on Pluto* is an example of accented cinema which, through the central character, creates a Thirdspace, 'distinguished by an all-inclusive simultaneity ... subjectivity and objectivity, the abstract and the concrete, the real and the imagined...' (Soja 1996: 56–7, quoted in Naficy 2001: 213), and the impossibility of Kitten's desire for fixity, represented by his search for his mother, is metaphorized in the repeated shots of his catching sight of her travelling down an escalator to the underground while he is travelling in the opposite direction.

As Martin McLoone observed, 'there is nothing in *The Butcher Boy* that would allow for empty "heritage" nostalgia' (2000: 217) and in fact the 'careful evocation of small-town rural life' which he notices is a hallmark of a type of political cinema for which postmodern intertextuality and play with surfaces is not an option. The importance of the referent, the illusionistic detail which insistently points to an exterior context, and at the same time the visual and performative excess produce a heightened reality which forces an interpretation of the image (Wood 2005a: 109).

Pat O'Connor's adaptations of literary works set in small-town or rural Irish pasts also engage with oppressive traditional social models which cast a long shadow into the present via the lived memories of those who experienced them. *Circle of Friends* (Ireland/UK/USA, 1995), set in the 1950s, uses the story of Bernadette 'Benny' Hogan (Minnie Driver) and a historical moment when girls were entering higher education and encountering dilemmas of personal choice, in order to explore women's struggle to reconcile tradition and modernity. Benny and her friends embody this clash, Benny in her voluptuous figure and intelligence, Nan (Saffron Burrows) in her willowy looks and willingness to use a sexual relationship to trap into marriage the cold Englishman, Simon Westwood (Colin Firth), and, when that fails, Benny's boyfriend Chris. Benny's version triumphs at the end in her successful combination of traditional modesty and goodness, with the promise of sensuality and an equal partnership. Nan's employment of the few strategies traditionally open to women to snare status men links her firmly to the past, but *Circle* and *Dancing at Lughnasa* (Ireland/UK/USA, 1998) are both interesting for the presence of people watching the protagonists, performing the panoptic function of social control. In the latter film, which splits the feminine principle into the five Mundy sisters, the character of Kate (Meryl Streep) performs the function of self-discipline in acceptance of social norms and gender templates. As Foucault observed (1977: 202–3) in his study of the panopticon, force is unnecessary when the subject is aware of his/her visibility. The disciplined body interiorizes the power relation, thereby becoming 'the principle of his own subjection'.

The Magdalene Sisters (Peter Mullan, Ireland/UK, 2002) takes social surveillance into the prison of the Magdalene laundries, asylums set up by the Catholic Church to punish and police women deemed disruptive to patriarchal order. Mullan's film delivers the 'we-feeling' of outrage at the plight of girls punished for being too feisty and self-confident, for inconveniently reporting rape as well as for producing children out of wedlock. The mental and physical cruelties meted out by the nuns shock by their willing acquiescence in the role of policing patriarchy, and the spectre of the holocaust which they evoke. Although attempts have been made to identify an Irish version of heritage cinema, the films themselves reveal that the impetus to construct a unitary and authentic version of the past is fraught with difficulty. Indeed, as Colin Graham proposes, authenticity in the Irish case prompts the question, 'whose authenticity?' (2001: 140–1). Not only are Irish historical films the results of international co-productions – mainly with the primary colonizing powers of the last and present centuries – but their spectacular visuals provoke the thought that they are merely reproducing a postmodern simulacrum for consumption by international audiences. As this section has shown, in common with some other European cinemas, the psychic investment of attempting to reconcile chaos and difference opens them up to the depth and complexity totally absent from the theme park.

Television and low-budget film production

As Lance Pettitt has intimated, television drama is not made in a creative free space but is a product of the economic, political and cultural forces around at the time (2000: 228). As Chapter Six explored, contemporary feature films are increasingly made with TV co-production finance, but the context of state television's financing from tax payers' money generates levels of uncertainty about future commitment to producing feature films. Radio Telefis Éireann (RTÉ) is the Republic's state TV channel, which following 1993 media legislation was forced to devote a proportion of its budget to the commissioning of independently produced programmes. Paddy Barrett claimed that although RTÉ's name appeared on half of the features supported by the Irish Film Board, its contribution was extremely modest – as little as I£500,000 ($800,000) a year from 1994, although a massive worldwide market for Irish drama and willing co-financiers had been identified (1997: 24). With the addition of commercial TV stations to the Irish media map, there were already considerable worries at the end of the 1990s about the future of RTÉ and the viability of domestic financing of feature films. Barrett's anxieties have been borne out in the 2000s when the strength of the euro against the dollar has made it less attractive to film in Ireland.

Films made in Ulster about the Troubles started to change in the mid-1990s with writers Graham Reid's *Life After Life* (Tim Fywell, UK, 1995) and *Love Lies Bleeding* (Michael Winterbottom, UK, 2003). The former explored the mismatch between IRA rhetoric and contemporary reality via the figure of Leo Doyle (Lorcan Cranitch), who is released from prison on licence after many years and finds himself regarded as a political dinosaur. The young are more interested in joyriding in stolen cars than throwing bombs and his former girlfriend is married and working in a supermarket whose trollies with their coin mechanism are a total puzzle to him. The latter film uses another prisoner on licence's quest to find the murderer of his girlfriend to delineate a moment of internecine leadership struggles leading up to the start of the peace process. Conn (Mark Rylance) witnesses the evolution of an 'acceptable face' to Sinn Fein leadership and realizes that, under the 'new' rhetoric, lie the same levels of violence as before. Although his subsequent £6 million BBCNI TV drama about the 1916 uprising used a love story to tease out the different players in North and South, Bennett received much abuse from the right-wing English press as if it were a political tract for the nationalists (Bennett 2000).

In the early 1990s sectarian violence made filming in Northern Ireland an unattractive option, but the defusing of political animosities in the late 1990s, and jealous looks at the Republic's film funding, led to the setting up of the Northern Ireland Film Commission in 1997 and the Northern Ireland Film Production Fund, supported by the European Union, in 1999. Funds from the British National Lottery have also been crucial as Northern Irish films can access funding from both the Arts Councils of England and Northern Ireland. The major player in Ulster was BBC Northern Ireland, whose Head of Drama, Robert Cooper, has had a pivotal influence. The turning point in engagement with contemporary reality came with Robert Cooper's optioning of a cult novel by Colin Bateman, *Divorcing Jack* (David Caffrey, UK, 1998), a hilarious dark comedy co-produced by the BBC and Scala Pictures for £3 million. A European co-producer (Ima Films) and an international sales deal with Winchester Films contributed to the production package, but lottery grants of £200,000 ($340,000) from the Arts Council of Northern Ireland and £800,000 ($1.036 million) from the Arts Council of England enabled the film to be shot in Ulster. The film differs from dark films about the Troubles in embedding its political moments in a fast-paced and surrealist black comedy. Filmed in 1997, but set in a vision of a fictional Ulster on the verge of independence in 1999, the protagonist, Dan Starkey (David Thewlis), is a hard-drinking and unfaithful journalist covering the election of Ulster's first Prime Minister. Thrown out by his wife, Dan finds his girlfriend, Margaret (Laura Fraser), murdered and embarks on his investigation into her death through the murky world of corruption and sectarian politics. In this he is helped by the American journalist, Parker (Richard Grant), and Lee (Rachel Griffiths), a nurse who doubles as a strippergram nun by night. *Divorcing Jack* is notable for Ulster accents and depiction of the normality of life in the province as well as the convoluted political situation. None of the protagonists lives in a red-brick terraced house and the film's *mise-en-scène* reveals that Northern Irish drama has reached the stage where the cramped, working-class interiors have been left behind and a range of middle-class interiors can be portrayed without signalling them out for comment.

More recent Irish films play with the stereotypes and turn them on their head. *The Most Fertile Man in Ireland* (Dudi Appleton, UK/Ireland, 1999) features Eamon (Chris Marshall), a young man working for a small-town detective agency who discovers the potency of his sperm and is persuaded by his colleague Millicent (Bronagh Gallagher) to market himself to infertile Irish women. The course of this marketing opportunity does not run smooth, due to the competing charms of Eamon's love interest, Rosie (Kathy Kiera Clarke). In effect, the splitting of the female characters between the sassy and entrepreneurial Millicent and traditional and religious Rosie embodies the contradictions for women in the formation of an image of contemporary Irish modernity, which finds expression in the saturated colours of the *mise-en-scène*, primary reds, blues and greens being present with the vivid orange of Eamon's hair. These draw attention to the film as fantasy in its construction of a new entrepreneurialism and the repetition of orange in the hair of many resulting babies, no small embarrassment to Eamon, signals the fact that business success has not been successfully incorporated into national myth.

When Brendan Met Trudy (Kieron J. Walsh, UK/Ireland, 2000) was co-produced by BBC Films and two Irish companies with IFB support, the BBC presence guaranteeing wider distribution outside Ireland. The DVD promotional campaign used good British and American reviews and internet sales companies clearly identified it as appealing to a diaspora audience by offering it at a discount with another Irish title. The improbable love affair between conservative Brendan and burglar Trudy provides a narrative twist to the romance, and for the conflict of tradition and modern life to be worked out in comedy. *About Adam* (Gerard Stembridge, Ireland/UK/USA, 2000) is another co-production with the BBC, with the presence of Miramax attracting a larger budget, and IFB support. A romantic comedy bearing resemblances to *Belle Époque* in Adam's (Stuart Townsend) conquest of three sisters, it differs in including their brother in the seductions, thus aiming at a young audience unoffended by sexual frankness and used to the TV complexities of *Sex and the City*. The interesting oscillation between postcard views of Irish countryside and images of modern 'swinging Dublin' reveals the international aims of this type of comedy.

Other IFB financial support has been for cross-border Irish co-productions, but most are small genre films which will appeal to the multiplex and TV audiences, with a potential life on DVD and TV in diaspora communities. They include crime films such as *Intermission* (John Crowley, Ireland/UK, 2004), horror and zombie flicks, black comedies and romances, family, music and football films, and a fast-paced comedy, *Inside I'm Dancing* (Damien O'Donnell, Ireland/UK/France, 2004) about two young disabled men, marketed as 'by the producer of *Billy Elliot* and the director of *East is East*'. The Republic's demographics include a large youth audience, which the existence of these popular films shows has been clearly identified by the IFB.

Conclusion

It is hard to avoid Ruth Barton's implied criticism of highlighting the usual suspects when discussing Irish cinema by looking only at *The Butcher Boy* or The Troubles films (2004: 3–4), but such films are interesting because they are so much products of their time. Ten years ago Hugh Linehan, a film critic for *The Irish Times*, wondered:

> What meaning and resonance do films like *Some Mother's Son, Nothing Personal* or *Michael Collins* hold for fans of *Trainspotting* and *Independence Day*? In Ireland they are major events, but elsewhere they are curiosities, postcards from a small country which, for a variety of reasons, has a disproportionately large presence on the international stage.
>
> (1996: 21)

Films of the 2000s have answered his question by, as Pettitt suggests, getting away from narrow considerations of Irishness and embracing 'the potentially liberating ideas of multiple identities (regional, federal, communal)' (2000: 18) in a vibrant contemporary world.

Ireland's politics lack resolution, but the concerns of the island have moved on. Ken Loach's *The Wind That Shakes the Barley* (Germany/Italy/Spain/France/Ireland/UK, 2006) is one of only a handful of films since 2000 to address political issues. Its funding by the IFB and Irish TV3 is part of Loach's usual complex financial package which includes distributors who have had previous success with his films, confirming his authorial status. Politics and the past have been superseded by politics without a capital letter, epitomized by *Pavee Lackeen* (Perry Ogden, Ireland, 2005), a study of Ireland's racial 'others', the traveller community, via engagement with the life of Winnie Maughan, whose traveller family are the butt of racial abuse and institutional interference and who live in conditions resembling 'Third World' poverty. It is significant that Irish culture is beginning to address those it has victimized, rather than itself as colonial victim. *Pavee Lackeen* won the London Film Festival's Satjajit Ray award.

As I have demonstrated in this chapter on the cinema of Ireland, the responses of this small country to the globalization of contemporary media are complex. The Republic has invested heavily in national funds to build and maintain an indigenous film industry so that its population will hear their own voices on the screen, and Ulster has responded with its own measures. The films examined show the difficulties of achieving a unitary voice and, since 1994, an accommodation with the institutions of Northern Ireland, which has resulted in more nuanced films reflecting the island's contested identities. Both the Republic and Ulster have become adept at accessing EU and MEDIA subventions in the pursuit of their aims. Although the number of established film directors is small, Irish actors are a great resource, explaining the absence of authorial cinema but the richness both of international-quality production (which wins prizes) and a vibrant low-budget sector of popular films. Ireland differs from Europe's bigger nations in not being a platform for concerted competition to Hollywood, instead using national funds to lure big-budget productions to the island in order to support the local industries. Ireland has enough conflicts of its own and enough contested history to provide narrative subjects, but the psychic investments of its different communities in Irish history prevent the evolution of a spectacular, 'heritage' take on it. The relentless pull towards referentiality of much Irish film-making indicates that there is too much at stake not to attempt to make sense of the past but, at the start of the new millennium, film-makers use contemporary stories to confound the stereotypes and work towards a new sense of Irish modernity.

The Irish Film Board is keenly embracing digital technology on the basis that digitizing film distribution is 'a manageable concept, roughly $50 million' in a small country and, in the case of *Man About Dog*, a digital release would have given a cheaper picture of the film's appeal in rural or urban Ireland than traditional 35mm distribution (Nahra 2006: 59–60). As this chapter demonstrates, institutional, political and commercial changes have delivered both big-budget international films and a solid bedrock of small, local films which speak to the multiplex audience in Irish accents.

Notes

1. Speech at the National Film Theatre, London, October 1995.
2. http://www.filmboard.ie/section_481.php (accessed 28.2.2005).

Conclusion

My study of contemporary European cinema has taken a long journey through the different cultural spaces available to the continent's film-makers. During the time that I have been teaching, researching and writing about this area, the film industries have evolved considerably and are set to develop further in the next few years – until the oil runs out at least.

In the Introduction I showed that European cinema has always been international in its scope, choice of subjects and distribution. I used globalization theory to introduce the question of the commercial imperatives of the world's prime provider of films, the USA, and the logical (in business terms) nature of its aims of vertical integration, global reach and the maximizing of marketing opportunities. In this current climate of commodification of films as products, studying the economic, commercial and legislative, as well as the artistic and cultural, context of European cinema is essential for a full understanding of a film's specificity and its very existence. Chapter One looked at the structures of the European film industries, how films are financed and exploited, and the role of the European Union in establishing a countervailing tendency to the global ambitions of American media capitalism. The globalizing tendencies of the EU have been set against the localizing ambitions of the regions of Europe, leading to tensions both in the production contexts of films and within the discourses of the films themselves.

Europe has always been characterized as producing a directors' cinema, of privileging the director as artist and source of meanings in filmic texts. Chapter Two examined the persistence of theories of authorship and art cinema, rejecting them as inadequate to explain the current situation. Recent films by directors who, according to the theoretical positions of the late 1970s and early 1980s, ought to be regarded as *auteurs*, that is, film-makers exerting control over their productions and maintaining a relationship with 'their' audience, demonstrate the difficulties of occupying the position of famous director at the start of the new millennium. When moderately successful directors are marketed on their names, why has it been so difficult to achieve *auteur* status? The answer is complex. The figure of the director is a commercial category which, like screenwriters, cinematographers, set designers and now CGI engineers and companies specializing in computer graphics, is taken into account when assessing a proposed film's budget and financing. Another factor which has to be considered is the increased speed of contemporary communications. A director like Michael Winterbottom responds very quickly to world – not national – events and cultural trends and produces a very varied filmography, which critics and academics then have difficulty in drawing together because his films do not show a neat progression of genre or theme.

Moreover, to make a truly auteurist, personal film reflecting the artistic aims of one person, a director either has to make low-budget, alternative or avant-garde films dependent on public subsidy, or get a commission from a television company. There are plenty of film-makers who choose the former and who become adept at using the calendar of grant applications. Either they stay in that sector or they move on. With the low price and accessibility of digital camera and sound equipment, an increasing number of film-makers are starting by gaining multi-tasking skills in micro-budget, personal films, which can then reach a wider public and establish a constituency via the internet. This type of cinema is not World Cinema in Elsaesser's sense of not-national, aimed at international markets and exploited by TV, DVD and other media (2005: 499–500). It more closely resembles Third Cinema in rejecting the parochialism of national or 'great European' cinema and in its desire to explore the relationships between the cultural and the political and to 'exceed the limits of both national-industrial cinemas' and Western cultural theory (Willemen 1989: 3). The more ambitious Third Cinema films do the festival rounds and if, like *This is Not a Love Song* (Bille Eltringham, UK, 2002), some nominations for awards are garnered, then a DVD release may result. Eltringham filmed in two weeks with a tiny budget, the film's style of production justifying her exploration of the possibilities and beauties of the DV format (Taylor and Hayden 2002: 41). Responding to the violent demonstrations at the G8 Summit in Genoa and to the shooting of Carlo Giuliani on 20 July 2001, Francesca Comencini's 75-minute documentary *Carlo Giuliani, a Boy* (*Carlo Giuliani, ragazzo*, Italy, 2002) is an example of an unsuccessful attempt to take political discussion into the cultural sphere. The film did the festival rounds, but had to wait until 2006 for mainstream DVD release. Using witness statements, still photographs and video footage shot on the day, Comencini's film attempts a careful reconstruction of events leading up to the shooting, identifying the shots as coming from a beleaguered police van. She includes a measured interview with Giuliani's mother, rejecting the suggestion that he was a no-global terrorist. It is a well-made film by an established film-maker, but it was buried – except for the invective and accusations of bias on the IMDb website. Significantly, its release has come with that of documentaries of other, no-global films, reflecting identification of an aggregate audience.

European cinema always traded on its quality, its craft traditions which guarantee a look to European cinema often exceeding budget restrictions. Chapter Three defined quality film, a sector of the film industry mostly despised by film critics and academics for accepting the economic imperatives of global media competition. In effect, quality cinema is an extension of the auteurist tendency in European cinema in that the director is used to validate the quality experience of the film. I discussed how the commercial strategies of the Miramax company favoured the consolidation of this sector and how some directors have become trapped within it. Very few have succeeded in returning to lower-budget film-making, and I examined how those who have have managed to do this and the attractions of downsizing. Currently Pedro Almodóvar occupies a dominant position in the quality sector and I used him as a case study of a director who has managed to manipulate the commercial and legislative context to build a career.

A few European films achieve big-budget international success in the market dominated by Hollywood films. Chapter Four examined how some films have done this and also reasons for the contemporary pattern of American investment in co-productions with a variety of European countries. I was particularly interested in what European film-makers brought to the high-concept package which is the Hollywood blockbuster template, and how and why they were able to incorporate local characteristics into a cinematic form destined for the global mainstream. The dangers of going down the American commercial road were also considered. The industry sectors discussed in Chapters Two and Three show an interesting evolution of the relationship with Hollywood, which cannot be neatly explained by the cultural imperialism paradigm. These big-budget European films are not so much competing with Hollywood in its own domestic market as competing with American cinema in the non-US market with great success. There is an evolving pattern of Hollywood financing of European films which will appeal not only in the lucrative European market but in Asia, the Far East and Australasia. *A Very Long Engagement* (*Un long dimanche de fiançailles*, Jean-Pierre Jeunet, France/USA, 2004) looks and sounds French, and *About a Boy* (Chris Weitz/Paul Weitz, UK/USA/France/Germany, 2002) looks and sounds English, but their funding reflects Hollywood's product differentiation, using the allure of European quality and culture to reach new audiences.

Yet there exist whole rafts of films which achieve success with low budgets in their national markets and which are rarely exported. Chapter Five considered the range of local tastes in Scandinavia, Britain, France, Spain and Italy. It also looked briefly at the micro-niche markets which Eastern Central European film-makers have been able to salvage from the ruins of their film industries after the collapse of the Berlin wall. Interestingly, the most successful of 'local' films are those which have adopted American film-making practices, particularly the franchise film and the notion of seriality. The *Taxi* films (made by Luc Besson's company) and Italy's *Christmas* comedies are examples. The case of the *Bronzés* franchise is interesting in illustrating how European film-making has changed. *Les bronzés* (Patrice Leconte, France, 1978) was a hugely popular comedy, full of puns and local jokes, set in a ClubMed holiday village and based on the writing team from the Splendide comedy theatre. It was followed a year later by *Les bronzés font du ski* (Patrice Leconte, France, 1979), with the same team now having holiday adventures in a ski resort. International DVD release of the latter film paved the way for *Friends Forever* (*Bronzés 3: Amis pour la vie*, Patrice Leconte, France, 2006), a co-production with the most popular French terrestrial TV channel, TF1, with the participation of satellite channel TPS, and which achieved 10 million admissions in France in the three months after its release. It is therefore positioned to benefit from the release patterns explored in Chapter Six.

Television has, particularly in Britain, been regarded as the sphere in which European cinema is alive and well. Chapter Six showed how the development of the continent's television industries, and TV channels' insatiable appetite for films to attract viewers and subscribers, have changed the balance of power for ever. French cinema has been used as a case study to show how TV companies' control of the end user has given them power to influence the forms and genres of future productions. Successive audiences represented by movement from a film's exhibition in cinemas, to transmissions on pay-TV, satellite subscription channels and exploitation in other media are carefully controlled and monitored, and successful formats feed into demands for similar products. Television commodifies cinema. This chapter also investigated two strategies to resist this commodification, represented by films featuring children, which explore desires for a society fit for future generations to inherit, and the sector which produces films for children.

Chapter Seven moved onto the study of content, particularly how European films have engaged with a civil war on their margins in the former Yugoslavia. Violence and visual excess have expressed the difficulties of reconciling cinematic representations of marginal peoples and events with notions of Europe as modern and civilized. I also considered how representations of the Balkans have evolved, tropes of marginality and otherness being used to attempt to make sense of the recent influx of populations from Eastern Central Europe whose presence disturbs ideas of unitary national identities. In the contemporary context of images and information from outside national territories being experienced simultaneously within the domestic space, the idea of borders becomes increasingly redundant, although the plethora of European films concerned with these liminal spaces testifies to a continued desire for fixity and stability.

Costume drama and films set in the past are considered to be what Europe does best. Chapter Eight looked at the so-called heritage cinema and the recent spate of war films to tease out the uses to which versions of the past are put. The tensions between the desire for stasis and the excitement of chaos and lack of resolution result in pleasurable narratives whose excessive spectacle, visual beauty, emotion, nostalgia and erotic content metaphorize the difficulties of evolving new ways of making sense of the contemporary world. I argued that, rather than being 'theme park' films, historical film fictions provide spaces for the rehearsal not only of questions of class and gender – who is being invited to join the national 'family' – but of what bodies of knowledge and behaviours are ethically appropriate for participation in the contemporary, multi-ethnic and multicultural world.

Irish cinema has been an interest of mine for over ten years. The final case study was included in order to explore the issues and patterns raised in earlier chapters in relation to the cinema of a small island on the margins of Europe. Ireland has a large, worldwide diaspora population and experience of being colonized by Britain. It also took part in Britain's eighteenth- and nineteenth-century colonial adventures. It is a country of powerful mythic formulations of identity, many of which are difficult to square with the Republic of Ireland's present status as a 'Celtic tiger' economy, the global movement of populations and the presence in the island of the disputed territory of Northern Ireland, which is part of the United Kingdom. Measures taken to build an indigenous film industry both sides of the border are examined. I also looked at the evolution of these measures and their success in generating images and ideas which speak with an Irish voice.

At the time of writing, we in Europe stand on the cusp of new developments in digital technology. The battle for technical supremacy has already started, with Technicolor Digital signing a deal with the US cinema chain Century Theatres to install digital projection systems in up to 120 of its screens (anon 2006). With the advance of DVD, distributors' back catalogues have become increasingly valuable, with a huge variety of old films being digitally remastered and released, to the profit of whoever holds the rights. This gives the exploitation of a film a very much longer 'tail' than the standard quick release and pass down the TV and satellite food chain. The technology already exists to add the streaming of a film over mobile phones to the five windows of film exploitation (cinema, video/DVD rental and retail, pay-TV Box-Office, pay-TV subscription channels, and free-to-air TV), although when this was tried in Italy too near the cinema distribution, the exhibitors pulled the film (Rodier 2005). It also enables European films marginalized by lack of release to find an audience through online DVD publishers, and for independent film-makers to find their constituency over the internet. Vittorio Moroni won prizes for his films at festivals, but desperation forced him to try new ways of distributing his work, inviting people to buy shares on his website, entitling them to a ticket to see the film when it is shown (Bolognini 2005: 48). Moroni claims that 20,000 people saw *Tu devi essere il lupo* (Italy, 2004) in the first three months of its release and his website, http://www.tudeviessereillupo.it, gives details of where it is to be shown. Just as 14–21-year-olds are 'blogging their way to a publishing revolution' (Gibson 2005: 9), the potential exists for young film-makers to do the same. After all, young graphic artists have been using the full resources of the internet for years, from personal sites to competitive entry to highly regarded virtual galleries of work.

But these are currently interstitial responses to the global domination of American media products. What this study has shown is that, for the most part, European cinemas accommodate to the hegemonic provider, adopting American business practices, taking advantage of the shelter which American finance, technology and distribution provides, taking ideas and formats which are of interest to create something more European. Audiences may be unaware of the existence of the European Union's MEDIA programme, but creative people and those involved in the European film business have been thinking transnationally, and out of the national box, for years. Their task of negotiating and accessing the different funding mechanisms is usually hidden from critical view, but the MEDIA programme is crucial to the new ways of working in the film industry. However much industry professionals and film-makers may complain about restricted opportunities, what we see on our various screens is marked by the tensions of the different images of possible identities and modes of life and conduct with which we are bombarded. Whether or not you believe that postmodernism exists, the visual excess, heightened spectacular beauty, the demonstration of virtuosity, violence, monstrous characters and situations, asymmetry and exuberance, complexity and chaos which are characteristic of the neo-Baroque in European cinema all testify to the fact that European film-makers are well up to the task of expressing the excitement and anxieties of a contemporary world in a transitional period of flux and uncertainty.

Bibliography

ADDONIZIO, A., CARRARA, G., DE SIMONE, M., LIPPI, R., PREMUDA, E., ROMANO, M. and SPINA, P. 2000: *Il dogma della libertà: Conversazioni con Lars von Trier*. Palermo and Florence: Edizioni della Battaglia, 2nd edition.

ALLEN, T. 1999: Perceiving contemporary wars. In Allen, T. and Seaton, J. (eds), *The Media of Conflict: War Reporting and Representations of Ethnic Violence*. London and New York: Zed Books, 11–42.

ALLINSON, M. 2001: *A Spanish Labyrinth: The Films of Pedro Almodóvar*. London and New York: I. B. Taurus.

AMELIO, G. 1994: *Amelio second oil cinema: Conversazione con Goffredo Fofi*. Rome: Donzelli.

ANDERSON, B. 1991: *Imagined Communities: Reflections on the Origin and Spread of Nationalism*. London: Verso, revised edition.

ANDERTON, S. 1996: Pride and perennials in Darcy's garden. *The Times/Weekend*, 30 November, 5.

ANON. 2006: Technicolor enters battle for digital dominance. *Screen International*, 4 January. http://www.screendaily.com/storyid=24639 (accessed 15.3.2006).

__2004: Rohmer films get Gallic shrug. *Screen International*, 27 February, 8.

__2000: Miramax films: les derniers nababs. www.ecran-noir.com/dossiers/miramax/chiffres.htm (accessed 12.4.2000).

__2000: Int'l shrinks for studios, boosts indies. *Screen International*, 26 July, 6.

ANNAUD, J–J. 2002: Les rapports insolites d'un cineaste européen avec Hollywood. In Paris, T. (ed.) *CinémAction*, Hors–série, 36–9.

APPADURAI, A. 1999: Disjuncture and difference in the global cultural economy. In Featherstone, M. (ed.), *Global Culture: Nationalism, Globalization and Modernity*. London, Thousand Oaks, New Delhi: Sage, 295–310.

APRÀ, A. and PISTAGNESI, P. (eds) 1986: *Comedy, Italian Style 1950–1980*. Turin: ERI.

AUSTIN, G. 1996: *Contemporary French Cinema: An Introduction*. Manchester: Manchester University Press.

BALMFORTH, J. 1995: Upwardly mobile. *TV World*, July/August, 13–14.

BARKER, C. 1999: *Television, Globalization and Cultural Identities*. Buckingham and Philadelphia: Open University Press.

BARRETT, P. 1997: The trying game. *Screen International*, 29 February, 21–4.

BARRON, F. 1971: Interview with Eric Rohmer. *Take One*, 4, 1, January, 4–5.

BARRY, P. 1995: *Beginning Theory: An Introduction to Literary and Cultural Theory*. Manchester: Manchester University Press.

BARTHES, R. 1970: Le troisième sens. *Cahiers du Cinéma*, 222, July, 12–19.

BARTON, R. 2004: Introduction. In Barton, R. and O'Brien, H. (eds), *Keeping It Real: Irish Film and Television*. London: Wallflower Press, 1–5.

BAUDRILLARD, J. 1993: *The Transparency of Evil. Essays on Extreme Phenomena*. London: Verso, trans. J. Benedict.

BECK, U. 2000: *What is Globalization?* London: Polity Press.

__2005: Quando la catastrofe diventa globale. *La Repubblica*, 10 January.

BENNETT, R. 2000: Why this witch-hunt won't stop me writing on Ireland. *The Observer*, 3 December. http://www.guardian.co.uk/Archive/Article/0,4273,4099837,00.html (accessed 19.3.01).

BERGFELDER, T. 2000: The nation vanishes: European co-production and popular genre formula in the 1950s and 1960s. In Hjort, M. and Mackenzie, S. (eds), *Cinema and Nation*. London and New York: Routledge, 139–52.

BERGHAHN, D. 2005: *Hollywood Behind the Wall: The Cinema of East Germany*. Manchester: Manchester University Press.

BHABHA, H. 1994: *The Location of Culture*. London and New York: Routledge.

BIZERN, C. and AUTISSIER, A-M. 1998: *Public Aid Mechanisms for the Film and Audiovisual Industry in Europe: Comparative Analysis of National Aid Mechanisms Vol.1*. Paris/Strasbourg: Centre National de la Cinématographie/European Audiovisual Observatory.

BIZIO, S. 2002: *Cinema Italian Style: Italians at the Academy Awards*. Rome: Gremese.

BLANEY, M. 2001: Producing hits. *Screen International*, 5 October, 9.

__2002a: Germans seek to retain local cash. *Screen International*, 9 August, 8.

__2002b: German funding falls. *Screen International*, 15 November, 6.

__2006: End of the line for 'silly money'. *Screen International*, 14 July, 5.

BOGGS, C. and POLLARD, T. (eds) 2003: *A World in Chaos: Social Crisis and the Rise of Postmodern Cinema*. Lanham, MA: Rowman & Littlefield.

BOLOGNINI, L. 2005: Cari registi fate come me: i film distribuiteli da soli. *La Repubblica*, 22 April, 48.

BONDEBJERG, I. 2001: European media, cultural integration and globalisation: Reflections on the ESF-programme Changing Media – Changing Europe. *Nordicom Review*, 1, 53–64. www.nordicom.gu.se/reviewcontents/ncomreview/ncomreview101/bondebjerg.pdf (accessed 15.7.2004).

__2005: The Danish way: Danish film culture in a European and global perspective. In Nestingen, A. and Elkington, T. G. (eds): *Transnational cinema in a global context: Nordic cinema in transition.* Detroit: Wayne State University, 111–39.

BOOTH, W. 1961: *The Rhetoric of Fiction*. Chicago: University of Chicago Press.

BORDWELL, D. 1979: The art cinema as a mode of film practice. *Film Criticism*, 4/1, 56–64.

BOURDIEU, P. 1986: *Distinction*. London and New York: Routledge.

__1993: *The Field of Cultural Production*. Cambridge: Polity Press.

BRANDSTRUP, P. G. and REDVALL, E. N. 2005: Breaking the borders: Danish coproductions in the 1990s. In Nestingen, A. and Elkington, T. G. (eds): *Transnational cinema in a global context: Nordic cinema in transition.* Detroit: Wayne State University, 141–63.

BRANSTON, G. and STAFFORD, R. 1999: *The Media Student's Book*. London and New York: Routledge, 2nd edition.

BRETT, D. 1996: *The Construction of Heritage*. Cork: Cork University Press.

BROOKS, P. 1976: *The Melodramatic Imagination*. New Haven: Yale University Press.

BROOKS, R. 1996: Bottomley wants 'heritage' films. *The Observer*, 19 May, 12.

BROWN, C. 2000: The Rick Factor. *Screen International*, 23 June, 25–8.

__2001: Godardian grace notes. *Screen International*, 19 October.

BROWN, G. 1997: No real need to watch this space. *The Times*, 5 June, 37.

BRUNO, G. 2002: *Atlas of Emotion: Journeys in Art, Architecture and Film*. New York: Verso.

BRUZZI, S. 1997: *Undressing Cinema: Clothing and identity in the movies*. London and New York: Routledge.

BUCI-GLUCKSMANN, C. 1994: *Baroque Reason: The Aesthetics of Modernity*, London: Sage, trans. P. Camiller.

BUTLER, J. 1990: *Gender Trouble: Feminism and the Subversion of Identity.* London and New York: Routledge.

CALABRESE, O. 1992: *Neo-Baroque: A Sign of the Times*, Princeton, NJ: Princeton University Press, trans. C. Lambert.

CANNADINE, D. 1998: *Class in Britain.* Yale: Yale University Press.

CARREIRA, S. de J. 1999: Le cinema portugais. http://www.ecran-noir.com/dossiers/monde/portugal/ (accessed 12.4.2000).

CASE, B. 1998: Pussy galore: interview with Patrick McCabe. *Time Out*, 22–29 April, 22–3.

CASTELLS, M. 2000a: *The Information Age: Economy, Society and Culture, Vol. I, The Rise of the Network Society.* Malden, MA, Oxford and Carlton: Blackwell, 2nd edition.

__2000b: *The Information Age: Economy, Society and Culture, Vol. II, End of Millennium.* Malden, MA, Oxford and Carlton: Blackwell, 2nd edition.

__2004: *The Information Age: Economy, Society and Culture, Vol. III, The Power of Identity.* Malden, MA, Oxford and Carlton: Blackwell, 2nd edition.

CHARITY, T. 2000: Winding rogue. *Time Out*, 22–29 March, 78.

CHIBNALL, S. and MURPHY, R. (eds) 1999: *British Crime Cinema.* London and New York: Routledge.

CLOVER, C. J. 1992: *Men, Women and Chainsaws.* London: British Film Institute.

CNC 2006: *Bilan 2005:* 02 Les films et les fictions à la television, 1–11; 06 La production cinématographique, 1–13. www.cnc.fr/Site/Template/T8.aspx?SELECTID=1468&ID=867 (accessed 10.09.2006).

COATES, P. 2005: *The Red and the White: The Cinema of the People's Poland.* London and New York: Wallflower Press.

COLE, G. 2000: Short tips. *Screen International*, 1 December, 16.

Commission of the European Communities. 2003: *COM(2003) 725 final. Report on the implementation and the mid-term results of the MEDIA Plus and MEDIA training programmes (2001–2005) and on the results of the preparatory action "Growth and audiovisual: i2i audiovisual".* http://europa.eu.int/eur-lex (accessed 10.11.2005).

__2004: *COM/2004/0470 final. Proposal for a Decision of the European Parliament and the Council concerning the implementation of a programme for the European audiovisual sector (MEDIA 2007).* http://europa.eu.int/eur-lex/lex/LexUriServ/LexUriServ.do?uri=CELEX:52004PC0470:EN (accessed 10.11.2005).

COOK, J. and ELSAESSER, T. 1994: Definitions of quality. In Elsaesser, T., Simons, J. and Bronk, L. (eds): *Writing for the Medium: Television in Transition.* Amsterdam: University of Amsterdam Press.

COOK, P. 1996: *Fashioning the Nation: Costume and identity in British cinema*. London: British Film Institute.

COOPERS and LYBRAND. 1992: *European Film: Industry or art?* London: Coopers and Lybrand.

CORNER, J. and HARVEY, S. 1991: Mediating tradition and modernity. In Corner, J. and Harvey, S. (eds): *Enterprise and Heritage: Crosscurrents of National Culture*. London and New York: Routledge, 45–75.

CORRIGAN, T. 1991: *A cinema without walls: Movies and culture after Vietnam*. London: Routledge.

COWIE, P. 1999: *Straight From the Heart: Modern Norwegian Cinema*. Oslo: Norwegian Film Institute/Kom Vorlag.

CRANE, D. 2002: Culture and globalization: Theoretical models and emerging trends. In Crane, D., Kawashima, N. and Kawasaki, K. (eds): *Global Culture: Media, Arts, Policy and Globalization*. New York and London: Routledge, 1–25.

CRETON, L. 2002: Filière cinématographique, secteur télévisuel et industries de la communication: Les enjeux de la convergence. In Creton, L. (ed.): *Le cinema à l'épreuve du système télévisuel*. Paris: CNRS Éditions, 9–41.

CROFTS, S. 1998: Authorship and Hollywood. In Hill, J. and Church Gibson, P. (eds): *The Oxford Guide to Film Studies*. Oxford and New York: Oxford University Press, 310–24.

CROTEAU, D. and HOYNES, W. 2001: *The Business of Media: Corporate Media and the Public Interest*. Thousand Oaks, London, New Delhi: Pine Forge Press.

DALE, M. 1997: *The Movie Game: The Film Business in Britain, Europe and America*. London and Herndon, VA: Cassell.

__2006: Portugal. In Rosenthal, D. (ed.): *The Guardian International Film Guide*, 43rd edition. London, Los Angeles, Cannes: Guardian Books, 230–2.

DALTON, S. 2002: Still making new waves, *The Times*, 7 February, 23.

DAWSON, G. 1994: *Soldier Heroes: British Adventure, Empire and the Imagining of Masculinities*. London and New York: Routledge.

DAWSON, J. 2003: The comedian of errors. *The Times/Magazine*, 29 March, 14–19.

DEVEREUX, E. 2003: *Understanding the Media*. London, Thousand Oaks, New Delhi: Sage.

DONIGER, W. 2000: Can you spot the source? *London Review of Books*, 17 February, 26–7.

DONNAN, H. and WILSON, T. M. 1999: *Borders: Frontiers of Identity, Nation and State*. Oxford and New York: Berg.

DOYLE, G. 2002a: *Understanding Media Economics*. London, Thousand Oaks, New Delhi: Sage.

__2002b: *Media Ownership*. London, Thousand Oaks, New Delhi: Sage.

DRINNAN, J. 2001: Media Plus faces end of first development round with an embarrassing cash surplus. *Screen Finance*, 14 (16), 14 September, 1–2.

DYER, R. 1979: *Stars*. London: BFI.

__1991: Stars and society: Charisma. In Gledhill, C. (ed.): *Stardom: Industry of Desire*. London: Routledge, 57–9.

DYER, R. and VINCENDEAU, G. (eds) 1992: Introduction. In *Popular European Cinema*. London and New York: Routledge, 1–14.

DYJA, E. 2004: UK film, television and DVD/video: Overview. In Dyja, E. (ed.): *BFI Film Handbook 2005*. London: BFI, 16–63.

ECC. 1988: Resolution setting up a European support fund for the co-production and distribution of Creative cinematographic and audiovisual works: 'Eurimages' (88/15). http://culture.coe.fr/Infocentre/txt/eng/eres88_15.html (accessed 20.5.2002).

EDWARDS, R. and USHER, R. 2000: *Globalisation and Pedagogy: Space, place and identity*. London and New York: Routledge.

EIMER, D. 2004: When two tribes go to war. *TheTimes/The Eye*, 15–21 May, 14.

ELKINGTON, T. 2005: Costumes, adolescence, and dogma: Nordic film and American distribution. In Nestingen, A. and Elkington, T. G. (eds): *Transnational cinema in a global context: Nordic cinema in transition.* Detroit: Wayne State University, 31–54.

ELSAESSER, T. 2005: *European Cinema: Face to face with Hollywood.* Amsterdam: Amsterdam University Press.

European Audiovisual Observatory. 1997: *Yearbook 1997: Cinema, Television and New Media in Europe*. Strasbourg: European Audiovisual Observatory.

__2002: *Yearbook 2002, vol. 3*: *Film and Home Video*. Strasbourg: European Audiovisual Observatory.

__2003: *Yearbook 2003, vol. 3*: *Film and Home Video*. Strasbourg: European Audiovisual Observatory.

__2004: *Yearbook 2004, vol. 3*: *Film and Home Video*. Strasbourg: European Audiovisual Observatory.

__2005: *Yearbook 2005, vol. 1*: *Economy of the Radio and Television Industry in Europe*. Strasbourg: European Audiovisual Observatory.

Vol 2: *Household Audiovisual Equipment – Transmission – Television Audiences*.

Vol 3: *Film and Home Video.*

Vol 5: *Television Channels – Programme Production and Distribution.*

__2006: *World Film Market Trends: FOCUS 2006.* Strasbourg: European Audiovisual Observatory/Marché du Film.

EVANS, G. 2000: Against the wind: new Portuguese cinema. In: *Filmwaves*, 11, 28–31.

FERGUSON, M. 1992: The mythology about globalization. *European Journal of Communication*, 7, 69–93.

F.F. 2002: Gli italiani all'estero troppo poco visibili. *Giornale dello Spettacolo*, 30, 4.

FINNEY, A. 1996a: *The State of European Cinema: A New Dose of Reality.* London and New York, Cassell.

__1996b: *Developing Feature Films in Europe: A practical guide.* London: Routledge.

FISHER, A. 1987: Munich's Mr Hollywood: Bernd Eichinger, the West German producer, talks to Andrew Fisher. *Financial Times*, 19 January, 12.

FOREST, C. 2001: *Économies contemporaines du Cinéma en Europe: L'improbable industrie.* Paris: CNRS Éditions.

__2002: La frequentation des films en salles et leur audience à la television. In Creton, L. (ed.): *Le cinema à l'épreuve du système télévisuel.* Paris: CNRS Éditions, 177–95.

FOUCAULT, M. 1977: *Discipline and Punish: The Birth of the Prison.* London: Penguin Books, trans. A. Sheridan. Trans. of 1975: *Surveiller et punir: Naissance de la prison.* Paris: Gallimard.

FRANKLIN, A. 2003: Polish producer hopes for new blockbuster with *Old Tale.* www.screendaily.com/print.asp/storyid=11961, 14 April (accessed 30.4.03).

FREAN, A. 1996: Bra company toes the Empire line. *The Times*, 30 April, 8.

FRENCH, P. 2004a: A new nightmare on Elm Street. In: *The Observer/Review*, 15 February, 9.

__2004b: Keeping up with the Jones. *The Observer/Review*, 14 November, 9.

__2005: Loving the alien, *The Observer*, 22 May, 9.

FROW, J. 1995: *Cultural Studies and Cultural Value.* Oxford and New York: Oxford University Press.

GAUT, B. 2003: Naked film: Dogme and its limits. In Hjort, M. and MacKenzie, S. (eds): *Purity and Provocation: Dogma 95.* London: BFI, 89–101.

GIBBONS, L. 2005: Projecting the nation: cinema and culture. In Cleary, J. and Connolly, C. (eds): *The Cambridge Companion to Modern Irish Culture.* Cambridge: Cambridge University Press, 206–24.

GIBSON, O. 2005: Young blog their way to a publishing revolution. *The Guardian*, 7 October, 9.

GIDDENS, A. 1990: *The Consequences of Modernity*. Cambridge: Pluto Press.

__1991: *Modernity and Self–Identity: Self and Society in the Late Modern Age*. Cambridge: Polity Press.

GILLEN, K. 2006: A strange time of year for buying. *The Guardian/Technology*, 2 February, 3.

GODARD, J-L. and ISHAGHPOUR, Y. 2005: *Cinema: The Archaeology of Film and the Memory of a Century.* Oxford and New York: Berg, trans. J. Howe.

GÖKTÜRK, D. 2002: Beyond paternalism: Turkish German traffic in cinema. In Bergfelder, T., Carter, E. and Göktürk, D. (eds): *The German Cinema Book*. London: British Film Institute, 248–55.

GOODRIDGE, M. 2006: The gathering storm. *Screen International*, 28 July, 10.

GRAHAM, C. 2001: *Deconstructing Ireland: Identity, Theory, Culture*. Edinburgh: Edinburgh University Press.

GRANT, C. 2004: Home-Movies: The curious cinematic collaboration of Anne-Marie Miéville and Jean-Luc Godard. In Temple, M., Williams, J. S. and Witt, M. (eds): *For Ever Godard*. London: Black Dog, 100–17.

GREEN, J. 2001: Not like all the others. *Screen International*, 21 September, 11–16.

GUBBINS, M. 2005: Cine Expo: record releases reel in $100m overseas. www.screendaily.com/storyid=22607 (accessed 8.11.2005).

HAKE, S. 2002: *German National Cinema*. London and New York: Routledge.

HANNERZ, U. 1990: Cosmopolitans and locals in world culture. In Featherstone, M. (ed.): *Global Culture: Nationalism, Globalization and Modernity*. London, Thousand Oaks, New Delhi: Sage, 237–51.

__1996: *Transnational Connections: Culture, People, Places*. London and New York: Routledge.

HARDING, J. 2001: Going by the book. *Financial Times Creative Business*, 27 November, 8–9.

__2002a: A foot in both camps. *Financial Times Creative Business*, 19 March, 8–9.

__2002b: Building up momentum. *Financial Times Creative Business*, 19 March, 9.

HARRIS, S. 2004: The *cinéma du look*. In Ezra, E. (ed.): *European Cinema*. Oxford and New York: Oxford University Press.

__2005: A Very Long Engagement. *Sight and Sound*, February, 76, 78.

HARVEY, D. 1990: *The Condition of Postmodernity: An Enquiry into the Origins of Cultural Change*. Oxford and Maldon, MA: Blackwell.

HAWKINS, J. 1999/2000: Sleaze mania, euro-trash, and high art. *Film Quarterly*, 53/2, 14–29.

HAYWARD, S. 1993: *French National Cinema*. London and New York: Routledge.

__2002: Luc Besson. In Tasker, Y. (ed.): *Fifty Contemporary Filmmakers*. London and New York: Routledge, 51–9.

HEDGES, I. 1991: *Breaking the Frame: Film Language and the Experience of Limits*. Bloomington and Indianapolis: Indiana University Press.

HENLEY, J. 2001: Drunk revolutionaries? Pas du tout. *The Guardian,* 13 September, 20.

HIGSON, A. 1993: Re-presenting the national past: nostalgia and pastiche in the heritage film. In Friedman, L. (ed.): *British Cinema and Thatcherism: Fires were Started*. London: UCL Press, 109–29.

__1995: *Waving the Flag: Constructing a National Cinema in Britain*. Oxford and New York: Clarendon Press.

__1996: The heritage film and British cinema, 232–48, and Space, Place, Spectacle: Landscape and Townscape in the 'Kitchen Sink' film, 133–56. In Higson, A. (ed.), *Dissolving Views: Key Writings on British Cinema*. London: Cassell.

__2003: *English Heritage, English Cinema: Costume Drama since 1980*. Oxford: Oxford University Press.

HILL, J. 1986: *Sex, Class and Realism: British Cinema 1956–1963*. London: BFI.

__1994: The future of European cinema: The economics and culture of pan-European strategies. In Hill, J., McLoone, M. and Hainsworth, P. (eds): *Border Crossing: Film in Ireland, Britain and Europe*. Belfast: Institute of Irish Studies/University of Ulster/British Film Institute, 53–80.

HIRSCH, M. 2004: Luxembourg. In: Kelly, M., Mazzoleni, G. and McQuail, D. (eds): *The Media in Europe: The Euromedia Handbook*, 3rd edition. London, Thousand Oaks, New Delhi: Sage, 139–44.

HJORT, M. 2003: Dogma 95: A small nation's response to globalisation. In Hjort, M. and MacKenzie, S. (eds): *Purity and Provocation: Dogma 95*. London: BFI, 31–47.

__2005: From epiphanic culture to circulation: The dynamics of globalization in Nordic cinema. In Nestingen, A. and Elkington, T. G. (eds): *Transnational cinema in a global context: Nordic cinema in transition.* Detroit: Wayne State University, 191–218.

HJORT, M. and BONDEBJERG, I. 2001: *The Danish Directors: Dialogues on a contemporary national cinema*. Bristol and Portland, OR: Intellect.

HOFMANN, K. 2002: Ladies who launch. *Financial Times Creative Business*, 19 March, 11.

HOPKINS, N. 2004: Miramax's founding brothers in talks over their Disney futures. *The Times/Business*, 11 August, 36–7.

HORSTI, K. 2003: Global mobility and the media: Presenting asylum seekers as a threat. *Nordicom Review*, 1, 41–54. www.nordicom.gu.se/common/publ_pdf/26_041–054.pdf (accessed 3.2.2005).

HOSKINS, C., McFADYEN, S. and FINN, A. (eds). 1997: *Global Television and Film: An Introduction to the Economics of the Business*. Oxford: Clarendon Press.

HUNTER, A. 2002: Harry Potter and the Chamber of Secrets. *Screen International*, 15 November, 22.

ILOTT, T. 1992: UK film, television, video: Statistical overview. In Leafe, D. (ed.): *BFI Film and Television Handbook 1993*. London: BFI.

__1996: *Budgets and Markets: A Study of the Budgeting of European Film*. London and New York: Routledge.

IORDANOVA, D. 2000a: The cinema of dispersed Yugoslavs: Diasporas in the making. *CineAction*, 52, 68–72.

__2000b: Hoffman, Jerzy. In Taylor, R., Wood, N., Graffy, J. and Iordanova, D. (eds): *The BFI Companion to Eastern European and Russian Cinema*. London: BFI, 98–9.

__2001: *Cinema of Flames: Balkan Film, Culture and the Media*. London: BFI.

__2003: *Cinema of the Other Europe: The Industry and Artistry of East Central European Film*. London: Wallflower Press.

IOSIFIDIS, P., STEEMERS, J. and WHEELER, M. 2005: *European Television Industries*. London: BFI.

JÄCKEL, A. 2003: *European Film Industries*. London, BFI.

JÄCKEL, A. and CRETON, L. 2004: Business 1960–2004: A certain idea of the film industry. In Temple, M. and Witt, M. (eds): *The French Cinema Book*. London: British Film Institute, 209–20.

JAMESON, F. 1991: *Postmodernism, or, The Cultural Logic of Late Capitalism*. London and New York: Verso.

__1998: *The Cultural Turn: Selected Writings on the Postmodern, 1983–1998*. London and New York: Verso.

JENSEN, J. W. 2006: Denmark: New fruit. *Screen International*, 19 May, 30.

JOHNSON, M. 2000: Case study: *Villa des roses*. *Screen International*, 15 December, 22.

JOHNSTON, S. 2001: A French fairy tale. *The Times/Magazine*, 29 September, 40–2.

JULLIER, L. and MAZDON, L. 2004: Technology 1960–2004: From images of the world to the world of images. In Temple, M. and Witt, M. (eds): *The French Cinema Book*. London: British Film Institute, 220–9.

KALETSKY, A. 1989: Monument to media 'synergy'. *Financial Times*, 22 April.

KAPLAN, E. A. 2001: Melodrama, cinema and trauma. *Screen*, 42:2, 201–5.

KEARNEY, R. 1997: *Postnationalist Ireland: Politics, Culture, Philosophy*. London and New York: Routledge.

KELLY-HOLMES, H. 2000: 'Strong words softly spoken': advertising and the intertextual construction of 'Irishness'. In Meinhof, U. H. and Smith, J. (eds): *Intertextuality and the Media*. Manchester: Manchester University Press.

KENNEDY, M. 1996: Darcy's pride fuels record rise in history tours. *The Times*, 22 July, 8.

KIBAR, O. 2003: Zentropa to cut staff by 25%.
www.screendaily.com/print.asp?storyid=10906 (accessed 20 March 2003).

KINDER, M. 1993: *Blood Cinema: The Reconstruction of National Identity in Spain*. Berkeley, Los Angeles and London: University of California Press.

KITZINGER, J. 2000: Media templates: patterns of association and the (re)construction of meaning over time. *Media, Culture and Society*, 22:1, 61–84.

KUHN, A. 1999: Introduction. In Cook, P. and Bernink, M. (eds): *The Cinema Book*. London: BFI.

KUHN, M. 2002: *One Hundred Films and a Funeral*. London: Thorogood.

LALLI, F. 1998: Artemisia – passione estrema. *Film/Tutti i film della stagione*, 34, 41–2.

LANDY, M. 1991: *British Genres: Cinema and Society, 1930–1960*. Princeton, NJ: Princeton University Press.

__1996: *Cinematic Uses of the Past*. Minneapolis and London: University of Minnesota Press.

LANGE, A. and WESTCOTT, T. 2004: *Public Funding for Film and Audiovisual Works in Europe – A comparative approach*. Strasbourg: European Audiovisual Observatory/European Investment Bank.

LAWRENCE, S. 2004: Cutting Bridget down to size. *The Times/Screen*, 11 November, 11.

LEACH, J. 2004: *British Film*. Cambridge and New York: Cambridge University Press.

LEE, M. J. 1993: *Consumer Culture Reborn*. London and New York, Routledge.

LEIGH, J. 2002: *The Cinema of Ken Loach: Art in the Service of the People*. Directors' Cuts. London: Wallflower Press.

LICASTRO SCARDINO, S., SCHIAVONE PANNI DI NAPOLI RAMPOLLA, M. and TOSI PAMPHILI, C. 2004: *Travestimenti: L'inventiva della Sartoria Farani in 40 anni di cinema, teatro e televisione*. Milan: Mondadori Electa.

LINEHAN, H. 1996: Trouble movies. *The Big Issue*, 206, 4–10 November, 20–1.

LOCHHEAD, L. 1995: The shadow. *Sight and Sound*, 6, 14–16.

LUNDBERG, P. 2003a: Close up: Josef Fares. *Screen International*, 24 January, 22.

__2003b: Case study: *Kops*. *Screen International*, 24 January, 22.

LURIE, A. 1999: Not for muggles. *The New York Review of Books*, 46:20. http://www.nybooks.com/articles/264 (accessed 26/7/2006).

LYOTARD, J-F. 1984: *The Postmodern Condition: A Report on Knowledge*. Manchester: Manchester University Press, trans. G. Bennington and B. Massumi.

MacCABE, C. 2004: The commerce of cinema. In Temple, M., Williams, J. S. and Witt, M. (eds): *For Ever Godard*. London: Black Dog, 94–9.

MACMILLAN, S. 2003: Czech film gets a make-over. *Screen International*, 24 January, 21.

MACNAB, G. 1997: Smilla's Feeling for Snow. *Sight and Sound*, November, 52–53.

__2005: Homeward Bound. *The Guardian*, 25 November, 6.

__2006a: Trier hits 50 and decides to 'narrow down'. www.screendaily.com/print.asp?storyid=25120, 11 February (accessed 3.3.2006).

__2006b: Stormbreaker. *Screen International*, 28 July, 23.

McINTYRE, S. 1994: Vanishing point: feature film production in a small country. In Hill, J., McLoone, M. and Hainsworth, P. (eds): *Border Crossing: Film in Ireland, Britain and Europe*. Belfast: Institute of Irish Studies, 88–111.

McKAY, S. 2006: The spy who saved us. *The Observer/Review*, 18 June, 26.

McLOONE, M. 2000: *Irish Film: The Emergence of a Contemporary Cinema*. London: BFI.

McQUAIL, D. 2004: Introduction. In Kelly, M., Mazzoleni, G. and McQuail, D. (eds): *The Media in Europe: The Euromedia Handbook*, 3rd edition. London, Thousand Oaks, New Delhi: Sage, 1–3.

MAHER, K. 2005: Jack of all trades, master of most. *The Times/Screen*, 20 October, 15.

MALTBY, R. 1995: *Hollywood Cinema: An Introduction*. Oxford and Malden, MA: Blackwell.

MARWICK, A. 1998: Class of 98. *The Observer/Review*, 11 October, 14.

MATTELART, A. 2002: An archaeology of the global era: constructing a belief. *Media, Culture & Society*, 24 (5), 591–612.

MATTHEWS, P. 1999: Festen. *Sight and Sound*, 3, 39–40.

MAULE, R. 1998: De-authorizing the *auteur*: Postmodern politics of interpellation in contemporary European cinema. In Degli-Esposti, C. (ed.): *Postmodernism in the Cinema*. New York and Oxford: Berghahn, 113–30.

MEAUX SAINT MARC, F. 1998: The new element. *Screen International*, 6 February, 17.

MEDIA Programme Newsletter, 2000, 19, May.

MILLER, T., GOVIL, N., McMURRIA, J. and MAXWELL, R. 2001: *Global Hollywood*. London: BFI.

MINNELLA, M. E. 1998: *La legge del desiderio: Cinema erotico ed erotismo nel cinema*. Alessandria: Falsopiano.

MIRA, A. 2005: Belle Epoque. In Mira, A. (ed.): *The Cinema of Spain and Portugal*. London: Wallflower Press, 199–207.

MITCHELL, R. 2006a: Rabbit runs. *Screen International*, 31 March, 34.

__2006b: Baling out. *Screen International*, 1 September, 35.

MONK, C. 1995: Sexuality and the heritage. *Sight and Sound*, October, 32–4.

__1999a: From underworld to underclass: Crime and British cinema in the 1990s. In Chibnall, S. and Murphy, R. (eds): *British Crime Cinema*. London and New York: Routledge.

__1999b: Heritage films and the British cinema audience in the 1990s. *Journal of Popular British Cinema*, 2, 22–38.

__2000: Villa des Roses. *Sight and Sound*, 10, 60.

__2002: Bend It Like Beckham. *Sight and Sound*, 5, 38–9.

MOSLEY, P. 2000: *Split Screen: Belgian Cinema and Cultural Identity*. New York: State University of New York Press.

MULVEY, L. 1987: Notes on Sirk and Melodrama (1977–8). In Gledhill, C. (ed.): *Home is Where the Heart Is: Studies in Melodrama and the Women's Film*. London: BFI, 75–9.

__1990: Visual pleasure and narrative cinema (1975). In Erens, P. (ed.): *Issues in Feminist Film Criticism*. Bloomington and Indianapolis: Indiana University Press.

NAFICY, H. 2001: *An Accented Cinema: Exilic and Diasporic Filmmaking*. Princeton, NJ: Princeton University Press.

NAGIB, L. 2005: João de Deus trilogy. In Mira, A. (ed.): *The Cinema of Spain and Portugal*. London: Wallflower Press, 188–97.

NAHRA, C. 2006: Where Ireland leads will Hollywood follow? In Rosenthal, D. (ed.): *The Guardian International Film Guide 2006*. London, Los Angeles, Cannes: Button Live Communications/Guardian Books, 59–61.

NDALIANIS, A. 2004: *Neo-Baroque Aesthetics and Contemporary Entertainment*. Cambridge, MA and London: The MIT Press.

NEALE, S. 1981: Art cinema as institution. *Screen*, 22/1, 11–39.

NEIIENDAM, J. 2003: Denmark speaks a different language. *Screen International*, 31 January, 18–20.

NESTINGEN, A. and ELKINGTON, T. G. (eds). 2005: *Transnational cinema in a global north: Nordic cinema in transition*. Detroit, MI: Wayne State University Press.

NOHRSTEDT, S. A., KAITATZI-WHITLOCK, S., OTTOSEN, R. and RIEGERT, K. 2000: From the Persian Gulf to Kosovo – war journalism and propaganda. *European Journal of Communication*, 15/3, 383–404.

NOWELL-SMITH, G. 1998: Introduction. In Nowell-Smith, G. and Ricci, S. (eds): *Hollywood and Europe: Economics, Culture, National Identity: 1945–95*. London: BFI, 1–16.

O'HEALY, Á. 2006: Paper delivered to the American Association of Italian Studies Conference, 24–28 May, Genoa.

O'SULLIVAN, C. 1999: Notting Hill. *Sight and Sound*, 6, 49–50.

PAJACZKOWSKA, C. 1990: 'Liberté! Egalité! Paternité!: Jean-Luc Godard and Anne-Marie Miéville's *Sauve qui peut (la vie)* (1980). In Hayward, S. and Vincendeau, G. (eds): *French Film: Texts and Contexts*. London: Routledge, 241–55.

PARKIN, J. 1996: A leaf out of the Regency book. *The Times/Weekend*, 24 February, 7.

PERRETTI, F. and NEGRO, G. 2003: *Economia del cinema: Princìpi economici e variabili strategiche del settore cinematografico*. Etas.

PERRIAM, C. 2003: *Stars and Masculinities in Spanish Cinema: From Banderas to Bardem*. Oxford and New York: Oxford University Press.

PETKOVIC, V. 2000: Case study *The Mechanism*. *Screen International*, 15 September.

PETLEY, J. 2002: Film policy in the Third Reich. In Bergfelder, T., Carter, E. and Göktürk, D. (eds): *The German Cinema Book*. London: BFI, 173–81.

PETRIE, D. 2000: *Screening Scotland*. London: BFI.

PETTITT, L. 2000: *Screening Ireland: Film and Television Representation*. Manchester: Manchester University Press.

PIDDUCK, J. 2004: *Contemporary Costume Film*. London: BFI.

POLLOCK, G. 1998: A hungry eye. *Sight and Sound*, 11, 26–8.

POZZATO, M. P. (ed.) 2000: *Linea a Belgrado: La comunicazione giornalistica in tv durante la Guerra per il Kosovo.* Rome: RAI–ERI, VQPT 177.

PYM, J. 1995: *Merchant Ivory's English Landscape: Rooms, Views, and Anglo-Saxon Attitudes.* London: Pavilion Books.

RAMPINI, F. 2003: Lara Croft, quanto sei cara; la Ue contro Hollywood. Monopolio e pay-tv: Monti apre un'inchiesta. *La Repubblica,* 16 January, 26.

RANTANEN, T. 2002: *The Global and the National: Media and Communications in Post-Communist Russia.* Oxford and Lanham, MA: Rowman & Littlefield.

READER, K. 2000: Subtext: Paris of Alexandre Trauner. In Konstantarakos, M. (ed.): *Spaces in European Cinema.* Exeter: Intellect: 35–41.

__2004: *Godard and asynchrony.* In Temple, M., Williams J. S. and Witt, M. (eds): *For Ever Godard.* London: Black Dog, 72–93.

RENOUARD, G. 1996: Éric Rohmer et Margaret Ménégoz. *Le film français,* 2631, 20 September, 18.

REPETTO, M. and TAGLIABUE, C. 2000: Alla ricerca dello spettatore perduto. In Repetto, M. and Tagliabue, C. (eds): *La vita è bella?: Il cinema italiano alla fine degli anni Novanta e il suo pubblico.* Milan: Il Castoro, 15–35.

RICE, J. and SAUNDERS, C. 1996: Consuming *Middlemarch*: the construction and consumption of nostalgia in Stamford. In Cartmell, D., Hunter, I. Q., Kaye, H. and Whelehan, I. (eds): *Pulping Fictions: Consuming Culture across the Literature/Media Divide.* London and Chicago: Pluto Press, 85–98.

ROBERTSON, R. 1990: Mapping the global condition: Globalization as the central concept. In Featherstone, M. (ed.): *Global Culture: Nationalism, Globalization and Modernity.* London, Thousand Oaks, New Delhi: Sage, 15–30.

ROBINS, K. 1997: What in the world's going on? In Du Gay, P. (ed.): *Production of Culture/Cultures of Production.* Milton Keynes: The Open University/Sage, 11–66.

ROCKETT, K. 1988: History, politics and Irish cinema. In Rockett, K., Gibbons, L. and Hill, J. (eds): *Cinema and Ireland.* London: Routledge.

RODIER, M. 2005: Italian exhibitors lift boycott after phone film rethink. http://www.screendaily.com/storyid=24146 (accessed 16.11.2005).

ROSSI, U. 1988: Cinema: da fenomeno di massa a fattore d'*élite*'. *Cinemasessanta,* 6/184, November/December, 4.

RYKAER, J. 2001: 10 years with MEDIA Salles. *European Cinema Journal,* 3/3, 1.

SAID, E. 1993: *Culture and Imperialism.* London: Vintage.

SÁNCHEZ-BIOSCA, V. 2000: Cinema spagnolo sotto il franchismo, 1939–75. In Brunetta, G. P. (ed.): *Storia del cinema mondiale, Vol. III, L'Europa: Le cinematografie nazionali*, Tomo primo. Turin: Giulio Einaudi, 547–81.

SAVARESE, R. 2000: Infosuasion in European newspapers. *European Journal of Communication*, 15/3, 363–81.

SBS, 1999: SBS Television reaches Australia's language communities. http://www.sbs.com.au/MARKETING/5a.html (accessed 17.12.1999).

SBS, 2002: Living diversity: Australia's multicultural future. http://www20.sbs.com.au/sbscorporate/index.php?id=547 (accessed 9.9.2005).

SCHWINKE, T. 2006: Running on Empties. *Screen International*, 12 May, 16.

Screen Digest 1995: European co-production and the role of Eurimages. June, 134–6.

Screen Digest 1997: The Fifth Element. May, 100.

SEGUIN, D. 2000: Round table. New European directors. *Screen International*, 15 September, 9.

SEGUIN, J-C. 1994: *Breve storia del cinema spagnolo*. Turin: Lindau.

SERENELLINI, M. 2002: Le grand bleu, il mio atto d'amore per gli abissi marini e i loro abitanti. *La Repubblica*, 13 September, 49.

SHAW, E. 1998: Guy Ritchie. In Hodges, M. *Contemporary British and Irish Film Directors*. London: Wallflower Press, 288–9.

SHEEHY, T. 2001: Round Table: The market-responsive *auteur*. *Screen International*, 18 November, 8.

__2002: Hidden territories, awkward statistics. *Screen International*, 15 March, 7.

SILVER, J. 2005: How to flog a turkey. *The Guardian/Media*, 3 October, 1–2.

SILVERMAN, K. 1994: Fragments of a fashionable discourse. In Benstock, S. and Ferriss, S. (eds): *On Fashion*. New Brunswick: Rutgers University Press, 183–96.

SMITH, P. J. 1994: *Desire Unlimited: The cinema of Pedro Almodóvar*. London and New York: Verso.

__2002. Only connect. *Sight and Sound*, July, 24–7.

__2004: *Belle Époque*. *Sight and Sound*, April, 38.

SNODDY, R. 2000: Stuffing lottery money into turkeys. *The Times/Times 2 Media*, 21 April, 12.

SOJA, E. 1996: *Thirdspace: Journeys to Los Angeles and Other Real-and-Imagined Places*. Oxford: Blackwell.

SOJCHER, F. 2002: Luc Besson, ou les contradictions du cinéma français. In Paris, T. (ed): *CinémAction*, Hors-série, 144–56.

SOLOMONS, J. and SMITH, D. 2004: That's enough actually. *The Observer*, 14 November, 3.

STONE, R. 2002: *Spanish Cinema*. Harlow: Longman.

__2004: ¡Victoria? A modern Magdalene. In Marsh, S. and Nair, P. (eds): *Gender and Spanish Cinema*. Oxford and New York: Berg, 165–82.

STONEMAN, R. 1998: Nine notes on cinema and television. In Hill, J. and McLoone, M. (eds): *Big Picture, Small Screen: The Relations between Film and Television*. Luton: John Libbey Media/University of Luton.

SWENGLEY, N. 1992: And now an Oscar for the wallpaper. *The Times Weekend*, 30 March, 6.

TAYLOR, P. and HAYDEN, M. (eds). 2002: *Regius London Film Festival Catalogue 2002*. London: BFI.

TELOTTE, J. P. 1991: *The Cult Film Experience: Beyond All Reason*. Austin, TX: University of Texas Press.

TEMPLE, M. and WITT, M. (eds). 2004: *The French Cinema Book*. London: British Film Institute.

TODOROV, T. 1984: *The Conquest of America: The Question of the Other*. New York: Harper and Row, trans. R. Howard, quoted in Kinder, M. 1993: *Blood Cinema: The Reconstruction of National Identity in Spain*. Berkeley, Los Angeles and London: University of California Press.

TOFFETTI, S. 1995: *Giuseppe Tornatore*. Turin: Lindau.

TOMLINSON, J. 1999: *Globalization and Culture*. Polity Press: Cambridge.

TURAN, K. 2002: *Sundance to Sarajevo: Film Festivals and the World They Made*. Berkeley, Los Angeles, London: University of California Press.

TURNER, G. 1986: *National Fictions*. Sydney: Allen and Unwin.

ULFF-MØLLER, J. 2001: *Hollywood's Film Wars with France: Film-Trade Diplomacy and the Emergence of the French Film Quota Policy*. Rochester, NY: University of Rochester Press.

VENTAVOLI, B. 2000: Ombre rosse: L'industria del cinema porno negli anni Novanta. In D'Agostino, P. and Della Casa, S. (eds): *Cinema italiano annuario 1999–2000*. Milan: Il Castoro.

VICENTE GOMEZ, A. 1990: Did you say business? *MEDIA 92 Newsletter*, 6, 7.

VINCENDEAU, G. 2000: *Stars and Stardom in French Cinema*. London and New York: Continuum.

WAYNE, M. 2002: *The Politics of Contemporary European Cinema: Histories, Borders, Diasporas*. Bristol: Intellect Books.

WESTWELL, G. 2006: *War Cinema: Hollywood on the Front Line*. London: Wallflower Press.

WHITE, P. and SANGEY, D. 1994: Factor 35 raises production temperature. *Screen International*, 8 July, 17.

WILLEMEN, P. 1989: The Third Cinema question: Notes and reflections. In Pines, J. and Willemen, P. (eds): *Questions of Third Cinema*. London: BFI.

WOOD, M. 2002: Bernardo Bertolucci in context. In Tasker, Y. (ed.): *Fifty Contemporary Filmmakers*. London and New York: Routledge, 41–51.

__2005a: *Italian Cinema*. Oxford and New York: Berg.

__2005b: The turbulent movement of forms: Rosi's postmodern *Carmen*. In Davies, A. and Perriam, C. (eds): *Carmen: From silent film to MTV*. Amsterdam and New York: Rodopi, 189–203.

__2006/7 (forthcoming): The dark side of the Mediterranean: Italian *film noir*. In Spicer, A. (ed.): *European Film Noir*. Manchester: Manchester University Press.

WYATT, J. 1994: *High Concept: Movies and Marketing in Hollywood*. Austin, TX: University of Texas Press.

ŽIŽEK, S. 2000: Dove finiscono i Balcani? In Grmek Germani, S. (ed.): *La meticcia di fuoco. Oltre il continente Balcani*. Turin: La Biennale di Venezia/Lindau, 29–30.

ZUCKER, C. and MOEN, K. 2000: Love and rage: Irish cinema of the 1990s. *Cineaction*, 51, 48–54.

Index

Film titles are in italics. Figures are denoted by f, eg 10f.

5 x 2 91
8 Women 91
24 Hour Party People 39–40
101 Reykjavik 17

Aalbaeck, Peter 12
Aardman Animation 113
About a Boy 171
About Adam 166
'accented' style 117–19
actors
  as directors 48
  Irish 158–9, 167
  as stars 80–1
admissions *see also* audiences
  art cinema films by 10f, 20–3
  box -office hits by 60–6
  European market 43
Ae Fond Kiss xvi
Agence Intergouvernementale de la Francophonie 9
airline market 74, 111
Akin, Fatih 127
Alexander 7
All About My Mother 58
Almodóvar, Pedro xx, 43, 54–8, 170
Amélie 53, 77, 79–80
Amelio, Gianni 7, 123
Amenábar, Julio xxiv
American cinema
  anxiety and violence xviii
  co-production with 68–9, 113
  competition from xi, 67–8, 171
  European markets 1–5
  globalization xiii
  influence on European 52
American Film Marketing Association (AFMA) 2
Angel 159
Anglaise et le Duc, L' 13, 31
animal films 112
animation 113
Anja and Viktor films 111
Annaud, Jean-Jacques xxiv
Appadurai, Arjun xv–xvi
Apted, Michael xxiv
ARD 4
Ardmore Studios 156
Argento, Dario 96
art cinema xix, xx, 18, 25, 27–8, 169 *see also auteur* film-making films by admissions 10f, 20–3
ARTE 50, 101, 106
Artemisia 142
Arts Councils, Britain 8, 165
As bodas de Deus 28
Asian communities xvi
Asterix and Obelix films 77
audiences xv
  female 139–40
  by genre 100–1f
  heritage films 139–40
  Ireland 152–3, 166
  middle classes xiii, 26, 29–32, 89–91, 105
  multiplexes 81
  Spanish 93
  young male 83–9
audio-visual sector 2–3
  market, European 3–5
  state aid 8
August, Bille 58
Australia xvii

auteur film-making xix, xx, 17, 40–1, 99, 169–70
  auteur theory 24–8
  Britain 38–40
  Denmark 35–7
  films by admissions 20–3
  France 29–35
  Italy 37–8
  Portugal 28–9
auteur theory xx, 24–8

Balkan film-making 128
Balkan Fund 9
Balkans conflict xxii, xxiii, 115–17, 128–9, 172
  British film-making 117–21
  Italian film-making 121–5
Baltic-Russian Development Fund for Documentaries 9
Basque identity 153–4, 161
Bavarian Film Fund 148
BBC (British Broadcasting Corporation) 4, 107–9, 120, 139, 165, 166
Bean: The Ultimate Disaster Movie 73–4
Beau Travail 106–7
Beautiful People 118–19
Before the Rain 117–18, 124, 130n
Being John Malkovich xiv–xv
Belle Époque 143
Bend It Like Beckham xvi
Beneix, Jean-Jacques 12, 52
Benigni, Roberto xxi, 48, 77, 80, 93
Bennett, Ronan 164–5
Berlusconi, Silvio xxi, 47
Bertelsmann xxi, 4, 100
Bertolucci, Bernardo 49, 52
Besson, Luc 52–3, 76, 92
Bevan, Tim 12
Bibi Blocksberg films 111
Billie Elliott 112
Black Book 52
Bloody Sunday 157
Blue Juice 88
Bluebird 109
Bollywood films xv
books, as basis for films 46–7
Borg, Dominique 77–8
box-office hits xx–xxi, 82
  British films 72–5
  co-production 68–72
  films by admissions 60–6
  French films 75–80
  Italian films 80
  nature of 67–8
  stars of 80–1
  television 102
Branagh, Kenneth xx, 38, 81
Bread and Roses xvi
Bread and Tulips 122
Breakfast on Pluto 162–3
Breaking the Waves 35, 36, 50
Bridget Jones films 7, 69, 71–2
British film-making xv, 38–40
  Balkans conflict 117–21
  box-office hits 72–5
  budgets 84
  children's films 110
  costume drama 134–42
  horror films 96
  and television 107–9
  war films 148–50
Brotherhood of the Wolf 77–9
Broughan, Peter 11
Bronzés, Les films 171
Buena Vista 2, 44, 56, 111
Bullet Boy 108–9
Butcher Boy, The 159, 160–1, 163
Byways 105

Cabaret Balkan 128
Callas Forever 48
Canal Plus xxii, 4, 48, 56, 77, 85, 100
  film-making, France 101, 102–6
Cannes film festival xix, 45, 50
capitalism xii–xiii
Capitol Films 6
Carax, Léos 45, 52
Card Player, The 96
Carla's Song xvi
Carlo Giuliani, a Boy 170
Carmen 5, 46
cartoons 113
Cavani, Liliana 48–9
Celebration, The 35–6
CGI (computer-generated images) *see* digitization

Chadha, Gurinder xvi
chaos xvii–xviii
Chicken Run 113
children xxii
  films about 107–9, 124–5
  films for 100–1f, 109–14
Choristes, Les 112
Chouchou 102
'Christmas' films 93–4
Chronicle of a Death Foretold 47
Ciby 2000 56
cinema du look xx, 43, 52–3, 79
Cinema Paradiso 144
cinema release *see* releases
cinematography xxi, 67, 75–7
Circle of Friends 163
classes, social
  Britain 140
  heritage films xxiii, 135–7, 139
  middle classes xiii, 26, 29–32, 89–91, 104
  social mobility xxiii, 84–5
  working class 87–8
CNC (Centre National de Cinématographie) xix, 8, 106
co-production xxi, 14–15
  Franco-Italian 68
  Germany 68–9
  Godard, Jean-Luc 34
  high-concept films 69–72
  Ireland 157
  Loach, Ken 16–17, 167
  television companies xxi, 83, 102–3, 171
  with USA 43, 68–72, 171
Cock and Bull Story, A 40
Code 46 39
Collectionneuse, La 29
colonialism 153–5
colour, use of 79
Columbia Tristar 2
Comédia de Deus, A 28
Comédies et proverbes 30
comedy 48, 73–4, 79, 92–5, 104
Comencini, Francesca 170
commercial influences 46–7
communications, developments in 102, 169–70
communism 146–7
computer games 110
Consequences of Love, The 49–50
Constantin Film 95, 148
Contes des quatres saisons 30
costs, of production xiv, 25f *see also* financing, film-making
costume design xxi, 77–8, 80, 82n
  Italy 143–4
costume drama xxiii, 52, 131–3 *see also* war films
  British film-making 134–42
  eroticism 137–8, 142–3
counter-cinema 49
criminal activity, attitude to 84, 87
crisis narratives xvii
Croupier 86–7
Crying Game, The 156, 159
culture xv–xvi, xviii, xxi
  and identities xiv, 8, 25–6
  protection of 2–3
Cyprus 11
Czech Republic 94, 145, 146–7

Dancer in the Dark 50
Dancing at Lughnasa 163–4
Danish Film Institute 8, 58, 111
Dark Blue World 146–7
Das Experiment 17
David's Summer 122
De Oliveira, Manoel 28
Denmark 35–7, 89
  Danish Film Institute 8, 58, 111
Depardieu, Gérard 81
Descent, The 96–7
diaspora communities xvii, 9
  Irish 153
Die Marquise von O 29–30
digitization xviii, xxi, 5, 167, 172–3
  special effects 67, 77
directors
  as auteurs 25–6, 28, 169–70
  Balkan 128
  quality cinema 44
  stylistic development 47
Dirty Pretty Things 105, 120–1
Disney Corporation 2, 4, 44–5
Distant Lights 126

distribution sector xxii, 2–3, 56
  bypassing of 97
  fragmentation of 4–5, 12–13
  MEDIA 2007 14
  Miramax 44–5, 139
Divorcing Jack 165
Dizdar, Jasmin 118–19
Dog Soldiers 96
Dogme95 35–7, 41n, 50, 90
Dogville 50–1
Domenica 109
Donati, Danilo 80
Downfall 17, 148
Dreamworks 113
Dutch film-making 9, 94, 109
DVD market xiv, 5, 102, 172–3

East Germany 94, 116
East is East xv
Eastern Central Europe 11, 12, 110, 116, 157
Eastern Europe xi, 94, 115, 145
economic pressures xiii, xiv, 12
Egoli Films 13
Eichinger, Bernd 95
Eltringham, Billie 170
End of The Affair, The 159
eroticism 137–8, 142–3
ethical dilemmas 150 *see also* Balkans conflict
ethnicity xv, xxii–xxiii
Être et avoir 12
Eurimages 14–15, 48, 58
  co-production 68, 77, 146
European Union xix, 17–18, 83, 169
  MEDIA programme 10–14
event movies *see* box-office hits
exhibition sector xxii, 5, 11
exploitation windows 8, 25, 173

Fares, Josef 88–9
Fassbinder, Edgar Reitz 148
Fellner, Eric 12
female
  audiences 139–40
  role 97, 100–1f
  struggle xvi, 118 (*see also* gender issues)
feminism xvi, 30, 138, 142, 160
Festen 36
festivals 45, 97, 110
  Cannes film festival xix, 45, 50
Field, The 158
Fifth Element, The 76–7
Film Four xvi, 159
Film Fund bodies 9
film institutes, national 8–9
film libraries xv
film noir 48–50, 59n, 123, 144
  neo-*noir* 87
FilmFernsehFonds 58
Filmförderungsanstalt 9, 68
financing, film-making xv, xxii, 52, 169
  costs, of production xiv, 25f
  DVD production 102
  European films 6–7
  France 102–4, 103f
  Germany 68–9, 94–5
  Italy 109
  multinational corporations 2
  problems with 51
  Spain 55, 59n
  success (*see* box-office hits)
Fine Line 2, 59n
Floris 94
Flying Classroom, The 111
Football Factory, The 87–8
France 2 102
France/tour/détour/deux/enfants 33
franchise film-making 114, 171
French film-making xx, 8
  box-office hits 75–80
  cinéma du look 52–3
  comedy 92
  directors 29–35
  historical films 142–3
  middle-class audience 91
  and television 101–7
  war films 147–8
Full Monty, The 7, 85

gangster films 86–8
Gaumont 5, 46
gender issues 49, 54–6, 57, 106, 127
  feminism xvi, 30, 138, 142, 160
  sexual identity 90, 139, 163
German film-making
  children's films 110, 111

co-production 68–9
comedy films 94–5
Turkish film-making 126–8
war films 148
Giordana, Tullio 124
Gleaners and I, The 34
Gleeson, Brendan 159
globalization xii–xvii, 36, 116–17, 169
definitions xii–xiii
local interests xxiii
'glocal' xvi, xx–xxi
Godard, Jean-Luc xx, 29, 32–4, 99
Gold Reel Award 7
Good Thief, The 159
Goodbye Lenin 13, 83, 94
Gosford Park 6, 139
Governess, The 136, 138, 139
Grant, Hugh 71, 72, 81, 137
Green Rays, The 30
Greengrass, Paul 157

Hallström, Lasse xxiv
haptic 78
Harry, He's Here to Help 104
Harry Potter 69–72
Hate 2 O 97
Hauer, Rutger 94
Head-On 127
Hear My Song 154
Heat's On, The 105
Hell's Kitchen 157, 159
Henry V 38
heritage cinema xxiii, 134–5, 172 *see also* costume drama
Hidden Agenda xv–xvi
Hideous Kinky 140–1
high-concept films 69–72
High Heels 55–6
Hilary and Jackie 141
Histoire(s) du cinema 33–4
historical films xxiii, 134, 150 *see also* costume drama; war films
Eastern Europe 145
French film-making 142–3
Ireland 160–4
Italian film-making 143–4
Spanish film-making 142–3
Hodge, Mike 86
Hollywood xiii, xix–xx, 1–5
majors 1–2, 18n
horizontal integration xiii, xiv–xv
horror films 77–9, 95–7
Ireland 159
Horseman on the Roof, A 142
Howard's End 136–7

I Went Down 159
identity issues xvii, xxii–xxiii, 49, 57, 122 *see also* Balkans conflict; classes, social; gender issues; racial tensions
Basque 153–4, 161
contemporary culture 88–9
Germany 160
Irish 153–5
national xix–xx, xxii–xiii
Il ladro di bambini 7
I'll Sleep When I'm Dead 86–7
I'm Not Afraid 109
immigration issues xv, xviii, 115, 116, 172
Balkan conflict xxii, 120–6
In Dreams 159
In Orange 109
Indian films xv
Institut National de l'Audiovisuel (INA) 33
international markets 46–7
internet 102, 170, 173
Interview with a Vampire: The Vampire Chronicles 159
Iraq, invasion of 145–6, 149
Irish Film Board (IFB) 9, 156, 164, 166, 167
Irish film-making xxiv, 152–3, 166–7, 172
colonial past 153–5
development of 155–7
historical films 160–4
Northern Ireland 164–6
television 164–5
theatrical traditions 158–9
Italian film-making xx
auteur 37–8
Balkans conflict 121–5, 129, 130n
box -office hits 80
children, films about 109, 124–5
children, films for 111
comedy 93–4
historical films 143–4
horror films 96, 97

pornography 97
quality cinema 46–52
and television 109
Italian for Beginners 90

Jalla! Jalla! 88–9
Jeunet, Jean-Pierre 27, 45, 52–3, 79, 147
Johnny English 74
Jordan, Neil 27, 45, 156, 159, 160–3
journalism, within films 117–18

Kaletsky, Anatole xii–xiii
Kamenak 94
King Arthur 7, 148–9
Kingdom of Heaven 7, 149–50
KirchMedia xxi, 4, 100
Kops 88–9
Kusturica, Emir 128

Labyrinth of Passion 54
Ladri di Saponette 13
Ladybird Ladybird xvi
Lagardère Média 4
Lamerica 123
Land and Freedom xvi
Länder 8, 95
language 5, 58
minority xxii, 3–4
Last Resort 107–8, 120
Last Tango in Paris 49
Leconte, Patrice 91
legislation, and film-making xxii, 1
European Parliament 2–3
France 75–6, 104
Germany 68–9
Luxembourg 100
Republic of Ireland xxiv, 156–7, 164
Leigh, Mike 52
Lemming 104–5
Life After Life 164–5
Life is Beautiful 48, 80
Lilya 4-ever 125–6
Live Flesh 57
Loach, Ken xv–xvi, 16–17, 167
local film 82, 83, 92–5, 171
location, film making xiv, 50
Lock, Stock and Two Smoking Barrels 86
Lola and Billy the Kid 127
Long Good Friday, The 155
López, Sergí 105
Love Actually 73
Love Lies Bleeding 159, 164–5
Lovers 142–3
luvvie 38, 42n
Luxembourg 100
Lyotard, Jean-François xii

Madrid 54, 56–7
Magdalene Sisters, The 164
majors, corporations 1–2, 4, 18n
male
audiences, young 83–9, 92–3, 95
identities (*see* Balkans conflict; gender issues)
Malèna 144
Malta 11
Man About Dog 154
Manderlay 51
Manitou's Shoe 95
Mansfield Park 136, 139
March of the Penguins 112
marketing xxii, 171
European 3–5
heritage films 139–40
smaller countries 152
MEDIA programme xi, xix, 1, 173
children's films 110
co-production 68
cultural diversity 3
development of 10–14
Republic of Ireland 157
subsidiarity funding 8
Mediaset 109
Mediterraneo 37
Memfis Films 89
merchandising 113–14
metanarratives xii, xviii
Michael Collins 162
middle classes xiii, 26, 29–32
as audience 89–91, 105, 140
portrayal in film 104
minorities *see* ethnicity
Miramax 2, 44–5, 67, 144
effect on marketing 47, 170
Mirò law 55, 59n
Monteiro, Joao César 28–9

Moodysson, Lukas 90, 125–6
Moretti, Nanni xx, 37–8
Moroni, Vittorio 173
Most Fertile Man in Ireland, The 165–6
Motion Picture Association of America (MPAA) 1, 2, 18n
movies *see* box-office hits
Much Ado about Nothing 38–9
multiculturalism xv, 117–21
multimedia corporations 4
multinational corporations 1–2, 4
multiplexes 58
  audience 81, 84
  Ireland 152
musicals 50
My Left Foot 156
My Name is Joe xvi, 16–17
My Summer of Love 108

Nanny McPhee 85
narratives xii, xviii, 158
nation states xiv, xxiii *see also* identity issues, national
National Lottery, British 85, 139, 165
National Trust 135
Navigators, The xvi
NBC companies 4, 100, 104
Nellis, Alice 94
neo-baroque elements xviii, 46, 49, 87, 173
  cinéma du look 52–3
  horror films 96–7
neo-realist films xix
New Line 2, 67
New Zealand 157
News Corporation 4, 100
niche markets *see* audiences
Nikita 53
Nine Songs 39
Nirvana 37
Nordic countries *see* Scandinavia
Nordic Film and TV Fund 9, 58
Northern Ireland xxiv, 152, 164–6, 167 *see also* Irish film-making
Notre Musique 34, 41n
Notting Hill xiv–xv, 72, 140
  'glocal' xvi
Nouvelle vague 29, 34–5

O'Connor, Pat 163
Odd Man Out 155
Oltra il confine 124
Once You're Born 124–5
One and Only, The 90
opera 39, 48
Others, The 92, 96
Ozon, François 91
Ozpetek, Ferzan 127

panopticon 18–19n, 160–1, 163–4
Pauline at the Beach 30
Pavee Lackeen 167
Pawlikowski, Pavel 107–8
Peerless Camera Company 80
Pepi, Luci, Bom 54
Perceval 29–30
Peter's Friends 38
Pieraccioni, Leonardo 93
Pinocchio xxi, 80
Pippi Longstocking films 111
piracy 45
Plunkett and Macleane xv
Poland 9, 145
politics and film-making xv–xvi, 94
  Italy 37, 46–7
Polleke 112
PolyGram xiv–xv, 4, 86
PolyGram Filmed Entertainment (PFE) xiv–xv, 73
Pornographic Affair, A 105
pornography 97, 100–1f
Portuguese cinema 28–9
postmodernism xii
  neo-baroque 46
  terrorism xvii
propaganda 116–17
public bodies, funding 8–9
Pusher films 125

quality cinema xx, 43–4, 58–9, 170
  definition of 44
  distribution 44–5
  France 52–3
  Italy 46–52
  Spain 54–8
Quo Vadis 145

racial tensions xvi, 112, 122, 127, 136, 167
Raining Stones xvi
Red Satin 105–6
Refn, Nicholas Winding 125
regional state-funded bodies 8
releases xiii–xiv, 9f, 10f
  and production 25–6, 26f
religious conflict 118
Republic of Ireland xxiv, 152–7, 167 *see also* Irish film-making
Reservoir Dogs 86
Revolver 86
Riff-Raff xvi
Ripley's Game 48–9
Ritchie, Guy 86
Rob Roy 11, 67, 74
Rohmer, Eric xx, 29–32, 41n, 91
Room with a View, A 135
Roses and Guns 123
Rosi, Francesco 5, 46–8
Rozema, Patricia 139
RTÉ (Radio Telefis Éireann) 164
Run Lola Run 94

sales agents 6–7
Salvatore Giuliano 46
Salvatores, Gabriele xx, 37, 38, 45, 109
satellite channels xxii, 99, 100
  partnerships xxi, 77 (*see also* Canal Plus)
  supply by genre 100–1f
Saving Private Ryan 157
Scandinavia xiv, xix, 88–91
  children's films 110, 111
school stories 112
Schpaaa 111
Seagram xiv–xv
Sense and Sensibility 136
set design xxi, 78
sexual issues *see also* gender issues
  eroticism 137–8, 142–3
  pornography 97, 100–1f
  sex trafficking 124–7
Sexy Beast 86
Shakespeare, William 38–9
Shakespeare in Love 45
Shallow Grave 84
Sheridan, Jim 159
short films 40, 42n
Short Sharp Shock 127
Show Me Love 90
Six Contes Moraux 29
slate funding 11–12
Smilla's Sense of Snow 58
Snatch 86
social class *see* classes, social
social context xi, xvii
  class mobility 84–5
  globalization xii–xvii
SOFICAs 75–6
Sony companies 1–2, 4, 139
Sophie Scholl 148
Sorrentino, Paolo 49–50
soundtrack 79–80
Spanish film-making xx, 43, 54–8, 59n
  comedy 92–3
  historical films 142–3
  horror film 96
stars, actors 80–1
state-supported film industry xi, xix–xx, 8–10
  annual releases and market share 9f, 10f
  Eurimages 14–15
  France 75–6
  Italy 37–8
  MEDIA programme 10–14
  Scandinavia 89–90
  television 99
Stealing Beauty 49
stereotypes 72–5, 80, 81
  French 105, 107
  of gender 112
  Irish 85, 154–5, 165
  Italian 122
  Welsh 85
Storaro, Vittorio xxiv
Stormbreaker 113
Summer - 27 Missing Kisses 13
Sverák, Jan 146, 151n
Sweden 88–9, 111
Switzerland xxii

takeovers, corporations xiv–xv, xxii, 4
Talk to Her 57
Tarantino, Quentin 45, 86
Taxi film series 92, 107
Tea with Mussolini 48

Technicolor Digital 172
technological changes xi, xiv, xv *see also* communications; digitization
television xxi–xxii, 99, 100–1, 171–2
  Balkans conflict 121
  British film-making 107–9
  children's films 109–14
  co-production xxi, 83, 114
  companies, European 4
  deregulation xiii, 46
  French film-making 101–7
  German film-making 127
  Irish film-making 164–6
  Italian film-making 109
terrorism xvii, 149, 170
Third Cinema 170
This is Not a Love Song 170
Tie Me Up! Tie Me Down 55
Time to Leave 91
To Forget Palermo 47
Together 90
Topsy Turvey 52
Tornatore, Giuseppe 144
Torrente films 93
tourism 135
training programmes 11–12, 40
Trainspotting 84
Trilogy of John of God 28
Triple Agent 31
Troska, Zdenek 94
Troy 7
Truce, The 47
Turkey 13, 126–8
Turkish Bath, The 127–8
Two Brothers 112
Tykver, Tom 12
typologies, national cinema 158

UGC 53, 56
UK *see* British film-making
Ulster *see* Northern Ireland
uncertainty xvii–xviii
Universal 2, 73, 100

Varda, Agnès 29, 34–5
Vera Drake 141
Verdone, Carlo 93
Verhoeven, Paul 52, 94
vertical integration xiii, xxi, 59
  American multinationals xiv–xv, 1–2
  Spain 56
Very Annie Mary 85
Very Long Engagement, A 16, 28, 53, 147–8, 171
Viacom 2, 4
Villa des roses 15–16
violence 117–18, 159, 172
  American cinema xviii
Visconti, Luchino 48
Vita è Bella, La 48, 80
Vivendi companies xv, xxi, 4, 100, 103–4
von Trier, Lars xx, 12, 35–6
  quality cinema 43, 50–2

Waking Ned 85
Wales xv, xxii, 85
Wallace and Gromit films 113
war films xviii, xxiii–xxiv, 134, 145–50 *see also* Balkans conflict
Warner Bros. 2, 70–1
Warriors 120
Way of Life, A 108–9
Weinstein Company 114
Welcome to Sarajevo 119–20
What have I done to deserve this? 54–5
When Brendan Met Trudy 166
Wilbur Wants to Kill Himself 90
Wimbledon 72–3
Wind That Shakes the Barley, The 167
Winterbottom, Michael xx, 12, 39–40, 88, 119, 169–70
With Fire and Sword 145
women, role of 97, 100–1f
Women on the Verge of a Nervous Breakdown 55
Wondrous Oblivion 112
working class 87–8 *see also* gangster films
Working Title 73, 74

X-Filme Creative Pool 94–5

Yugoslavia *see* Balkans conflict

ZDF (Zweites Deutsches Fersehen) 127
Zeffirelli, Franco 48
Zentropa companies 51, 59n, 90